Immigration, Nationality an

D0530233

Immigration, Nationality and Asylum under the Human Rights Act 1998

Nicholas Blake QC
of the Middle Temple, Barrister

Laurie Fransman
of the Middle Temple, Barrister

TWO GARDEN COURT

CHAMBERS

Butterworths
London, Edinburgh, Dublin
1999

United Kingdom	Butterworths, a Division of Reed Elsevier (UK) Ltd, Halsbury House, 35 Chancery Lane, LONDON WC2A 1EL and 4 Hill Street, EDINBURGH EH2 3JZ
Australia	Butterworths, a Division of Reed International Books Australia Pty Ltd, CHATSWOOD, New South Wales
Canada	Butterworths Canada Ltd, MARKHAM, Ontario
Hong Kong	Butterworths Asia (Hong Kong), HONG KONG
India	Butterworths India, NEW DELHI
Ireland	Butterworth (Ireland) Ltd, DUBLIN
Malaysia	Malayan Law Journal Sdn Bhd, KUALA LUMPUR
New Zealand	Butterworths of New Zealand Ltd, WELLINGTON
Singapore	Butterworths Asia, SINGAPORE
South Africa	Butterworths Publishers (Pty) Ltd, DURBAN
USA	Lexis Law Publishing, CHARLOTTESVILLE, Virginia

© Reed Elsevier (UK) Ltd 1999

All rights reserved. No part of this publication may be reproduced in any material form (including photocopying or storing it in any medium by electronic means and whether or not transiently or incidentally to some other use of this publication) without the written permission of the copyright owner except in accordance with the provisions of the Copyright, Designs and Patents Act 1988 or under the terms of a licence issued by the Copyright Licensing Agency Ltd, 90 Tottenham Court Road, London, England W1P 0LP. Applications for the copyright owner's written permission to reproduce any part of this publication should be addressed to the publisher.

Warning: The doing of an unauthorised act in relation to a copyright work may result in both a civil claim for damages and criminal prosecution.

Any Crown copyright material is reproduced with the permission of the Controller of Her Majesty's Stationery Office.

A CIP Catalogue record for this book is available from the British Library.

ISBN 0 406 92745 6

Printed by Hobbs the Printers Ltd, Totton, Hampshire

Visit us at our website: http://www.butterworths.co.uk

Foreword

by Ian Macdonald QC

This book has grown out of a seminar organised by 2 Garden Court Chambers in the summer of 1998. The seminar dealt with the impact on immigration, nationality and asylum law of the Human Rights Act 1998. Since then things have moved on. The seminar papers have been developed and revised. More importantly the Immigration and Asylum Bill (IAB) has been presented to Parliament and debated. It is the New Labour project for immigration law in the new millennium. And what a project! It rewrites great chunks of the immigration law we have known for the last 30 years. In particular, it does away with one of the key human rights elements of immigration law, the right of appeal on merit against a decision to deport. At a time when people are getting excited about the incorporation into UK law of specific European Convention on Human Rights (ECHR) provisions, the IAB is proposing to reduce rights; appeal rights are being scaled down to the bare minimum required by the ECHR.

This is a salutary lesson. Immigration law has always kept in close contact with international human rights law, a course I have tried to chart with Nick Blake in successive editions of *Macdonald's Immigration Law and Practice*. The latest interaction, caused by the enactment of the Human Rights Act (HRA), is of course the most momentous and far reaching and has an import far beyond the subjects addressed by the various papers in this book. It affects the whole of British law. But the point I wish to make is that the ECHR was already shaping the development of immigration law before the HRA came along. The Convention is therefore familiar terrain to many who have been concerned with our immigration laws.

That familiarity grew first in the colonies before the mass migrations of the late 1950s and early 1960s gave rise to modern immigration law. Immigrants had already invoked the right of individual petition to the European Commission by the time of the Commonwealth Immigrants Act 1968; this undoubtedly influenced the Wilson Committee and the government of the day and led to the Immigration Appeals Act 1969, which introduced the immigration appeal system as we currently know it.

The Convention was adopted under the auspices of the Council of Europe set up after World War II. The UK was one of the founder members. All members of the Council, says the founding statute, 'must accept the principles of the rule of law and of the enjoyment by all persons in its jurisdiction of human rights and fundamental freedoms ...'[1]. The ECHR was the first step towards the fulfilment of these principles.

---

1   Statute of the Council of Europe (1949 Cmnd 7778), art.3. See generally *A.H. Robertson, v Council of Europe* (2nd Edn).

The Cold War was then at its height and undoubtedly the stimulus for these developments was the recent experience of the Nazi regime in Germany and a fear of totalitarian Communism on the other hand. Democracy was contrasted with dictatorship[2]. The signatories are to be 'governments of European countries which are like minded and have a common heritage of political traditions, ideals, freedom and the rule of law'. They are also to share a 'profound belief in an effective political democracy as the cornerstone of human rights and fundamental freedoms'.

More concretely, the aim of ECHR was to secure 'the universal and effective recognition and observance' of the rights set out in the UN's Universal Declaration of Human Rights (UDHR) of 1948. But unlike the Declaration, which was not much more than an expression of pious hope, the European Convention imposed legal obligations on the state parties to ensure that their laws were in conformity with the Convention, and set up the European Court of Human Rights and the Commission as an enforcement mechanism to ensure compliance. It also provided for states to recognise the right of individuals to petition the Commission and to accept the compulsory jurisdiction of the Court.

The development of this machinery took place in stages. When the ECHR first came into operation in 1953 the Commission became competent only to receive state applications. The Court was not operative. Individual petitions to the Commission were first allowed in 1955, but at that time only six countries accepted the arrangement. It was not until 3 September 1958 that the Court achieved competence. Obviously the most important development was the right of individual petition. Once it was introduced the number of individual applications far exceeded the number of inter-state cases[3].

It took nearly sixteen years from the ratification of the Convention before Britain recognised the right of individual petition and the compulsory jurisdiction of the Court[4]. During this period the matter of individual petition and compulsory jurisdiction was raised either in debate or in the form of questions no fewer than 11 times between May 1956 and February 1965. On each occasion the matter was side-stepped by the government of the day. Various excuses were made, such as:

(i)　that 'the Law of this country has always been in advance of the laws of most other countries in regard to human rights'

(ii)　that 'a flood of fatuous or insincere applications would roll in on them, causing them extra work and adverse publicity'[6]; and

(iii)　that 'the State and not the individual is the proper subject of international law'[7].

But the main reason seems to have been Britain's colonial situation. At the international level the UK had extended its obligations under the Convention to 42 colonial territories in 1953[8]. That in itself had been something of an embarrassment. Up to May 1960 colonial unrest had led to no fewer than 10 derogations from article

---

2　See A.H. Robertson 'the Political Background and Historical Development of the European Convention on Human Rights' 1965 ICLQ Supp No.11.

3　ECHR, Council of Europe Directorate of Press and Information (1975) p13.

4　This was first done on 14.01.66: see (1966) 15 ICLQ 539.

5　See HC Official Report (5th Series) 20th Nov 1950 Col 16.

6　HC Official Report (5th Series) 23rd May 1960 Col 174.

7　Ibid Col 180.

8　1953 (Cmnd 9045).

5 of ECHR (the right to liberty and security of the person)[9]. The handling of the Cyprus emergency had been the subject of complaint by Greece, which one Minister thought had been brought 'unfairly and for propaganda purposes'[10]. Dr Hastings Banda had tried to get Iceland to bring a complaint against the UK over his imprisonment without trial in Nyasaland (Malawi)[11] and in 1960 the government was induced to give an assurance that powers to detain persons and to impose forced labour in the colonies would only be exercised in accordance with article 15 of the Convention[12].

The colonial situation undoubtedly played an important part in delaying the full application of the Convention. When one MP commented that the reason why the government 'might look askance at the right of individual petition is the fear lest it should be necessary constantly to derogate from the Convention in respect of the right when disturbed conditions arise in any colony', the Minister replied that 'among emerging communities political agitators thrive and one may well imagine the use which political agitators would make of the right of individual petition'[13].

There is no doubt that the easing of the colonial situation, with nearly half of the 42 colonies becoming politically independent, paved the way for the eventual recognition of the right of individual petition in 1966. One irony of the colonial situation was that, having steadfastly refused to give individual human rights guarantees to the people of the colonies while they were under British rule, the UK Government was only too willing to see such guarantees inserted in their new constitutions when they became independent, a process starting with Nigeria in 1959[14].

The invocation of the Convention during the period when colonies gained independence gave rise to a group of lawyers who became familiar with the provisions of ECHR. When many of these same people came to deal with the harshness and unfairness of the Commonwealth Immigrants Act after 1962 it is not surprising that they were among the first to invoke these same fundamental rights when a new European forum for individual complaints became available. The very first case where the individual right of petition was exercised was that of a Commonwealth immigrant. This was a father complaining over the refusal of admission of his 13 year old son. After his application was admitted by the Commission it led to a friendly settlement[15]. In the next case the applicant was not so successful, the Commission holding that the son was by then an adult and had lived apart from his father for too long a period to establish family life within the meaning of article 8[16].

As stated, the fact that individual immigrants were already invoking the right of individual petition by 1967 undoubtedly had an influence on the course of events that followed and in 1969 the Labour government of the day introduced a comprehensive system of immigration appeals upon the recommendation of the Wilson Committee[17]. The Immigration Appeals Act 1969 is, in my opinion, the one great gesture to human rights in the development of UK immigration law from 1962 to the present day.

---

9 HC Official Report (5th Series) 23 May 1960 Col 174.
10 Ibid Col 181.
11 Ibid Col 176 and 180.
12 HC Official Report (5th Series) 19th May 1960 Written Answers Cols 133-134.
13 HC Official Report (5th Series) 23 May 1950 Cols 174 and 182.
14 See Nigeria's Independence Constitution, Chapter I, set out within a Westminster statutory instrument.
15 *Mohammed Alam v UK* 2991/66 (1967) Times, 12 October.
16 *Harbahjan Singh v UK* 2992/66 (1967) Times, 12 October.
17 1967 Cmnd 3387.

The Convention has also shaped the approach of successive governments to the issue of family rights. During the 1970s there was a see-saw in the formulation of successive domestic Immigration Rules on the ability of husbands to join their wives in the UK. Wives had always been allowed to come to the UK for marriage. Marriage to a British husband also conferred on women (prior to 1983) a right to register as UK citizens themselves. The Rules on husbands were never as liberal. Eventually a petition to Strasbourg over the in-built discrimination was made in the case of *Abdulaziz, Cabales and Balkandali v UK*[18]. The Court held that the current Immigration Rules breached the Convention and were discriminatory on grounds of sex contrary to article 8 read with article 14. The British government had a choice of placing the rights of husbands on the same basis as wives. Instead they chose to level down, so that the rights of women were reduced.

This process of achieving equality by levelling rights down to the minimum possible will, as this book shows, be a feature of the HRA and the IAB.

In the introductory chapter Laurie Fransman deals with the basic concepts of Convention law and provides an overview of rights and freedoms made directly enforceable in UK law by the HRA.

Strictly speaking the Act does not incorporate the Convention or the rights it contains, but is a very British compromise which makes human rights justiciable in the courts and allows the courts to make a declaration of incompatibility where there is a conflict between UK statute and an 'incorporated' Convention right. Nevertheless the UK courts will in future use both domestic and Convention case law to interpret and apply the Convention. Laurie Fransman points out the potential pitfalls and conflicts between UK traditions of interpretation and precedent and the purposive and wider ranging approach of Convention jurisprudence.

There is some overlap between the various papers presented. Both he and Nick Blake highlight the entirely novel interpretation rule introduced by the HRA, namely that courts and Tribunals should strive to reach an interpretation of any legislative provision to achieve conformity with incorporated Convention rights.

Because immigration law operates in a vibrant social and political context, it offers a fruitful field of conflict between the new approach to construction enjoined by the HRA and the more traditional attitude to interpretation. Decisions of the immigration appellate authorities and the courts will be awaited with interest.

Immigration practitioners tend to view the traditional approach of UK courts to their interpretative task as cautious, narrow and conservative, and tend to suppose that this will continue to be the case. But, as Laurie Fransman points out, there is double scope for a flowering of judicial creativity. First, he joins Nick Blake and the increasingly large chorus who point out that the restraints of the European Court in Strasbourg imposed by the 'margin of appreciation' doctrine has no application to domestic law. Therefore, there may be opportunities to revisit domestically cases which have failed in Strasbourg. Second, under section 2 of the HRA European Court precedent is not strictly binding and there is, therefore, scope for enlarging rights and freedoms. For example, the narrow European Court interpretation of 'civil rights' in article 6 might be a case in point.

In the field of immigration there is already in place in the UK a long standing and elaborate appeal system with its own case law, and a well developed judicial review jurisdiction. Bringing the ECHR home affects the procedures of immigration law as much as substance, and this topic is explored in detail in a paper by Fran Webber and Raza Husain.

In judicial review cases the potential class of applicant is wider than the mere 'victims of a violation' preferred by the ECHR. Where this makes a difference, a solution may lie in the widening practice of UK courts to allow interventions by public interest organisations in judicial review proceedings. Nick Blake's paper also touches upon this area. The Webber and Husain paper looks at the jurisdiction of the immigration appellate authorities to consider breaches of the Convention. Problems arise under the present restricted jurisdiction in asylum appeals under section 8 of the Asylum and Immigration Appeals Act 1993 and in restricted deportation appeals under section 5 of the Immigration Act 1988. The solution to these jurisdictional questions is in fact to be dealt with in the government's new Bill, the IAB.

A key objection that is made and emphasised in more than one of the papers concerns the proposed loss of the existing deportation appeal. Admittedly, since section 5 of the Immigration Act 1988 commenced it has been restricted in the case of persons here less than seven years, but as regards the rest at least it allowed the appellate authority to revisit the merits of every deportation and to weigh up the competing claims of a public policy of strict enforcement on the one hand and the personal and community circumstances of the proposed deportee on the other hand. Whereas the 1988 Act cut inroads into this right of appeal, now under the IAB it will disappear altogether and appeal rights will be front-loaded onto the appeal against a refusal to extend a leave to enter or remain.

In place of the full-blown rights of a deportation appeal, the only safeguard will be the newly incorporated ECHR rights. It is not quite the same thing, as Nick Blake points out. In his rigorous analysis of the likely new terrain he comments that it is unfortunate that the minimum standards of human rights obligations are intended to replace a significant aspect of the immigration appeal system, which was designed to give appellate scrutiny of the compassionate merits of individual deportation cases. A levelling down to core obligations is not a purely British phenomenon; he points out that it is happening, it seems, all over Europe.

Rick Scannell deals with asylum seekers. He identifies a growing gap between the number of asylum applicants and the number falling within the 1951 Convention definition of a refugee. This 'protection gap', as he calls it, is partly caused by the actual scope of the 1951 Convention and partly by restrictive interpretations of the Convention adopted by certain decisions of UK courts. However, he is optimistic that the gap can be filled by the incorporation of ECHR rights and analyses the very important Strasbourg case law, especially on article 3.

The area of immigration law in which the ECHR has been most engaged prior to incorporation is the one concerning family and other relationships. As I have already pointed out, this is the area in which the first individual right of petition was exercised. There is an enormous body of existing ECHR case law at Court and Commission level. It is the part of ECHR law with which immigration lawyers are most familiar.

In his paper Duran Seddon analyses this case law in detail and highlights how it applies to various recurring relationships. Incorporation, he argues, will provide greater scope to immigration practitioners and their clients to invoke and develop their rights to family and personal relationships.

The incorporated rights under ECHR are all to be read with article 14, the anti-discrimination provision of the Convention. As Stephanie Harrison points out in her paper, article 14 does not provide a general, comprehensive, free-standing protection, since it is restricted to protecting persons against discrimination only in respect to rights and freedoms contained in the Convention. In her paper she looks at the limitations of this important incorporated right and sets out the case law on the definition of discrimination contained in it. She then looks at its possible impact after incorporation and points out that article 14 jurisprudence needs to complement, not replace, that of the Sex and Race Discrimination Acts.

Nuala Mole then takes us to the relationship between the HRA and the rights of free movement of persons under Community law. She sets out the relevant provisions of Community law with clarity and detail and discusses the impact of each legal order on the other, drawing attention to all the relevant case law in the process. She concludes that the ECHR will serve to assist immigration practitioners in reinforcing Community law arguments before our national authorities.

Finally, Laurie Fransman presents a second paper, this on the impact of incorporation on British nationality, and offers (*inter alia*) the mouth-watering prospect of non-Protocol 4 challenges to UK exclusions and expulsions of own nationals.

The papers presented in this book provide a scholarly and extensive coverage of the likely impact of the HRA in the immigration law field. Because of uncertainties in the exact scope of the IAB, there are inevitably large areas in which we can only await developments. However, the book is, we hope, a timely pre-taste of what the key issues are likely to be.

I A Macdonald QC
2 Garden Court Chambers
Temple
August 1999

Preface

When the immigration team at 2 Garden Court Chambers first considered the proposals of the Human Rights Bill to incorporate ECHR rights into domestic law, it was clear to us that from commencement of the new law there could no longer be a discreet category of human rights experts within the legal profession as human rights expertise will be required in every field of practice, immigration certainly being no exception. Some members of the team drafted discussion papers identifying the human rights law we shall be applying post-incorporation and how that application may change the practice of immigration in terms of the procedural and substantive arguments we might bring to bear in representing our clients. We realised the changes could be extensive and that we should be sharing our thoughts with a wider group of practitioners.

So 2 Garden Court Chambers joined with the Aire Centre and the Public Law Project and on 1 June 1998 held a seminar on the impact of the Human Rights Act (HRA), then still in passage, on domestic immigration, nationality and asylum law and practice. We presented our papers and an Aire Centre paper to a cross-section of regular Chambers' users and the exercise was well received. We hope to hold more seminars in due course, so as to accommodate everyone with an interest and so as to maintain the creative momentum while at the same time taking account of related developments.

There has, since the seminar, been one particular development which multiplies the changes coming to immigration practice and the corresponding need for progressive discussions. On 27 July 1998 the White Paper *Fairer, Faster and Firmer - A Modern Approach to Immigration and Asylum* was published and on 9 February 1999 the resultant Immigration and Asylum Bill (IAB) was introduced in the House of Commons. The Bill virtually rewrites UK immigration law and practice; from the giving of advice, to the making of applications, to the bringing of appeals, little will remain familiar once the IAB and HRA are fully in force by the autumn of 2000. The Bill will not only change the domestic immigration terrain over which the HRA will be casting the incorporated rights and freedoms of the ECHR, but also will create an appeal right expressly for human rights challenges under the HRA.

So when Butterworths Tolley asked to publish our seminar papers we agreed in the reinforced belief that the changes that are coming must be discussed as widely as possible. In revising our papers for publication we therefore took account wherever appropriate of the contents of the IAB. However, the papers essentially remain outlines to demonstrate the potential of the HRA in immigration practice. They aim to identify possibilities rather than sketch out fully developed argument. In an environment where a purposive approach to construction is required, and the purpose is the constantly developing one of a practical application of developing human rights norms, it can be said that most things are possible and very little is forbidden.

The result is a book which we hope is instructive and thought-provoking, and which, though a final product in one sense, can only be a first study of what immigration-*cum*-human rights practice will be in the new millennium.

The materials we have included are the HRA, the ECHR itself (as in force following the commencement of Protocol 11 on 1 November 1998) and clause 59 of the IAB (as published on 28 July 1999 on emerging from Committee in the House of Lords). There are also useful Hansard excerpts, including some relating to the Special Immigration Appeals Commission Act 1997, a measure largely prompted by the UK's need to remedy the ECHR violations found by the Strasbourg Court in the *Chahal* case. Two documents pertinent particularly to chapter 2 appear at the end of that chapter.

The entire immigration team at 2 Garden Court has been involved in the process leading up to the book even though not all are authors of individual chapters. We particularly acknowledge Ian Macdonald QC, who, in addition to providing the foreword (and presenting a seminar paper), read and commented upon every chapter. Owen Davies QC has provided technical assistance and Val Easty is another who contributed to the seminar. Sonali Naik and Patrick Lewis assembled the Hansard materials.

Chambers' immigration team wish to express their gratitude to the Aire Centre (especially Nuala Mole and Navtej Ahluwalia, for contributing to the founding seminar and chapter 7) and the Public Law Project (especially Helena Cook, for her oral presentation at the seminar). We are also indebted to Judy Ware, 2 Garden Court Administrator, for her assistance with the conference, and would like to thank the Butterworths Tolley editorial team for their enthusiasm for our work. The royalty due from the publishers is being donated to an immigration/human rights related charity.

We have tried to ensure the book is up-to-date to 15 August 1999.

Nicholas Blake QC & Laurie Fransman
Temple
August 1999

Contents

Table of Statutes and Statutory Instruments

Table of European and International Legislation

References in this Table are to page. Where a page number appears in **bold** type this indicates that the provision is set out in part or in full.

Table of Cases

**Decisions of the European Court of Justice are listed below numerically.
These decisions are also included in the preceding alphabetical list.**

CHAPTER 1

The European Convention on Human Rights (ECHR)

Laurie Fransman

1. Introduction to the ECHR and sources of Convention law

1.1 The Council of Europe (sponsor of the ECHR)

The Council of Europe is based in Strasbourg, France, and was established[1] after the Second World War 'to achieve a greater unity between its Members'[2] and thereby reduce the risk of future wars. The fundamental purpose of the subsequently established European Communities[3] was similar, but whereas the Communities were supra-national in character and derived competence over member states by those states assigning aspects of their sovereignty, the Council of Europe was and remains an inter-governmental organisation in which representatives of its member states come together in a Parliamentary Assembly[4] and a Committee of Ministers[5] to make resolutions and recommendations and adopt treaties. The member states are only bound if they choose to implement a recommendation or ratify a treaty.

The Council of Europe has a substantial web site at www.coe.fr which includes a short history of the organisation, its founding Statute (ie constitutional basis) and all the treaties concluded under its auspices[6].

---

1   By 10 states: Belgium, Denmark, France, Ireland, Italy, Luxembourg, the Netherlands, Norway, Sweden and the UK. There are now, in 1998, 40 member states: Albania, Andorra, Austria, Belgium, Bulgaria, Croatia, Cyprus, Czech Republic, Denmark, Estonia, Finland, France, Germany, Greece, Hungary, Iceland, Ireland, Italy, Latvia, Liechtenstein, Lithuania, Luxembourg, Malta, Moldova, Netherlands, Norway, Poland, Portugal, Romania, the Russian Federation, San Marino, Slovakia, Slovenia, Spain, Sweden, Switzerland, the former Yugoslav Republic of Macedonia, Turkey, Ukraine and the UK.
2   The Statute of the Council of Europe (signed in London on 5 May 1949), art 1a. See also the preamble and arts 1-4 and 10-12.
3   The European Coal and Steel Community (ECSC) established 18 April 1951, the European Economic Community (EEC – renamed the European Community *simpliciter* by the 1992 Maastricht Treaty on European Union) established 25 March 1957 and the European Atomic Energy Community (EAEC or Euratom) also established on 25 March 1957.
4   Whose members are appointed by the national parliaments of each state.
5   At which the Foreign Ministers of the member states meet at least twice a year and for the rest of the time are represented by Permanent Representatives.
6   Including the ECHR as amended to date and, in the section on Public and International Law (subsection: Movement of Persons), the 1963 and 1997 Nationality Conventions.

1.2   The ECHR – a mandatory Bill of Rights for Council of Europe members

The Council of Europe treaty that is best known and has had greatest impact is the ECHR – the European Convention on Human Rights (or, in full, the European Convention for the Protection of Human Rights and Fundamental Freedoms 1950). It was signed in Rome on 4 November 1950, the UK ratified it on 8 March 1951 and it came into force on 3 September 1953[7]. It has been directly applicable within contracting states with monist legal systems but, unless incorporated, not within dualist states like the UK, Ireland or certain Scandinavian countries. However, the Court has held that it is not necessary for the Convention to be incorporated into domestic law[8]. The European Union is not a party to the Convention and for the time being cannot become one[9], but does import the Convention into its jurisprudence[10].

The ECHR has been supplemented or amended by 11 subsequent Protocols[11] (and see also the two Agreements on the persons participating in proceedings before the Commission/Court[12]).

As one of the earliest Council of Europe treaties the ECHR serves to clarify certain of the Council of Europe's membership requirements. To join, the 1949 Statute of the Council of Europe provides a state must subscribe to 'the rule of law' and everyone within it must enjoy 'human rights and fundamental freedoms'[13]. The rights and freedoms set out in the ECHR may be viewed as the minimum required to be respected by the domestic laws of states applying for membership. The inference is that states on joining the Council of Europe are expected to accede to the ECHR and this has generally come to be regarded as a 'political obligation'[14].

As a result, the ECHR:

'... has evolved into a European bill of rights, with the European Court of Human Rights having a role akin to that of a constitutional court in a federal legal system'[15].

1.3   Other human rights treaties and the ECHR compared

The Convention in article 53 clarifies that it does not oust any other right or freedom domestically in force in a state or (and this is more significant in the case of the UK) to which the state is otherwise bound internationally. This is particularly relevant in

---

7   But the 'right of individual petition' and 'compulsory jurisdiction of the Court' provisions (for which see below) only commenced on 5 July 1955 and 21 January 1959, respectively.
8   *Lawless v Ireland (No 3)* (1961) 1 EHRR 15; *Ireland v United Kingdom* (1978) 2 EHRR 25.
9   In Opinion 2/94 [1996] ECR I-1759 the ECJ took the view the EU cannot become a party to the ECHR under the current treaties.
10   Treaty on European Union 1992, art F(2).
11   As of 1 November 1998 the 11th Protocol altered the institutional structure established under the Convention and the layout of the Convention itself (see below).
12   The European Agreement relating to Persons participating in Proceedings of the European Commission and Court of Human Rights, signed in London on 6 May 1969 (ETS No 67); the European Agreement relating to Persons participating in Proceedings of the European Court of Human Rights, signed in Strasbourg on 5 March 1996 (ETS No 161).
13   Statute, art 3.
14   Harris, O'Boyle and Warbrick, *Law of the European Convention on Human Rights*, 1995, p 1.
15   Harris *et al*, p 2.

view of the omission of some rights from the ECHR, such as rights relating to asylum which are dealt with by the separate Refugee Convention drafted at about the same time[16]. It also provides an opening for arguments in cases under the Human Rights Act (HRA) 1998[17] to be supported by provisions of other key treaties such as:

- The Universal Declaration of Human Rights 1948,
- The International Covenant on Civil and Political Rights 1966, and
- The Convention against Torture and other Cruel, Inhuman or Degrading Treatment or Punishment 1984.

The ECHR's coverage of rights and freedoms is based upon that of the Universal Declaration of Human Rights 1948[18] and it is the European equivalent of the ICCPR (the International Covenant on Civil and Political Rights 1966)[19], another UN treaty. The ICCPR and ECHR are not identical, though, and so on some points the protection provided by the former is superior[20]. The UK has ratified the ICCPR[1] but as with the ECHR (until now) has not incorporated it into domestic law. As an equivalent to the ECHR's right of individuals to apply to the Strasbourg Court[2], the ICCPR has a right of individual communication whereby individuals may complain to the ICCPR's Human Rights Committee[3], but it is available in an optional protocol and the UK has not ratified it.

The UN's Convention against Torture and other Cruel, Inhuman or Degrading Treatment or Punishment 1984 is referred to as the Convention against Torture, or CAT, for short. It entered into force on 26 June 1987 and the UK ratified it on 8 December 1988. The body established under this treaty to monitor the period reports of the state parties and adjudicate in individual cases is the Committee against Torture, but the right of individuals to access the Committee is optional and the UK has not opted in[4]. Article 3 of CAT and article 3 of the ECHR similarly prohibit torture.

---

16 1951 Convention Relating to the Status of Refugees 189 UNTS 137 (drafted under the auspices of the United Nations rather than the Council of Europe).
17 On this point see pp 54-55.
18 GA Res 217a (III).
19 UKTS 6 (1977); 999 UNTS 171. As an equivalent to the ECHR's right of individual petition (see below) the ICCPR has a right of individual communication whereby individuals may complain to the ICCPR's Human Rights Committee, but it is optional and the UK has not accepted it.
20 For example, art 26 prohibits discrimination more effectively because the ECHR equivalent, art 14, can only be relied upon incidentally (see below).
1   On 20 May 1976.
2   See section 7.3 on p 27, below.
3   The 'Human Rights Committee' should not be confused with the 'Human Rights *Commission*', which is the UN's main human rights body meeting inter-governmentally to make political decisions. The ICCPR's 'Human Rights *Committee*' and the CAT's '*Committee* against Torture', on the other hand, are established under particular treaties and they comprise experts sitting in an individual capacity and not as country representatives serving a national interest. They monitor country reports that must be submitted periodically by the state parties under the treaty concerned and adjudicate in cases brought by individuals in those of the states that have accepted individual right of access to that enforcement machinery. The UN's human rights organisations are based in Geneva where they share a single secretariat (ie civil service) known as the Human Rights Centre.
4   See previous footnote.

CAT should not be confused with the Council of Europe's European Convention for the Prevention of Torture and Inhuman or Degrading Treatment or Punishment 1987[5], the language of which is lifted from article 3 of the ECHR. Under this Convention is established the European Committee for the Prevention of Torture and Inhuman or Degrading Treatment or Punishment. This Committee has unrestricted access to individuals in detention, so as to try prevent ill-treatment, but no equivalent to the ECHR Court or even the UN Committees' power to adjudicate in individual cases. On the other hand, the ECHR has no such preventative function.

The ECHR is virtually exclusively concerned with civil and political rights but is complemented by other Council of Europe treaties on human rights, such as the European Social Charter. The Charter complements the ECHR in much the same way as the UN's International Convention on Economic, Social and Cultural Rights complements the ICCPR. Finally, a recent and relevant addition to the Council of Europe's catalogue of treaties is the 1997 European Convention on Nationality[6], which is not yet in force or ratified by the UK but should be taken into account whenever considering ECHR references to nationality.

The Human Rights Act 1998 has now put the possible incorporation of at least some of these other UK international obligations onto the agenda.

1.4 Sources of Convention law

The most important resources for the practitioner are naturally the Convention itself and accompanying Protocols (and the Council of Europe's own guidance on their contents – the original working papers and explanatory notes – can be very helpful). The next most indispensable resource in case law. In the UK Sweet & Maxwell's European Human Rights Reports (EHRR) are more relied upon than Strasbourg's official reports as the latter can be harder to find and less user friendly and, annoyingly, have no uniform citation style. The EHRR is excellently complemented by Sweet & Maxwell's European Human Rights Law Review (EHRLR) and these together with Internet access to the invaluable Council of Europe web site will provide the practitioner with most normal resource requirements. Details of these (and some other sources) now follow.

The Convention and Protocols, travaux and explanatory notes

The ECHR (as amended on 1 November 1998) and its Protocols are reproduced at the end of this book and are available on the Internet at www.dhcour.coe.fr complete with signature, ratification and commencement dates.

The Convention should be read together with the working papers relating to the treaty text; these are published as *The Collected Edition of the Travaux Préparatoires of the European Convention on Human Rights* (Martinus Nijhoff, 1975).

Further, on the earlier Protocols see *The Explanatory Reports on the 2nd to 5th Protocols*, H(71)11 (1971), available on request from the Council of Europe.

5 ETS 126.
6 See chapter 8.

Cases

Official reports: Series A and Series B and the new RJD; CD and DR

The official Court reports (for Commission reports, see next) are referred to as Series A (which contain judgements and decisions) and Series B (the written pleadings, oral arguments and related documents). Series B is very out of date and little referred to in practice. Since 1996 the official reports are referred to as Reports of Judgements and Decisions, or RJD (and now include Commission reports; see next).

The official Commission reports covering 1959 to 1974 is the Collection of Decisions of the European Commission of Human Rights, or CD for short. Since 1975 the series (published quarterly) has been called the Decisions and Reports of the European Commission on Human Rights, or DR (and sometimes D&R) for short. The DR series is now being incorporated into the RJD series.

The Digest and the Yearbook

The Digest of Strasbourg Case-Law Relating to the European Convention on Human Rights contains article-by-article summaries of Court and Commission case law since 1984. Some case law can also be found in the Yearbook of the European Convention on Human Rights.

The EHRR

The European Human Rights Reports (EHRR) are published in the UK by Sweet & Maxwell and report Court and Commission cases. In practice it tends to be this series that is most relied upon and cited by UK lawyers.

Cases on the Internet

There is now a huge database of case law available at www.dhcour.coe.fr. It includes the text of judgments, decisions, reports and resolutions, an article-by-article digest of cases (in 'Case-Law Information Notes' within 'General Information'), lists of recent judgements and pending cases and also press releases (some of which, on recent decisions of note, are very helpful). Also try www.beagle.org.uk/echr.

Other case sources

Other ECHR case sources include the invaluable though out-of-date resource *The Case Law of The European Convention on Human Rights Relating to Immigration, Asylum and Extradition*, Joanna Stevens, September 1992 (an ILPA/Law Society publication). Relevant Commission and Court cases are listed with extracts.

The Rules of Court

The Rules of Procedure of the European Court of Human Rights now current came into force on 4 November 1998 and are available at www.dhcour.coe.fr. They describe the constitution of the Court and its procedures.

Other materials

The EHRLR

The European Human Rights Law Review (EHRLR) is published in the UK by Sweet & Maxwell (six issues a year) and contains case summaries, articles and new items. It is widely used by UK lawyers as a companion to the EHRR.

Yearbook

The Yearbook (see above) includes, for example, resolutions of the Parliamentary Assembly.

2.   What one needs to know of the Convention to run Human Rights Act cases

2.1   An immediate need to know a novel jurisprudence

The incorporated provisions of the ECHR have the force of law in our domestic system. This means that from the commencement of the HRA there is suddenly a bill of rights against which the courts and tribunals in this country have to check the validity of acts and decisions of public authorities and the provisions of law under which those acts and decisions are taken. This immediately requires a detailed knowledge of the full catalogue of incorporated rights. However, that is not all: a state which simply enacts a novel bill of rights will then set about developing a jurisprudence of it, but the UK by contrast is incorporating a bill of rights that has been in force since 1953 and consequently has over 40 years' worth of case law clarifying the rights and how they are to be applied. The courts and tribunals here are not to set about defining and applying the incorporated articles *de novo*, but in the light of all Strasbourg jurisprudence. Section 2(1) of the HRA imposes the obligation to import that jurisprudence: it provides that a court or tribunal determining a question which has arisen under the Act must, so far as it is relevant to the proceedings, take into account any:

- judgment, decision, declaration or advisory opinion of the Court;
- opinion[7] or decision[8] of the Commission;
- decision of the Committee of Ministers.

There is therefore a warehouse full of jurisprudence that is immediately to be digested, and it includes not only case law clarifying the scope of each incorporated right, but unfamiliar terminology, concepts, rules of construction and judicial techniques.

2.2   The nature of the Convention, rules of interpretation, method by which to apply a right and content of the incorporated rights themselves

For present purposes the Strasbourg jurisprudence is presented in four categories. In the first, concepts going to the nature of the Convention are explained and, in the process, the terms 'state responsibility', 'subsidiary' (in relation to the Court's role), 'positive and negative obligations' and 'vertical vs horizontal' effects. The second category concerns the rules developed by the Court for interpreting the Convention

---

7   In any Report under art 31 of the Convention (see above).
8   In connection with arts 26 or 27(2) (see above).

and the third comprises an analysis of the method or approach the Court takes when applying a specific right to an established set of facts. This analysis clarifies the doctrines of 'proportionality' and the 'margin of appreciation'. In the fourth category is an article by article summary of the scope of each incorporated right.

Throughout, the tendency is to view and explain the jurisprudence from the perspective of a UK immigration and nationality practitioner.

3.   Nature of the Convention: the key concepts of state responsibility, the subsidiary role of the Court, positive and negative obligations, and vertical vs horizontal effect

Article 1 of the Convention provides that the:

'... Contracting Parties shall secure to everyone within their jurisdiction the rights and freedoms defined in Section 1 ...'

One might say that this article imposes positive and negative obligations on states and is a basis of the concept of state responsibility, which in turn defines the relationship between the Court and each state party and leads to a distinction between horizontal and vertical applications or effects of the Convention rights.

This last sentence would be incomprehensible to a UK practitioner unfamiliar with the Convention. It is packed with concepts that illustrate that while the UK has slowly been moving towards a political decision to incorporate, the jurisprudence of the Convention has been developing, requiring us, upon incorporation, immediately to familiarise with a matured jurisprudence. Unpacking the sentence, though, and explaining each concept in turn is not difficult.

First, state responsibility as evidenced by article 1 is the responsibility of a state to secure the rights and freedoms protected by the Convention and to be their primary protector. This means that the Strasbourg Court has only a subsidiary function. The point was made over 20 years ago in *Handyside*[9]:

'The Court points out that the machinery of protection established by the Convention is subsidiary to the national systems safeguarding human rights ... The Convention leaves to each Contracting State, in the first place, the task of securing the rights and liberties it enshrines. The institutions created by it make their own contribution to this task but they become involved only through contentious proceedings and once all domestic remedies have been exhausted.'

Harris[10] puts it this way:

'The overall scheme of the Convention is that the initial and primary responsibility for the protection of human rights lies with the contracting parties. The Strasbourg authorities are there to monitor their action, exercising a power of review comparable to that of a federal constitutional court over conduct by democratically elected governments or legislatures within the federation.'

---

9   (1976) 1 EHRR 737 at para 48.
10   Harris *et al* at p 14.

State responsibility involves what Convention jurisprudence refers to as positive and negative obligations. A negative obligation requires the state not to interfere with an individual's enjoyment of a right and in short is an obligation to do nothing. A positive obligation requires the state to take steps to protect an individual's rights; in short, to do something. Article 3, for example, imposes a negative obligation on the state to refrain from subjecting individuals to torture or inhuman or degrading treatment or punishment, but also imposes a positive obligation to protect individuals from such acts. So in *Ireland v United Kingdom*[11] the UK was in breach of article 3 for subjecting prisoners to degrading treatment contrary to the negative obligation, while in *Chahal*[12] the Court found the UK's proposed deportation would breach article 3 as being contrary to the positive duty to prevent torture. The Court in *Stubbings*[13], concerned with article 8 (right to respect for private and family life), made the point succinctly:

'… although the object of Article 8 is essentially that of protecting the individual against arbitrary interference by the public authorities, it does not merely compel the State to abstain from such interference: there may, in addition to this primary negative undertaking, be positive obligations inherent in an effective respect for private or family life.'

A positive duty may be express, such as in article 2 (right to life), or may be found by the Court to be implied, such as in article 8. Either way, the positive obligation doctrine means it is possible to succeed against the state on the ground that it has failed to take steps to protect rights.

A further aspect of the concept of state responsibility is that it requires an allegation of breach to be levelled against the state rather than an individual or non-state organisation. The Convention applies vertically (between the state and an individual), not horizontally (between individuals). It is for this reason that it is only the acts of a 'public authority' that may be challenged under the HRA[14].

However, where positive obligations are in play the Convention can in practice have a horizontal application. This is because where a positive obligation requires the state to protect an individual's rights, the state may have to protect them from the acts of another individual. So an individual might proceed against the state under article 3 for failing to protect him or her from torture or inhuman or degrading treatment or punishment by another individual. In *A v United Kingdom*[15], for example, the UK was found to be in breach of article 3 for not protecting a child from corporal punishment meted out by the child's step-father at home. The breach was by the UK of a positive obligation in article 3, though may appear to have been by the parent. The Court in *Stubbings*[16] (to continue the quote above) phrased it more elegantly:

'These obligations [positive obligations] may involve the adoption of measures designed to secure respect for private life even in the sphere of the relations between individuals themselves.'

11 (1978) 2 EHRR 25.
12 (1996) 23 EHRR 413.
13 (1996) 23 EHRR 213 at 235.
14 HRA, s 6; see chapter 2, section 2.4 at p 33, below.
15 [1998] 3 FCR 597. See also *Y v United Kingdom* (1994) 17 EHRR 238.
16 (1996) 23 EHRR 213 at 235.

Before turning from the nature of the Convention, it is notable that the extent to which Convention jurisprudence has been able to develop has been limited by the Convention's nature as an inter-governmental treaty binding only the states that ratify it. Regarding the protection of individuals from other individuals, for example, rights have been applied with horizontal effect only as a consequence of state responsibility. However, incorporated into domestic law the Convention's rights and accompanying jurisprudence may have the opportunity to develop without reverence for the state responsibility concept. This may free the courts and tribunals here to be bolder and, for example, consider applying Convention rights horizontally.

4. The rules for interpreting the Convention

Interpreting the broad guarantees of the Convention is done with reference to a number of approaches and principles.

4.1 Teleological (or purposive) approach and the dynamic (or evolutionary) approach – a departure from the domestic norm

The teleological or purposive approach[17] is undoubtedly the principal rule of interpretation used in Convention jurisprudence and it gives priority to the purpose of the Convention[18], namely the protection of rights and freedoms. It is supported by article 31 of the Vienna Convention on the Law of Treaties 1969[19].

The dynamic or evolutionary approach may be applied in tandem and derives from *Tyrer v United Kingdom*[1], perceiving the Convention to be a:

'... living instrument which ... must be interpreted in the light of present day conditions'.

The much more recent case of *Loizidou v Turkey*[2] confirms this approach:

'That the Convention is a living instrument which must be interpreted in the light of present-day conditions is firmly rooted in the Court's case-law. ... Such an approach, in the Court's view, is not confined to the substantive provisions of the Convention, but also applies to those provisions, such as Articles 25[3] and 46[4], which govern the operation of the Convention's enforcement machinery. It follows that these provisions cannot be interpreted solely in accordance with the intentions of their authors as expressed more than forty years ago ...'

---

17 Eg see *Wemhoff v Germany* (1968) 1 EHRR 55, at para 8.
18 See its Preamble.
19 UKTS 58 (1980).
1   (1978) 2 EHRR 1 at para 31.
2   (1995) 20 EHRR 99, at para 71.
3   Concerning the right of individuals to bring cases. Since 1 November 1998 (the Protocol 11 changes) the corresponding provision is art 34.
4   Concerning the compulsory nature of the Court's jurisdiction. Since 1 November 1998 still within art 46.

Consequently the meaning of a provision may evolve in keeping with the changing morality and standards of the day, so an act may be outlawed which at the Convention's inception may have been considered acceptable, such as corporal punishment.

These approaches are largely unfamiliar to UK domestic law. The rule in *Pepper v Hart*[5] does enable a court of tribunal to look to the purpose of a piece of legislation but only in cases of ambiguity. Otherwise it has been the ordinary and natural meaning that usually prevails. In HRA cases traditional domestic interpretative techniques must give way to the Strasbourg techniques.

4.2   Freedom from the doctrine of precedent

A further adjustment to be made in HRA cases concerns the approach to precedent. It follows from the dynamic approach that the strict doctrine of precedent is in conflict with Convention case law, as a given provision cannot have a meaning that is fixed for all time. Accordingly, previous decisions that are on point are to be assessed for value rather than unquestioningly obeyed as precedent in the UK sense. Recent decisions will weigh more than old ones[6]. Very old ones, in Strasbourg jurisprudence, are not even necessarily overturned but may simply be rendered otiose by the passing of time.

The strict precedent doctrine is also at odds with the context-specific meanings attributed to Convention provisions in Strasbourg case law. That is to say, in Convention jurisprudence the meaning given to a provision is derived from the specific context of the case. Accordingly the criteria emerging from a judgement may need to be adapted in a different factual context.

As the precedent doctrine does not apply, a decision in a given Convention case is therefore only strictly binding upon the parties to that case, just as has always been true of cases before the statutory immigration appellate authorities.

Notwithstanding the inapplicability of strict precedent, as a matter of common-sense and of the certainty principle an existing decision should be followed where there are no cogent reasons to depart from it[7].

4.3   Autonomous meanings and historical analysis

The meaning of a particular term or expression is not necessarily the same in Convention jurisprudence as that exact term or expression in domestic law; it may instead be given an autonomous meaning[8], such as 'civil rights and obligations' in article 6[9].

Further, in deriving a meaning Strasbourg jurisprudence permits an examination of the Convention's *travaux préparatoires*, though it is possible that the dynamic approach may of course negate the original intent underlying a right.

---

5   [1993] AC 593.
6   Whether a decision was unanimous and of the full Court also goes to weight, and any Court decision counts more than a Commission decision.
7   *Cossey v United Kingdom* (1990) 13 EHRR 622, at para 35.
8   Eg *Adolf v Austria* (1982) 4 EHRR 313, at para 30.
9   In English law the expression covers rights and obligations in public law, but not in Convention jurisprudence where it is largely confined to private law rights. See art 6 at pp 21-22, below.

4.4 Other approaches

It may also be appropriate to consider the grammatical approach (comparing the English and French authentic texts), a systemic method (analysing where the provision lies within the Convention and where it ends and the next begins), a consensual approach[10] (finding the common standard among member states) and even the literal interpretation method (giving a provision its ordinary meaning).

Of course, account may also be taken of other Council of Europe treaties, resolutions and recommendations and even non-Council of Europe treaties and non-ECHR case law.

5.   The method by which to apply a Convention right

5.1   Six stages

When considering whether there has been a violation of one of the Convention rights on an established set of facts the Strasbourg jurisprudence requires various issues to be addressed. This general approach and the nature of the issues to be addressed are not set out in the Convention or any Protocol or even in the Rules of Court, but emerge from case law. As a result, different commentators group the issues in different ways and so their number and even the order in which they are to be considered can vary. For present purposes six issues are identified, each marking a new stage in the consideration of a given case. These are:

1.   Whether a right guaranteed by the Convention or a Protocol is *prima facie* engaged;
2.   Whether any exceptions are permitted in respect of that right or whether any reservation or derogation applies;
3.   If an exception is permitted, whether it is provided for in the state's domestic law;
4.   Whether the state has a legitimate objective in applying the exception;
5.   Whether applying the exception is necessary to achieve that legitimate objective – ie the limitation on or interference with the right must be in proportion to the objective to be achieved;
6.   Whether the state is to be permitted some leeway in exercising its discretion – ie a margin of appreciation – even though the above requirements, including proportionality, are satisfied.

These are now considered in turn (but see also pp 53-55 for a re-statement of the stages with an immigration focus and chapter 5 as a whole for the appreciation of the stages in an article 8 context).

5.2   Whether a right guaranteed by the Convention or a Protocol is *prima facie* engaged

Whether an established set of facts *prima facie* engages one or more of the rights depends primarily on the scope of each right, as to which see below.

10 Eg *Tyrer v United Kingdom* (1978) 2 EHRR 1, at para 31.

The right must also be available in the sense that a state can only be in breach of the Convention and Protocol provisions it has ratified. So article 3(2) of the Fourth Protocol (no one shall be deprived of the right to enter the territory of the state of which he is a national) was not engaged in *East African Asians v United Kingdom*[11] as the UK had not (and still has not) ratified that Protocol.

However, there may be some scope for engaging an *un*incorporated right via Community law. Where, for example, a UK court or tribunal makes an article 177[12] reference to the European Court of Justice (ECJ), the ECJ may draw on a provision of the Convention and Protocols as forming part of its jurisprudence[13]. At the time of writing, therefore, in *R v Secretary of State for the Home Department, ex p Kaur*[14] the High Court has referred questions on the position of British Overseas citizens and the ECJ will be invited to take account of article 3(2) of the Fourth Protocol in answering them.

5.3   Whether any exceptions are permitted or whether any reservation or derogation applies

The great majority of the rights are not absolute, which means that even where the right is *prima facie* engaged there will be no violation if the act or omission complained of falls within a permitted exception, reservation or derogation.

A derogation is possible under article 15 (derogation in time of emergency), save in respect of certain specified articles including, notably, article 3. The UK has made one article 15 derogation and it is set out in the HRA, Sch 3, Pt I. It concerns article 5(3) and Northern Ireland. Regarding reservations, article 57 permits them to be made at signature or ratification and the UK made such a reservation when ratifying the First Protocol. The reservation is set out in the HRA, Sch 3, Pt II and concerns education.

Of far greater practical importance are the exceptions, also referred to as limitations, interferences or restrictions, that the articles conferring a right mostly include in their individual wording. Article 2(1), for example, provides 'No one shall be deprived of his life intentionally *save in the execution of a sentence of a court ...*' (emphasis supplied) and further express exceptions are set out in article 2(2).

Articles 8 to 11, inclusive, are particularly notable where exceptions are concerned because they are stylistically identical: each has two paragraphs, the first of which sets out the right and the second of which sets out the permitted exceptions by means of a formula that varies only slightly from article to article.

Where the articles list permitted exceptions, those lists are exhaustive and no others can be implied[15]. However, where no express exceptions are listed in an article, it is possible they may be implied[16]. If an exception is not express and cannot be implied, the article is referred to as absolute, ie. giving an absolute guarantee. This

---

11   (1973) 3 EHRR 76.
12   Of the EC Treaty.
13   Eg see the Treaty on European Union 1992, art F(2) requiring respect the fundamental rights as guaranteed by the ECHR, though this applies to the EU rather that the EC. See also chapter 7.
14   Decision of Lightman J on 11 December 1998 to make an art 177 reference; questions actually referred in April 1999.
15   See *Golder* (1975) 1 EHRR 524, at para 44 (on art 8(2)).
16   As has been done, for example, in respect of art 14 and Protocol 1, art 1.

is so in respect of article 3, the prohibition on torture, etc, and there cannot even be an exception based on the individual being a terrorist[17].

The availability of exceptions to one degree or another – or their unavailability – is not arbitrary but an attempt by the drafters of the Convention to attain a balance between the rights of an individual and the compromises that must be made living in a democratic society. For example, one of the article 10(2) exceptions to the article 10(1) right to freedom of expression is where the 'protection of the reputation or rights of others' is at stake, so a free press must be balanced against a right to privacy. Finding the right balance between the rights of the individual and demands of the surrounding democratic society underlies the entire approach to the Convention's application[18], and as its application is 'dynamic' (changing with the moral and other conventions of the day – see rules of interpretation, below), that balance is liable to shift in time.

5.4   If an exception is permitted, whether it is provided for in the state's domestic law

Where an article conferring a right permits exceptions to it, a state relying on such an exception must provide for it in its domestic law. The rule of law is one of the Council of Europe's membership requirements and it flows from this that a state must act in accordance with its own laws in purporting lawfully to deny a right.

Many of the articles make this requirement overtly: for example, articles 8(2) to 11(2) provide there can be no interference with the rights 'except such as is in accordance with the law' or 'as are prescribed by law'. These expressions are synonymous.

Domestic law in this regard may include the common law but must be accessible and comprehensible. Individuals must have 'an indication that is adequate in the circumstances of the legal rules applicable' and those legal rules must be 'formulated with sufficient precision to enable the citizen to regulate his conduct'[19].

It is unusual for there to be a contentious issue as to this requirement.

5.5   Whether the state has a legitimate objective in applying the exception

To be justifiable an exception must be applied to achieve a legitimate objective. So where the state wishes to interfere with a right, a legitimate purpose in doing so must be stipulated. Again it is articles 8 to 11 that best illustrate this, expressly referring to the interests of public safety, national security, and so on. These are so broad it would be very unlikely for a government to fail to advance a legitimate objective and so this stage of the consideration of a case is not a significant one in practice.

---

17   *Chahal* (1996) 23 EHRR 413.
18   As the Court said in *Soering* (1989) 11 EHRR 439: 'inherent in the whole of the Convention is a search for a fair balance between the demands of the general interest of the community and the requirements of the protection of the individual's fundamental rights'.
19   *Sunday Times v United Kingdom* (1979) 2 EHRR 245, at para 49.

5.6 Whether the exception is necessary to achieve the objective – 'proportionality'

The principle of proportionality is used extensively in European law and in the present context applies particularly where there is a balance to be struck between the enjoyment of rights and freedoms and justifiable interference with their enjoyment. It is by no means limited to articles 8 to 11, but most breaches of these provisions are on proportionality grounds given the balance to be struck between the first and second paragraphs of each of those articles[20]. The second paragraph of each requires the rights in the first to be balanced against such interference, limitations or restrictions as are 'necessary in a democratic society'[21]. This means the interference with or limitation on the right must be no greater than is necessary to achieve the legitimate objective. In other words, it must be proportionate to the legitimate aim pursued.

An early case applying the proportionality doctrine in terms is *Handyside v United Kingdom*[1], concerning The Little Red Schoolbook, seized by the police under the Obscene Publications Act. The UK argued there was no violation of the right to freedom of expression in article 10(1) as its action was necessary for the protection of morals under article 10(2). The Court said at paragraph 47 that it must investigate whether:

'... the protection of morals[2] in a democratic society necessitated the various measures taken against the applicant'.

In the Court's view the case:

'... brought to light clear-cut differences of opinion on a crucial problem, namely, how to determine whether the actual ... [interferences] ... complained of by the applicant were "necessary in a democratic society", "for the protection of moral"'.

In paragraph 48 the Court said:

' ... whilst the adjective "necessary", within the meaning of Article 10 paragraph 2, is not synonymous with "indispensable" ... neither has it the flexibility of such expressions as "admissible", "ordinary", ... "useful" ... or "desirable"'.

Rather, it implies a 'pressing social need'.
In paragraph 49 the Court said its:

"... supervisory functions oblige it to pay the utmost attention to the principles characterising a "democratic society". Freedom of expression constitutes one of the essential foundations of such a society. ... This means, amongst other things, that every ... [interference] ... in this sphere must be *proportionate to the legitimate aim pursued*' (emphasis supplied).

In short, the doctrine is that the state's interference with a right must not be excessive in all the circumstances – it cannot use a sledgehammer to drive in a pin.

20 For further discussion see p 54.
21 Arts 8(2), 9(2), 10(2), 11(2).
1   (1976) 1 EHRR 737.
2   Note that this was the legitimate objective identified by the UK.

In *Dudgeon*[3] safeguarding vulnerable members of society was held to be a legitimate aim of anti-gay legislation, but it was held not to be proportionate to this aim to criminalise the actions of consenting adults in private:

> 'Although members of the public who regard homosexuality as immoral may be shocked, offended or disturbed by the commission by others of private homosexual acts, this cannot on its own warrant ... penal sanctions'.

In *Moustaquim*[4] the Court expressed it in terms of a balancing exercise:

> '... it appears that, as far as respect for the applicant's family life is concerned, a proper balance was not achieved between the interests involved, and that the means employed was therefore disproportionate to the legitimate aim pursued. Accordingly there was a violation of Article 8'.

In all cases it must be 'convincingly established'[5] by the state that its interference is proportionate to the legitimate aim pursued and to do so its reasons for the interference have to be 'relevant and sufficient'[6].

An interference is not only disproportionate if it is wider than the minimum necessary to achieve the aim, but also if it obliterates the rights altogether. In *F v Switzerland*[7] the prohibition of marriage in certain circumstances obliterated the article 12 right to marry.

In some more obvious cases the Court does not expressly refer to proportionality, but simply finds the interference is not 'necessary in a democratic society'. In the Spycatcher cases, for example, once the book was published in the USA and being imported into the UK, interference with a free press (trying to ban publication in the UK) was no longer 'necessary' for the purposes of article 10(2).

For a proposed rationalisation of the proportionality test, see the Advocate General's Opinion in the ECJ case of *Grogan*[8].

Proportionality can be an important tool in applying the Convention. It is likely to arise extensively in HRA cases and effectively will take the place of rationality challenges in judicial review cases[9]. The rationality test refers to:

> '... a decision which is so outrageous in its defiance of logic or accepted moral standards that no sensible person who had applied his mind to the question to be decided could have arrived at it'[10].

However, under the Convention the starting point is that a protected right should not be violated and that any departure from this should be strictly limited to instances where it is necessary in a democratic society. This is a harder test in the sense that the

---

3   (1981) 4 EHRR 149.
4   (1991) 13 EHRR 802, at para 46.
5   *Barthold v Germany* (1985) 7 EHRR 383 at 403 (an art 10 case).
6   *Handyside*, para 50.
7   (1987) 10 EHRR 411.
8   [1991] ECR I-4685 at 4719.
9   See above for the subsidiary role of the Court giving it a supervisory function broadly corresponding to that of the High Court in judicial review.
10   *Council of Civil Service Unions v Minister for the Civil Service* [1985] AC 374 at 410 *per* Lord Diplock.

government will find it harder to justify a given breach as being proportionate than to defend the decision as being rational[11].

5.7 Whether the state is to be permitted a 'margin of appreciation'[12]

The proportionality requirement is subject to a leeway, known as the margin of appreciation, that the Court is sometimes willing to allow the states[13]. It means:

> '... the state is allowed a certain measure of discretion, subject to European supervision, when it takes legislative, administrative or judicial action in the area of a Convention right. ... the doctrine has its counterpart in the context of judicial review in national systems of administrative law and serves as a lubricant at the interface between individual rights and public interest'[14].

The case that established the margin of appreciation doctrine was *Handyside*[15], the Little Red Schoolbook case already referred to in the context of proportionality, above. The Court was wrestling with the moral requirements of the UK (such as they were 25 years ago) to test whether they necessitated an interference with the applicant's article 10(1) right to freedom of expression; ie to test the proportionality of the interference. Although the Court was in the best position to pronounce on proportionality, it acknowledged the UK was better positioned to know the country's moral requirements of the day and so had to be permitted some leeway in assessing whether they really required protection from the publication it found offensive. The Court said in paragraph 48:

> 'By reason of their direct and continuous contact with the vital forces of their countries, State authorities are in principle in a better position than the international judge to give an opinion on the exact content of these requirements[16] as well as on the "necessity" of ... [an interference] ... intended to meet them. ... . [I]t is for the national authorities to make the initial assessment of the reality of the pressing social need implied by the notion of "necessity" in this context. Consequently, Article 10 paragraph 2 leaves to the Contracting States a margin of appreciation. This margin is given both to the domestic legislator ("prescribed by law") and to the bodies, judicial amongst others, that are called upon to interpret and apply the laws in force ... '

In paragraph 49 the Court added 'Nevertheless, Article 10 paragraph 2 does not give the Contracting States an unlimited power of appreciation' as it is subject to the Court applying the proportionality requirement.

In short, the relevant authorities in a state have a discretion in judging what restriction on the exercise of a right is necessary to safeguard a legitimate interest and the extent of that discretion is the margin of appreciation. Depending on the

---

11 On the relationship between proportionality and *Wednesbury* unreasonableness, see *Salah Abdadou* (1998) 6 March (Court of Session), reported in Immigration Law Update, Vol 1, no 9 (8 May 1998).
12 See *The Problem of the Margin of Appreciation* [1997] EHRLR 380, by Nicholas Lavender. See also chapter 2, section 2.1 at p 31. See p 109 for the position in Community law.
13 Some reverse this, saying the margin of appreciation is subject to proportionality – see the next section.
14 Harris *et al*, pp 12, 14-15.
15 (1976) 1 EHRR 737.
16 Ie the moral requirements of the state.

case (including the state's legitimate objective), at one extreme there may be a very narrow margin and, at the other, a virtual *carte blanche*[17].

The doctrine particularly, but not exclusively, applies to proportionality. Harris[18] states:

> '... in assessing the proportionality of the state's acts, a certain degree of deference is given to the judgement of national authorities when they weigh competing public and individual interests in view of their special knowledge and overall responsibility under domestic law ...'

and as proportionality arises most frequently in respect of the article 8 to 11 rights, interference with which may be justifiable on broad grounds, so does the margin of appreciation. However, a margin of appreciation may also be permitted, for example, in respect of articles imposing a positive obligation to act, in the context of article 1 of the First Protocol (which uniquely permits a 'public interest' justification) and in other instances where the state must make an assessment or exercise its judgement (like article 14). The doctrine does not apply, though, to article 3, being an absolute right.

The doctrine's rationale as explained in *Blackstone's Guide to the Human Rights Act 1998*[19] is that:

> 'The Convention is an international human rights instrument, policed by an international court. The Strasbourg institutions have to be sensitive to the need for "subsidiarity", that is, to ensuring that the member states' own political and cultural traditions are respected. For example, what may offend religious sensitivities in one country may be an aspect of free speech in another.'

In HRA cases it is not clear how the margin of appreciation doctrine will translate into domestic law. It is suggested it should not apply at all to the interpretation in UK courts and tribunals of the incorporated Convention rights. The doctrine is appropriate as a tool of the Strasbourg Court as there an international treaty has to be applied with approximate uniformity across states with differing traditions and legal systems, but under the HRA the incorporated rights are simply provisions of UK domestic law and the doctrine should have no place. If this is right and the doctrine is not to apply, there will be opportunities to revisit domestically cases that have failed as a result of its application in Strasbourg.

5.8 The inter-connections between legitimate objectives, proportionality and the margin of appreciation

Some say proportionality is subject to the margin of appreciation and others that the margin of appreciation is subject to proportionality, but this is a difference of perspective not substance. In *Handyside* it was said the state makes the 'initial assessment' applying a margin of appreciation and the Court then exercises its

---

17 *Rasmussen v Denmark* (1984) 7 EHRR 371 at 380: it depends on the circumstances, the nature of the case and background.
18 Harris *et al*, at p 13.
19 Wadham and Mountfield (1999) at 16.

supervisory function and checks the proportionality requirement, but this just refers to the chronological sequence of administrative decision followed by judicial challenge and does not dictate the order in which matters are to be considered within that challenge. Proportionality and the margin of appreciation are really two sides of the same coin, or two aspects of the same consideration. In the text above, the margin of appreciation is dealt with last to emphasise that it can apply to more than just proportionality; whether there is a legitimate objective in play can benefit from a margin of appreciation too. Indeed, the nature of the objective identified may have an effect on the overall extent of the margin of appreciation allowed. In particular, where the objective concerns national security, public morality or other areas where there can be widely inconsistent approaches among the states, the extent of the margin of appreciation is likely to be greater.

Legitimate objectives, proportionality and the margin of appreciation are not necessarily referred to in those terms in each and every judgement where they arise. Nor are they consistently referred to as the discreet, sequential, issues suggested by the text above. This is symptomatic of the flexibility with which the concepts are applied. No hard and fast rules have emerged regulating their use and there can be an interplay between them[20].

6.   The incorporated rights and freedoms and who enjoys them

6.1   Who enjoys the rights and what can they challenge as a result

The incorporated[1] rights extend to everyone in the jurisdiction[2] regardless of their nationality or immigration status but only a victim or potential 'victim' of a breach of one of those rights may rely on it in taking a case to Strasbourg[3] or in HRA[4] cases (such as before adjudicators, the Tribunal or on judicial review). It is not just individuals who may be victims, but 'any person, non-governmental organisation or group of individuals'[5]. This means legal persons (ie limited companies)[6] are included as are organisations and groups such as unincorporated associations, political parties and churches. The significance of this in the sphere of immigration practice includes the fact that whereas immigration applicants (ie those seeking entry clearance or leave) are individuals, work permit applicants tend to be companies. An intervenors such as an NGO, may be a third party in a case brought by a victim but cannot bring a case on a victim's behalf.

---

20   For a helpful UK case dealing helpfully with this interplay and *Wednesbury* unreasonableness, see *Salah Abdadou* (1998) 6 March (Court of Session), reported in Immigration Law Update, Vol 1, no 9 (8 May 1998).
1   The incorporated rights are the same as the ratified rights (ie. the rights and freedoms of the Convention and of the ratified Protocols), save for art 13 of the Convention which is ratified but not incorporated.
2   ECHR, art 1.
3   ECHR, art 34.
4   HRA, s 7(1), (6) importing art 34.
5   *Ibid.* An individual must also be a victim to have access to the ICCPR's Human Rights Committee and the CAT's Committee against Torture; see section 1.3 above.
6   Being expressly included in art 1 of Protocol 1 does not imply exclusion from the other provisions.

In a HRA case or in taking a case to Strasbourg the challenge may be to administrative decisions of the public authorities, actual provisions of law or a judgement of a court or tribunal.

Among the as yet *un*incorporated rights, immigration and nationality status can be relevant to the enjoyment of rights by individuals. Protocol 4, article 2, applies only to those 'lawfully' within the territory of a state and article 3 of the same applies only to one who is a 'national' of the state. Protocol 7, article 1, is by its nature and in terms limited to an 'alien lawfully resident' in the state.

Although the incorporated rights extend to everyone in the jurisdiction, an person's immigration or nationality status may nonetheless affect the application of the rights to that person; ie the degree to which the state may interfere with the individual's enjoyment of that right. An express example is provided by article 5(1)(f) which states no one shall be deprived of his or her liberty save in respect of:

> '... the lawful arrest or detention of a person to prevent his effecting an unauthorised entry into the country or of a person against whom action is being taken with a view to deportation or extradition'.

6.2 The rights likely to be most commonly relied upon in the immigration context

Article 2 (right to life) is potentially relevant but in practice article 3 (prohibition against torture, etc) has been relied upon in preference and will be a key provision. Article 4 (prohibition of slavery and forced labour) could possibly be helpful and article 5 (right to liberty) could be used to challenge detentions[7]. Article 6 (right to a fair trial) could be very significant if immigration matters can somehow be brought within 'civil rights' for the purposes of that provision[8] and might even be used to test the procedures of the Special Immigration Appeals Commission. Article 8 (right to respect for private and family life) will, like article 3, be another key provision if existing Strasbourg case law is any indication. Article 12 (the right to marry) is unlikely to be of assistance as it is not a right to enter to marry, but article 14 (prohibition of discrimination) will certainly have impact even though it needs to be pleaded in conjunction with one of the other rights. Article 2 of Protocol 1 (right to education) may be obliquely relevant.

The most sorely missed *un*incorporated provision will be article 3 of Protocol 4, guaranteeing the rights of entry and non-expulsion of a state's own nationals.

6.3 Summary of the rights (with an immigration emphasis)

Article 2 – Right to life

The provision protects human life. The state has a negative obligation not to take life and a positive obligation to safeguard it. However, this does not outlaw the death penalty – that is done by Protocol 6. The exceptions (in paragraph 2) include killing

---

7 Eg as in *Chahal* (1997) 23 EHRR 413.
8 See pp 21-22.

in self-defence. Virtually the only case finding a violation of article 2 is *McCann v United Kingdom*[9] (shooting of three IRA members in Gibraltar in 1988); the Court said that as human life is the subject of the article, the 'most careful scrutiny' is required.

Article 3 – Prohibition of torture

Article 3 is an absolute bar on torture, inhuman or degrading treatment or punishment. Article 3 permits no exceptions and there can be no article 15 (see below) derogation. However, it consequently has a high threshold[10]. Torture means deliberate inhuman treatment causing very serious and cruel suffering[11]. Treatment or punishment is inhuman if it causes intense physical and mental suffering, and degrading if it arouses in the victim a feeling of fear, anguish and inferiority capable of humiliating and debasing the victim and possible breaking his physical or moral resistance[12].

In the immigration context article 3 has been applied (alone or in conjunction with article 14) in respect of exclusions from the United Kingdom (*East African Asians v United Kingdom*[13]), extradition (*Soering v United Kingdom*[14]), deportation (*D v United Kingdom*[15]) and expulsion on national security grounds (*Chahal v United Kingdom*[16]). It will be engaged where there are substantial grounds for believing there is a real risk that removal will result in torture or inhuman or degrading treatment or punishment.

Article 3 is considered in depth and contrasted with the Refugee Convention and Protocol in Chapter 4.

Article 4 – Prohibition of slavery and forced labour

Article 4(1) imposes an absolute bar on slavery or servitude. The article 4(2) bar on forced or compulsory labour is subject to exception (work while in detention, military service, work in lieu of military service and emergency or normal civic service).

Article 4 has been little argued in Strasbourg jurisprudence.

Article 5 – Right to liberty and security

Article 5 has developed as a single right rather than two, one on liberty and another on security. It applies as a safeguard against the arbitrary deprivation of liberty by laying down three broad conditions. First, the deprivation of liberty requires a 'procedure prescribed by law'[17]. Second, the deprivation of liberty can only occur in the circumstances set out in article 5(1)(a)-(f) (the last of which concerns detention

---

9 (1995) 21 EHRR 97.
10 'Ill-treatment must attain a minimum level of severity if it is to fall within the scope of Article 3': *Ireland v United Kingdom* (1978) 2 EHRR 25, at para 162.
11 *Ibid*, para 167. In *Aydin v Turkey* (1997) 25 EHRR 251 rape and ill treatment in custody was held to be torture. See also *Aksoy v Turkey* (1997) 23 EHRR 553.
12 *Ibid*.
13 (1973) 3 EHRR 76 (citizens of the UK and Colonies prevented from joining their wives in the UK – the racial discrimination amounted to degrading treatment).
14 (1989) 11 EHRR 439 (extradition to the USA to wait an indefinite period on death row).
15 (1997) 24 EHRR 423 (unavailability of necessary treatment for an AIDS sufferer in the country to which the UK proposed removal).
16 (1996) 23 EHRR 413 (real risk of ill treatment of a terrorist in the country to which the UK proposed removal).
17 Art 5(1).

to prevent unauthorised entry into the country or with a view to deportation or extradition); the list is exhaustive and must be narrowly defined[18]. Third, a person must be told the reasons for his or her arrest[19] and be able to challenge the lawfulness of the detention[20].

In the immigration context it has been established that the obligation to submit to further examination can be an obligation within article 5(1)(b) and therefore a permitted exception[1]. However, detention under article 5(1)(f) can cease to be lawful if deportation or extradition is not carried out diligently or amounts to an abuse of power[2].

Article 6 – Right to a fair trial

The article 6 right has been the most litigated in Strasbourg. Whereas paragraphs 2 and 3 of the article are exclusively concerned with criminal matters, paragraph 1 additionally concerns 'civil rights and obligations'. This expression in our domestic law might include immigration matters, but so far in Strasbourg jurisprudence it has not. Case law confines 'civil' to the private law sphere only[3] and so includes matters such as family law, contract and probate but not rights and obligations in public law. Accordingly article 6 has been found not to apply to immigration issues such as entry and removal (*Uppal v United Kingdom*[4]), asylum (*P v United Kingdom*[5]), deportation (*Agee v United Kingdom*[6]), extradition (*Farmakopolous v Greece*[7]), nationality (*S v Switzerland*[8]) or entry for employment (*X v United Kingdom*[9]) .

However, for two reasons article 6 might still possibly become relevant in immigration practice. First, the traditional Strasbourg interpretation of 'civil' may be evolving. In *Stran Greek Refineries v Greece*[10] the Court said:

> '... it is enough that the outcome of the proceedings should be decisive for private rights and obligations'.

So the door is ajar where it can be argued that a public law right engages a civil right in some way and this has the support of some commentators[11].

Second, if public law proceedings cannot be 'civil' in article 6 there might be some prospect of them becoming 'criminal', at least in part. A matter classified as non-criminal by the state may be held to be criminal for the purposes of article 6[12], although Strasbourg has this far resisted such a classification of any immigration

---

18 *Winterwerp v Netherlands* (1979) 2 EHRR 387.
19 Art 5(2).
20 Art 5(4).
1 *McVeigh v United Kingdom* (1981) 25 DR 15.
2 *Lynas v Switzerland* (1976) 6 DR 141. See also *Zamir v United Kingdom* (1983) 40 DR 42 and *Chahal v United Kingdom* (1996) 23 EHRR 413.
3 *König v Germany* (1978) 2 EHRR 170, at para 95.
4 (1979) 3 EHRR 391. See also *X, Y, Z, V and W v United Kingdom* (1967) 25 CD 117 at 122-123.
5 (1987) 54 DR 211 at 211-212.
6 (1976) 7 DR 164, at paras 27-30.
7 (1990) 64 DR 52.
8 (1988) 59 DR 256.
9 (1977) 9 DR 224 at 226.
10 (1994) 19 EHRR 293, at para 39.
11 Eg Harris *et al* at pp 184-185.
12 See *McFeeley v United Kingdom* (1981) 3 EHRR 161.

case[13], distinguishing between purely criminal matters on the one hand and, on the other, administrative action which also founds criminal liability. The distinction may blur, though, as in the UK extradition is a criminal, not immigration, proceeding and the UK courts and tribunals will need to apply article 6 to it under the HRA.

For article 6 arguments in UK cases see, for example, *R v Secretary of State for the Home Department, ex p Canbolat*[14] and *R v Secretary of State for the Home Department, ex p Uzun*[15].

Article 7 – No punishment without law

One can only be punished if the act was a criminal offence at the time it was done. This guards against retrospective criminal laws.

Article 8 – Right to respect for private and family life

Article 8 is the first of a group of identically structured articles (articles 8 to 11) the first paragraph of which sets out the protected right(s) and the second the permitted exceptions. Article 8 concerns four discrete rights: the right to respect for private life, family life, home and correspondence. It arises often in the immigration context because essentially it is there 'to protect the individual against arbitrary interference by the public authorities'[16]. It imposes negative obligations not to interfere but may also involve positive obligations[17].

The right to respect for private life is a right to personal development and to establish relationships[18] and may be engaged in immigration cases[19]. It includes an individual's sexuality[20] and a right to respect for one's 'physical and moral integrity'[1]. The physical and moral integrity limb is a protection against a lesser level of harm than is required under article 3 and so is easier to establish. However, interference with it may be justifiable under article 8(2) (whereas article 3 admits to no exceptions).

The right to respect for family life has been particularly relied upon in the immigration sphere[2]. '(T)he mutual enjoyment by parent and child of each other's company' constitutes a fundamental element of family life'[3], which means that family life in Strasbourg jurisprudence is essentially about heterosexual couples and their children. Usually the family members must be living together to enjoy family life but there can be exceptions if there is frequent and regular contact[4]. Family life is certainly enjoyed by married couples and possibly by unmarried, cohabiting, couples[5] so long as they are of opposite sex[6]. However, there can only be an interference with family life if it cannot be enjoyed

---

13 A specific example being *Moustaquim v Belgium* (1991) 13 EHRR 802.
14 [1998] 1 All ER 161.
15 [1998] 1 Imm AR 314.
16 *Johnston v Ireland* (1986) 9 EHRR 203, at para 55. See also *Kroon v Netherlands* (1994) 19 EHRR 263.
17 *Johnston v Ireland, supra.*
18 See *Niemetz v Germany* (1992) 16 EHRR 97, at para 29.
19 *Boughanemi v France* (1996) 22 EHRR 228, at para 42.
20 See *Dudgeon v United Kingdom* (1981) 4 EHRR 149.
1   See Harris *et al*, at p 307 and *X and Y v Netherlands* (1985) 8 EHRR 235.
2   See *Constructive Deportation* [1995] EHRLR 63, by N Mole; *The concept of family life under the European Convention on Human Rights* [1998] EHRLR 15, by J Liddy.
3   *B v United Kingdom* (1988) 10 EHRR 87.
4   *Kroon v Netherlands* (1994) 19 EHRR 263.
5   See *X, Y and Z v United Kingdom* (1997) 24 EHRR 143.
6   *X v United Kingdom* (1997) 24 EHRR 143.

elsewhere than the UK[7] and there may be no violation if the disruption to family life has been brought about by the individual's breach of immigration controls[8].

The Immigration and Nationality Directorate implemented policy – DP2/93 – designed to prevent breaches of the family life limb of article 8. The policy, since updated, has only been tested in the UK courts on a judicial review basis so will need re-visiting under the HRA.

The right to respect for a person's home was engaged in *Gillow v United Kingdom*[9] and could have an immigration application. A couple were absent from their home in the Channel Islands for 18 years because of overseas postings and on return were refused a local residence permit. It was held the right to respect for home includes a right to 're-establish home life'.

Article 8 is considered in depth in Chapter 5.

Article 9 – Freedom of thought, conscience and religion

This comprises a right to have or change one's religion or beliefs (which is absolute) and a right to 'manifest' them (which is not, and may be limited on the grounds set out in article 9(2)).

Article 10 – Freedom of expression

This typically raises freedom of the press issues. For a classic statement of the right, including the exercise of it being able (subject to article 10(2)) to 'offend, shock or disturb', as such are the demands of 'that pluralism, tolerance and broadmindedness without which there is no "democratic society"', see *Handyside v United Kingdom*[10]. See also *R v Secretary of State for the Home Department, ex p Brind*[11], suggesting UK law is already compliant.

Article 11 – Freedom of assembly and association

This includes the right, subject to article 11(2), to have trade unions and political parties.

Article 12 – Right to marry

The right to marry and found a family applies only to 'the traditional marriage between persons of opposite biological sex'[12] and so are exercisable only conjunctively, not disjunctively. The right is in effective an aspect of family life under article 8 and does not import a right to enter the state in order to marry.

Article 13 – Right to an effective remedy

Article 13 has not been incorporated but is mentioned here as it may arise in HRA cases via the back door (given the section 2 obligation on courts and tribunals to have

---

7   *Abdulaziz v United Kingdom* (1985) 7 EHRR 471.
8   *X v United Kingdom* (1987) 11 EHRR 48.
9   (1986) 11 EHRR 335.
10 (1976) 1 EHRR 737, at para 49.
11 [1991] 1 AC 696, HL.
12 *Rees v United Kingdom* (1986) 9 EHRR 56, at para 49.

regard to all Strasbourg jurisprudence and the section 3 interpretative obligation). The article requires a state to provide an effective remedy if there is an arguable claim that Convention rights have been violated. The main issue for the UK has been whether judicial review is an effective remedy. It was held in *Soering v United Kingdom*[13], *Vilvarajah v United Kingdom*[14] and *D v United Kingdom*[15] that it is, but in *Chahal v United Kingdom*[16] that it is not. However, since the enactment of the Special Immigration Appeals Commission Act, *Chahal* might be decided differently[17].

Article 14 – Prohibition of discrimination

A claim that article 14 has been breached cannot stand alone, but must be pleaded as an adjunct to another breach. This is because the provision does not outlaw discrimination *per se*, but requires equal access to the Convention's protected rights. 'It is as though article 14 formed an integral part of each of the articles laying down rights and freedoms whatever their nature'[18]. However, it is not necessary to go so far as to show a breach of another article.

   Article 14 is considered in depth in Chapter 6.

Protocol 1, article 1 – Protection of property

An entitlement to the peaceful enjoyment of one's possessions. Subject to extensive savings it protects against state interference with, or state deprivation or control of a person's property.

Protocol 1, article 2 – Right to education

No person shall be denied the right to education (a muted version of 'everyone has the right to…') and the state shall respect the right of parents to have education conform with their religious and philosophical convictions.

Protocol 1, article 3 – Right to free elections

A guarantee of free elections at reasonable intervals by secret ballot.

Protocol 6, articles 1 and 2 – Abolition of the death penalty

This is an extension of article 2 of the Convention. In the UK the death penalty was generally abolished in 1965 but theoretically still available for treason and certain other uncommon offences. However, section 36 of the Crime and Disorder Act 1998 abolished the death penalty in those other cases as of 30 September 1998[19], leaving the way clear to incorporate this Protocol.

   Article 2 concerns exceptions in time of war.

---

13 (1989) 11 EHRR 439.
14 (1991) 14 EHRR 248. But see the view of the Commission of an appeal that is only exercisable after leaving the UK.
15 (1997) 24 EHRR 423.
16 (1996) 23 EHRR 413.
17 See also *Judicial review of discretion in human rights cases* [1997] EHRLR 391, by N Blake.
18 *National Union of Belgian Police v Belgium* (1975) 1 EHRR 578.
19 Crime and Disorder Act 1998 (Commencement No 2 and Transitional Provisions) Order 1998, SI 1998/2327, art 2(1)(g).

7.   The institutions and procedures established under the Convention and the remaining need for recourse to them post-incorporation

7.1   The remaining need to go to Strasbourg post-incorporation

The incorporation of the rights and freedoms of the Convention and Protocols ratified by the UK does not 'bring rights home' in the sense that there can be no more recourse to the European Court of Human Rights in Strasbourg. That recourse remains available on the same basis as before – ie following the exhaustion of local remedies – but the justiciability of the rights and freedoms in the UK courts and tribunals should mean there will be less need for recourse to Strasbourg as under the HRA compliance with the Convention should normally be attained in the process of exhausting the local remedies. On the other hand, the intense focus upon human rights points following the commencement of the HRA may at least in the early years send such a large wave of cases up through the judicial hierarchy that more, not less, than normal make it to Strasbourg.

Recourse to Strasbourg will still be necessary because full satisfaction in every case can never be guaranteed by the domestic courts (ie. they may fail to interpret and apply the Convention correctly) and also because the Act is a compromise between the power of the courts to ensure compliance with the Convention and the sovereignty of parliament and there is scope in that for there to be a shortfall of protection[20]. Further, challenging a derogation will require such recourse.

So as incorporation should reduce, may increase, but certainly will not eliminate the need to take cases beyond the UK's courts and tribunals and on to Strasbourg, practitioners must additionally be familiar with the Convention's institutions and procedures for accessing them.

7.2   The institutions established under the Convention – before and since 1 November 1998

The main institutions of the Council of Europe, established by the Statute of the Council of Europe, are the Parliamentary Assembly and the Committee of Ministers. Under the ECHR, just one of the Council of Europe's many treaties, the European Commission of Human Rights and European Court of Human Rights were established and the Council of Europe's already existing Committee of Ministers was also required by the ECHR to play a role specific to the Convention. Therefore of the three institutions engaged by the Convention to administer it – the Commission, the Court and the Committee of Ministers – two were established exclusively for a human rights function (the Commission and Court) while the other (the Committee of Ministers) was and remains a principal institution of the Council of Europe itself.

Originally the Commission and Court were not permanent, meaning they did not sit full-time. The Commission served as a clearing house in the sense that it received the cases, assessed their admissibility, established the facts and attempted to secure

---

20 HRA, s 3(2)(b): the validity and continuing operation of primary legislation is not affected by its incompatibility with the incorporated rights.

friendly settlements of those it found admissible, and then referred to the Court those it could not resolve. The Commission and Court were respectively served by commissioners and judges acting as individuals and not as representatives of any state.

On 1 November 1998 Protocol 11 came into force. It did not introduce additional substantive rights but made radical changes to the enforcement machinery in order to speed up the passage of Strasbourg cases (it was taking five years to conclude a case) and cope with more cases (as the new democracies of Central and Eastern Europe join the Council of Europe). At the same time it strengthened the machinery (states can no longer opt not to recognise the right of individual petition and compulsory jurisdiction of the Court – see below) and tidied up the appearance of the Convention as a document (such as by inserting headings).

Institutionally, Protocol 11 abolished the Commission altogether (save for a transitional period of a year to enable remaining pre-existing cases to be processed) and reconstituted the Court as a two-tier permanent Court; Chambers of seven judges at first instance and a Grand Chamber of 17 judges. Additionally, at the lowest level there are Committees (three judges) making admissibility decisions on most of the individual applications received. Effectively, the Commission (or rather, its work) has been merged into the Court. Protocol 11 also relieved the Committee of Ministers of its main human rights function under the Convention. It was that the Commission would send a report on the merits of the case to the Committee of Ministers who would take a decision on it after three months if during that period the case was not referred to the Court[1]. The Committee of Ministers no longer makes any merits decisions. However, the Committee of Ministers supervises the execution of the Court's judgements[2] and may request the Court to give advisory opinions on legal questions concerning the interpretation of the Convention and Protocols[3].

7.3　The procedural provisions before and since 1 November 1998

Past tense references to the Commission and its functions since 1 November 1998 should be read subject to its continued existence on and after that date for a transitional period of one year.

Jurisdiction restricted to the cases before it

As mentioned above, the Commission received complaints of breaches and those it found admissible, but was unable to resolve by friendly settlement, were then finally decided by the Court or, in default, the Committee of Ministers. The Court now carries out all these functions itself. The Commission and Court could not take unilateral action to try to prevent violations, but only act upon cases brought to them[4] and this remains true of the Court. Further, as before, the concern is only with present rather than future violations[5] but the Commission and Court could give a (non-binding)

1　A case might not be referred if, eg, it did not raise a new point on interpretation.
2　Art 46(2).
3　Art 47.
4　Unlike, eg, the Committee for the Prevention of Torture and Inhuman or Degrading Treatment or Punishment (referred to above).
5　However, the Court can rule to prevent a violation that would result from the applicant's extradition (*Soering v United Kingdom* (1989) 11 EHRR 439) or deportation (*Chahal v United Kingdom* (1996) 23 EHRR 413; *D v United Kingdom* (1997) 24 EHRR 423).

'Rule 36 indication'[6] regarding a proposed course of action by the state in a particular case[7] and this procedure is still available[8].

The 'right of individual petition' and 'compulsory jurisdiction of the court'

There are two ways in which a case can come before the Court. Any state party to the Convention may refer to the Court an alleged breach by another state party[9] or individuals may bring a case to the Court under article 34[10]. This 'right of individual petition', as it has been known, applies to any person, NGO or group of individuals[11] as has without doubt been the reason for the ECHR's success as an effective, dynamic and heavily used human rights instrument. The UK recognised the right of individual petition in 1966.

The recognition of the compulsory jurisdiction of the Court refers to the recognition of the Court as making binding decisions in all matters to do with the interpretation and application of the Convention without the requirement of further agreement by the state.

The right of individual petition and the Court's compulsory jurisdiction originally depended upon the state party accused of breach having declared that it recognised the competence of the Commission and Court in these respects[12]. All the states so declared. Since 1 November 1998, however, these have been mandatory features of the Convention and binding on all state parties without the need for declarations. The terminology has changed too: the Convention as amended now refers to individual 'applications'[13], rather than petitions, and the Court is said to have 'binding force'[14].

Admissibility decisions

All the individual applications received in Strasbourg are sifted through an initial admissibility procedure. If the application is incompatible with the Convention, manifestly ill-founded or an abuse, it is inadmissible[15] (such as where it offends the 'Fourth Instance' doctrine[16]). As indicated, originally the Commission was

---

6 Rule 36 of the Rules of the Commission and rule 36 as amended of the Rules of the Court as in force prior to November 1998.

7 Eg *Cruz Varas* (1991) 14 EHRR 1. If 'serious and irreparable harm' may result from a person's removal from the jurisdiction, the Court will request the state not to remove pending a merits decision on the case.

8 Rules of Court, r 39. See also pp 58-59.

9 Art 33. See *Ireland v United Kingdom* (1978) 2 EHRR 25, for example.

10 Previously art 25(1).

11 See section 6.1, above.

12 To introduce some element of control by states parties over the unprecedented powers given to the Commission and Court, the crucial elements – recognition of the right of individuals to bring cases and recognition of the Court's compulsory jurisdiction – require separate acceptance by the states parties. These usually takes the form of short-life declarations renewed every few years (but see Protocol 11).

13 Art 34.

14 Art 46.

15 See now art 35. Only 10% of petitions between 1955 and 1996 were admissible.

16 Which provides the Strasbourg Court cannot be used as a court of further appeal from the last domestic court (eg where the basis of the application is that the last domestic court made wrong findings of fact on the evidence).

responsible for admissibility decisions. Now it is the Court. A new application will be assigned either to a Committee or a Chamber for a decision on admissibility. The Committee may declare the application inadmissible by unanimous vote. Most individual applications are sifted by such Committees. Applications that are not declared inadmissible by the Committee are passed to a Chamber. Whether an application goes via a Committee or direct to a Chamber for an admissibility decision, the first instance decision on the merits of the application will be made by the Chamber. A Chambers decision on admissibility may be made by majority vote and must be reasoned and made public.

Basic procedure on an individual petition

Guidance notes on bringing a case are available from the Court and relevant information is also available at the Court's web site, www.dhcour.coe.fr. For a clear and practical guide to taking a case to Strasbourg see *European Human Rights: Taking a Case under the Convention*[17] by L J Clements.

- To start, the individual sends an application to the Court.
- All domestic remedies must have been exhausted.
- The application must be made within six months of the last domestic decision.
- The Court decides on admissibility and a decision of inadmissibility if final.
- If a petition is admissible the Court considers the merits and tries to broker a friendly settlement.
- The case on merits is dealt with at first instance by a Chamber unless it exceptionally relinquishes the case to the Grand Chamber. Where the Chamber determines the case on the merits at first instance, it may be appealed (referred) to the Grand Chamber within three months.
- Proceedings before the Court are in English or French and are public.
- The judgement on merits of the Chamber of Grand Chamber is final and binding. However, the Court cannot strike down provisions of national legislation. It interprets the Convention and in so doing may find a provision of national law to be in breach, but only the state may amend its domestic laws.

17 (1999) Sweet & Maxwell (at the date of writing this new edition has been withdrawn to be re-issued).

CHAPTER 2

The Human Rights Act 1998 and the Immigration and Asylum Bill of 1999

Nicholas Blake QC

1. Introduction

It was originally anticipated by practitioners that the Human Rights Act 1998[1](HRA) would come into force against the broad background of a statutory system of immigration appeals as had been developed since 1969[2]. This system grants rights of appeal against certain refusals of entry clearance, certain refusals of extensions of stay, refusals of asylum where there is a possibility of removal in breach of the Refugee Convention[3]and against deportation decisions.

It now appears that the HRA will be implemented against a significantly different background of immigration control, to be introduced by the Immigration and Asylum Bill 1999 (IAB) presented to Parliament in 1999. This chapter examines the key provisions of the HRA and discusses certain provisions of the IAB that will most directly raises human rights questions.

2. The scheme of the HRA 1998

The HRA represents a significant shift towards a rights based legal system in the United Kingdom. It does not purport to be an entrenched Bill of Rights of the sort that is frequently found in the Constitutions of Commonwealth and other countries, and neither is it the weakest form of rights legislation existing merely alongside other statutes[4] and leaving it solely to the courts to disentangle contradictions. Instead, the British model balances parliamentary sovereignty and the hegemony of fundamental rights[5].

---

1 The Act obtained Royal Assent on 9 November 1998 when ss 18, 19. 20 and 21(5) came into force.
2 Immigration Act 1971, ss 13-19; Immigration Act 1988, s 5; Asylum and Immigration Appeals Act 1993, s 8 amended by the Asylum and Immigration Act 1996; EEA Order 1994.
3 The Geneva Convention Relating to the Status of Refugees 1951 and Protocol.
4 In the extensive literature on constitutional entrenchment the New Zealand and Canadian models are frequently contrasted in this respect. For a recent decision on the results of entrenchment in a Caribbean constitution see *Browne v R* (1999) Times, 12 May, PC where a sentence of detention at the Governor General's pleasure provided under the 1873 statute was struck down as being inconsistent with the independence constitution of St Christopher and Nevis.
5 For a review of the debate see Emmerson 'This Year's Model – The Options for Incorporation' EHRLR (1997) Issue 4, p 313.

The HRA enacts articles 2-12 and 14 of the European Convention on Human Rights and articles 1 to 3 of Protocol 1 and Protocol 6 to the Convention[6]. This is subject to the UK's existing derogations and reservations[7]. In this essay these articles will be referred to as the incorporated rights; in the statute they are called 'the Convention rights'. Article 1 of the Convention is not incorporated because that is the article that urges signatory states to give effect to the Convention rights in their national legal systems and there is no doubt that the HRA does have this effect. More controversially article 13 has been omitted. The government argument was that the requirement to provide an effective remedy for other Convention rights is already provided for in the HRA, and that to incorporate article 13 as well would either be unnecessary or would give too much power to the UK courts to develop remedies inconsistent with those provided for in the HRA itself[8]. Under the European Convention on Human Rights, article 13 is not a free standing right and has to be prayed in aid together with another right afforded by the Convention. Nevertheless its omission is unfortunate and neither reason for its exclusion is ultimately convincing. Article 13 is itself a substantive right under the Convention and has been the subject of much important jurisprudence. The government recognised in debate[9] that the UK Courts will need to examine this case law in performing their statutory duties under the Act, and it is to be hoped that the interpretation of the other Articles will take on board pertinent observations deriving from this case law, so a victim of a violation will not be procedurally worse off in the UK than s/he would in Strasbourg. This is after all the HRA's aim[10]. The application of the Convention is not confined to the higher courts and judicial review proceedings[11]. It must be applied by every court, tribunal or appellate body throughout the land to any issues within its jurisdiction[12]. Some bodies will be unable to give remedies such as compensation if this is not within the scope of their existing powers[13].

The five principal features of the approach of the HRA are as follows:

(1) the requirement that the courts take into account the case law under the Convention in determining questions under the HRA[14];

(2) the requirement that the courts interpret national legislation in accordance with the parts of the Convention that are incorporated[15];

(3) the power of the Courts to declare primary legislation incompatible with the Convention when compatibility cannot be achieved by interpretation[16];

6   HRA, s 1(1), Sch 1, Pt 1.
7   HRA, ss 14, 15 and Sch 3.
8   See Lord Chancellor's comments during the passage of the Bill in the Lords Hansard 18th November 1997, col 475; Home Secretary 20 May 1998, col 979; see also Lord Chancellor's Tom Sargant Memorial Lecture December 1997.
9   See footnote 8 above for references.
10   Labour Party Consultation Document *Bringing Rights Home* (December 1996).
11   HRA, s 7(1)(a), (2) a person may bring proceedings in any appropriate court or tribunal to be determined by rules; a person may rely on the Convention in defending any proceedings brought against them (s 7(1)((b)).
12   HRA, s 8(1).
13   HRA, s 8(2).
14   HRA, s 2(1).
15   HRA, s 3(1).
16   HRA, s 4(2).

(4) the requirement on any public authority to act consistently with the Convention whether the act or decision took place before or after the passing of the HRA and the ability of the courts to give remedies in respect of failures to do so[17];

(5) the requirement on a promoting Minister to make a statement as to the compatibility of any new Bill with the Convention[18].

A person's reliance on an incorporated right does not restrict any other right or freedom s/he may enjoy in the UK[19].

2.1 The case law

A court or tribunal in the UK does not set about interpreting the Convention *de novo* but must do so by taking into account the existing jurisprudence developed under the Convention by the Strasbourg organs[20] .This means that where it is relevant to do so in applying the HRA, regard must be had to judgments, decisions, declarations or advisory opinions of the European Court of Human Rights; opinions and decisions of the Commission, and decisions of the Committee of Ministers. The language of the statute is not that the UK courts are bound by decisions of the Court, but it is difficult to imagine that a British court would take a contradictory approach to the meaning of a Convention right that had been conclusively elaborated by the Court. However, in the *application* of the Convention, the British courts may come to a different solution applying Convention principles. This will particularly be so as the doctrine of the margin of appreciation will not be applied by the domestic court[1]. This doctrine is an aspect of international deference to national standards in questions where discretion is permitted by the Convention on difficult moral and ethical issues. A wide margin of appreciation has been afforded contracting states in the fields of transsexualism, abortion, reproductive technology and the like[2]. The national court does not have to show similar deference because it is in a better position to review the evidence and take national sensibilities into account. Although there may be scope for permitting public authorities discretion, this will be directly and substantively reviewed by the national courts applying Convention standards[3].

2.2 Interpretation

At present the common law principles of statutory interpretation permit limited use of international instruments when interpreting legislation passed after the obligation

17　HRA, ss 6(1), 7(1), 8(1).
18　HRA, s 19(1).
19　HRA, s 11.
20　HRA, s 2(1).
1　See Lord Chancellor's remarks in his Tom Sargant Memorial Lecture December 1997; see also the observations of the divisional Court in *R v Stratford Justices, ex p Imbert* (1999) Times, 25 February. See also pp 16-17.
2　See *XYZ v United Kingdom* (1997) 24 EHHR 143 at para 44.
3　For the present limits on whether a measure interfering with private life is necessary see *R v Ministry of Defence, ex p Smith* [1996] QB 517.

in question, but only where the national statute is ambiguous[4]. A wholly new principle is brought into being by section 2 of the HRA that is much more dynamic and purposive. The Courts are required to interpret national legislation in accordance with the Convention *wherever possible*. This is the approach laid down in EC law to the interpretation of national law consistently with EC Directives and Regulations and the case law on that topic will prove instructive to interpretation under section 3 of the HRA[5]. The duty of interpretation applies to all legislation[6], whether primary or secondary, whenever passed[7], and will enable courts to reach a strained meaning of a term in order to give effect to compatibility. There is no need for ambiguity before applying this new rule of construction. It will thus become the first and primary canon of construction wherever a statute engages the subject matter of incorporated rights.

2.3   Declarations of incompatibility

Some statutes are so clear that they cannot be read down to afford a meaning consistent with the Convention. Although the decisions of the Scottish Parliament and the Welsh and the Northern Irish Assembly are liable to be struck down by the courts as incompatible with the Convention[8], the primary legislation of the United Kingdom Parliament cannot be declared null and void by the courts[9]. Secondary legislation is also protected but only to the extent that the enabling power required measures to be taken inconsistent with the Convention; if the power could have been exercised without contravening Convention rights the impugned decision that does contravene can be struck down as *ultra vires*[10]. For primary legislation incompatible with incorporated rights, however, the most that the Courts can do is to issues a declaration of incompatibility. This does not affect the validity of the legislation and is not binding on the parties[11]. It is therefore more the expression of a formal judicial opinion that has procedural consequences. When there is no further appeal in the domestic courts, the responsible Minister may make a remedial order amending the legislation by an order in Council[12]. Although there is no legal duty on the Minister to make such an order this is to be expected as the normal course where the promoting Minister had previously considered that the legislation was compatible with the Convention. A remedial order may have effect from a date earlier than the date it is made and may include a power to amend or repeal primary or subordinate legislation[13]. A draft of any such order must be approved by Parliament unless it must be made urgently[14]. Alternatively the Minister can refuse to amend the law. In those circumstances the aggrieved individual will have to re-litigate the issue before the

---

4   See *R v Secretary of State for the Home Department, ex p Brind* [1991] 1 AC 696.
5   *Marleasing* [1990] ECR 1-4135.
6   For the meaning of 'legislation', see HRA, s 21(1).
7   HRA, s 3(2)(a).
8   Their decisions are considered subordinate legislation: HRA, s 22(1)(b)–(e).
9   See *Bringing Rights Home*; HRA, s 4(6).
10 HRA, s 4(3) and (4)(b).
11 HRA, s 4(6).
12 HRA, s 10(1)(a), (4) and Sch 2.
13 HRA, Sch 2, para 1; but this power cannot be used to make a retrospective criminal offence (para 1(4)).
14 HRA, Sch 2, para 2.

Strasbourg Court and if successful obtain such remedy as is available there. In these circumstances the Minister may again wish to make use of the powers to make a remedial order as opposed to correcting the deficiency by ordinary legislation. Out of deference to normal Parliamentary proceedings a remedial order can only be made if a Minister considers that there are compelling reasons for doing so[15]. The existence of an intended legislative incompatibility should normally amount to such compelling reasons. The alternative to correcting the inconsistency would be to make a derogation[16]. In England, Wales and Northern Ireland only the High Court or above[17] can issue a statement of incompatibility, and, if considering doing so, the court must give notice to the Crown who may be joined as a party[18]. An inferior tribunal will be restricted to identifying the problem and presumably granting leave to appeal where there is potential incompatibility.

2.4   Incompatible acts of public authorities

It is unlawful for a public authority to act in a way that is incompatible with a Convention right, unless it is acting as required by a provision of primary legislation[19]. The intention has been to give a wide definition to public authority. It applies to any person who performs functions of a public nature[20]. This clearly includes central government (including executive agencies), local government, the police, the CPS, immigration officers and others exercising public functions[1]. It is likely that it will include all the bodies whose decisions are presently capable of challenge by judicial review, but it remains to be seen whether distinctions will emerge.

In one respect, the definition is wider. It includes all courts and tribunals. Thus superior courts of record whose decisions are presently excluded from judicial review may be acting unlawfully and be capable of challenge in the future. This has particular implications for compensation for unlawful detention[2]. Parliament is not however a public authority and so again its sovereignty is kept intact[3]. The established churches can be a public authority but their measures are not subject to a remedial order[4], and great emphasis was devoted to religious belief in debate during the passage of the Bill where it was concluded that practices inconsistent with religious doctrine will not have to be adopted. The position of the Press Complaints Commission was also the subject of much debate in Parliament and special considerations apply where the court is minded to give relief that affects freedom of expression[5].

---

15   HRA, s 10(2).
16   HRA, s 14; s 15 for reservations; Sch 3 for existing derogations and reservations. All existing derogations or reservations have to be reviewed within five years, and will cease unless renewed. New orders making a derogation or a reservation also last for five years unless renewed: ss 16 and 17.
17   HRA, s 4(5); in Scotland it is the High Court of Justiciary sitting otherwise than as a trial court.
18   HRA, s 5(1).
19   HRA, s 6(1) and (2).
20   HRA, s 6(3).
1   See *Bringing Rights Home*; Hansard, 16 November 1997, col 1231.
2   HRA, s 9(3) and see below.
3   HRA, s 6(3).
4   HRA, s 10(6).
5   HRA, s 12.

Purely private persons and corporations are not public bodies unless they are exercising public functions. Private security firms who are detaining immigrants under contracted out powers would certainly appear to be a public authority in respect of these functions. It remains to be seen whether airlines and other carriers exercising functions of reporting passengers to immigration officers and adopting measures to comply with Carriers Sanctions are public authorities. Merely obeying a statutory duty may not be exercising a public function, but assisting the prevention of illegal entry by the adoption of practices approved by the immigration service could be. In some cases corporations will themselves be litigating to enforce respect for their human rights.

Where it is alleged that a public authority has acted inconsistently with a Convention right, the matter can be litigated in any legal proceedings brought by or on behalf of that authority, or alternatively the affected person can bring proceedings against the public authority[6]. The ability to secure enforcement of the duty by judicial review proceedings is limited however. The applicant is to be taken to have a sufficient interest in relation to the unlawful act only if he, or she is, or would be , a victim of that act[7]. Victims are confined to those who are considered 'victims' under the existing Convention jurisprudence applying article 34 of the Convention[8]. This is a narrower class of persons than those who are considered to be sufficiently interested parties to bring judicial review proceedings[9]. The victim in Strasbourg jurisprudence is limited to the person directly affected by the violation, which may extend to affected family members, and in some cases the personal representatives or others considered to be the indirect victim[10]. Voluntary organisations will not be able to bring judicial review proceedings determining that a public authority has violated its s.6 duties. This is a weakness considering the absence of a Human Rights Commission, the precarious state of legal aid at present and the costs and uncertainty in vindicating rights. The government did contemplate that such organisations might intervene to assist the court in proceedings brought by victims however[11].

The position is complicated where a person seeks judicial review of a decision on the ordinary grounds of legality, and relies on the section 3 interpretation principle to interpret the statutory duty in question and cites Convention case law. The relief sought would be *certiorari* rather than one of the remedies developed under section 8 of the HRA. The issue would be whether the decision is lawful rather than whether a public authority had violated Convention obligations. In those circumstances, the general law on standing for the purpose of Order 53 should remain unchanged. If that is so, one needs to be a victim not so much to have locus to institute judicial review but to obtain a form of relief and a section 6 ground for that relief that was not otherwise available. All that was needed was that relief on section 6 grounds be confined to victims.

Relief under the HRA in relation to any act or proposed act of the public authority is such relief or remedy, within its powers, as the court considers just and appropriate[12].

---

6   HRA, s 7(1).
7   HRA, s 7(2) and (3) for Scotland.
8   HRA, s 7(7).
9   Hansard, 24 November 1997, col 830.
10 Hansard HC, 20 May 1998 col 1084; Harris *et al*, *Law of the European Convention On Human Rights*, pp 630–638. The state of the law may make a whole class of persons victims see *Dudgeon v United Kingdom*.
11 Hansard, HL 24 November 1997, col 830. For Third Party Interventions see the report of the Working Party for JUSTICE/Public Law Project (1996) chaired by Sir John Laws. See also review Article in Northern Ireland Legal Quarterly Autumn 1997.
12 HRA, s 8(1).

Damages can only be awarded by a court that has power to award damages or compensation in civil proceedings[13]. Convention principles of necessity to afford just satisfaction is the criterion for the award of damages[14].

2.5 Statement of compatibility

All new Bills introduced after 9 November 1998 will have to contain a statement from the Minister of the Crown to the effect that the legislation is, in his or her view, compatible with the incorporated rights[15], or that no such statement can be made, but nevertheless the government wishes to pursue the legislation[16]. The Parliamentary scrutiny of such statements will be an important part of the process of legislation where Bills clearly have a human rights impact. The difficulty is that in the absence of a Human Rights Commission or a specialist advisory committee whose views have to be first obtained, Parliament may not have all the material it needs to make an independent assessment. A bare Ministerial assertion of compatibility is likely to evoke the celebrated response of Mandy Rice-Davis[17].

3. The HRA and the IAA

When the HRA was being enacted immigration practitioners were concerned that it did not readily vest jurisdiction in a statutory tribunal whose functions were so narrow as to exclude questions of the compatibility with the Convention of administrative decisions. There would be little problem where a tribunal could decide whether a decision was in accordance with the law[18] as the law would now include the section 6(1) duty of a public authority to act consistently with the Convention. However, in asylum appeals for example, the special adjudicator is restricted to considering whether removal would contravene the terms of the Refugee Convention rather than whether the decision is in accordance with the law[19]. So the fact that the decision was illegal on some other ground than breach of the Convention would not be relevant, and breaches of article 3 would have to be pursued by the unsatisfactory vehicle of judicial review rather than in the same hearing as the asylum appeal. It was also unclear how human rights questions would be raised in deportation appeals restricted by section 5 of the Immigration Act 1988. The Government's response was to enact what is now section 7(11) of the HRA whereby the Minister responsible for exercising the rule-making power of statutory appellate bodies (most usually the Lord Chancellor) would promote amendments to the procedure rules, enabling HRA issues to be ventilated in the course of such appeals[20].

---

13 HRA, s 8(2).
14 HRA, s 8(3).
15 HRA, s 19(1)(a).
16 HRA, s 19(1)(b).
17 'He would wouldn't he?' Oxford Dictionary Quotations, 4th edn, 540-6.
18 Immigration Act 1971, s 19(1) as applied in *Abdi v Secretary of State for the Home Department* [1996] Imm AR 148.
19 *R v Secretary of State for the Home Department, ex p Mehari* [1994] QB 474. See also p 61 *et seq*.
20 See Annex 2 for the letter of explanation.

Events have now moved on. No timetable was announced for the implementation of the bulk of the HRA. In May 1999, the Government announced that the HRA will come into force in October 2000. However in the meantime immigration decisions continue to be taken and appeals heard and a considerable period of ambiguity remains. Although section 22(4) of the HRA is now in force, it demonstrates that it is only the decisions of public authorities taken after the date of commencement of sections 6 and 7 that will enable a victim to institute proceedings alleging that the decision is unlawful as contrary to section 6. As we have seen, different rules apply where proceedings are instigated by or on behalf of a public authority. In those circumstances where the HRA is in force, complaint can be made in any subsequent appeal of decisions taken before implementation.

This has clear application in the context of criminal law. An offence may be investigated in 1998 and brought to trial in 1999 with an appeal against conviction in the year 2000. Although the HRA was not in force at the first and second stages of this scenario, a complaint that the investigation breached the Convention can be made in the course of an appeal against conviction if the HRA is in force by then. The Divisional Court[1] has recently concluded that in the interim a public authority such as the DPP has an administrative law duty to consider the likely effect of the HRA on a subsequent appeal when deciding whether to initiate or maintain criminal proceedings. It remains to be seen whether this decision will encourage the government to name the day for implementation and reduce the gap between potential and actual judicial accountability of public authorities for human rights.

It might be thought that this decision is of relevance in deportation and other expulsion decisions. Such decisions are certainly proceedings for the purpose of judicial review challenges and stays of removal can be obtained against the execution of such proceedings pending challenge[2]. However, section 7(1)(b) and (6) of the HRA refers to legal proceedings rather than just proceedings. It remains to be seen whether the IAA or the courts will consider that a deportation decision is a legal proceeding because it is clear that it will result in an appeal from that decision. If it did, then it could immediately consider compatibility with the Convention in such decisions on the basis that the general law requires the public authority to contemplate the future impact of its decisions. This is particularly the case in deportation appeals, where the order is due to last well beyond the expected date of commencement. Alternatively, the IAA will have to rely on the concept of legitimate expectation to apply a legality review of the decisions of the immigration service[3]. This is easier in the context of article 3, where there are numerous statements of the government's intention to act in conformity with the *Chahal* decision, than article 8, where present policy envisages a narrow interpretation of the *Berrehab*[4] case. Where there is no countervailing policy statement, however, legitimate expectation of conformity with

---

1   *R v DPP, ex p Kebilene* [1999] 3 WLR 175, CA; pending appeal to the House of Lords.
2   *R v Secretary of State for Education, ex p Avon County Council* [1991] 1 QB 558. This decision has since been doubted by the Privy Council.
3   The concept has been given a boost by the decision of the Court of Appeal in *R v Secretary of State for the Home Department, ex p Ahmed and Patel* [1998] INLR 570 at 583 to 584 approved by the Privy Council in *Thomas and Hilaire v Baptiste* [1999] 3 WLR 249 ((1999) Times, 23 March not on this point)
4   *Berrehab v Netherlands* (1988) 11 EHRR 322.

international obligations may still have a function in immigration appeals until the incorporated rights come into direct play on commencement[5].

Even when the HRA does come into force, there remains the problem of chronology and whether an adjudicator can regard as incompatible with the HRA an immigration decision taken on an earlier occasion when the HRA is not in force. Whether or not an immigration appeal is a proceeding brought by or on behalf of a public authority in the same way that a criminal charge or expropriation proceedings may be, the IAA should have no difficulty in applying Convention standards to such immigration decisions. The solution to the question of IAA jurisdiction to deal with pre-HRA decisions, is the recognition that expulsion is part of a continuing process of which appellate review is a step. Since the IAA is itself a public authority within the meaning of the HRA it has its own public duty to prevent the prohibited consequence: namely expulsion in breach of incorporated rights.

This feature of the HRA should prove influential in the elaboration of the jurisprudence applying the Act to immigration control. The principles involved go beyond a dispassionate examination of the actions of others, but requires the IAA itself to act in a manner consistent with the ECHR in all aspects of its decision taking and regulating its own procedure. Challenges to the procedure rules, poorly reasoned decisions, practice directions and the like will all have to be judged from the point of view of what is needed to reach a consistency with international standards.

One of the inadequacies of the present appellate system is the absence of legal aid in the statutory appeal system, and the shortage of properly qualified immigration asylum lawyers to service growing client demand. This is a problem that is likely to exacerbate in the year 2000 when the introduction of franchising will reduce the number of immigration solicitors able to give advice and assistance, and the government proposals for dispersal of asylum seekers throughout the country may make regional access to experienced advisers even more difficult than at present[6]. Whilst the ability to get appropriate advice may diminish, the importance of having it at the outset is significantly increased. Many asylum practitioners are familiar with the argument that access to proper advice at the outset can save considerable delays and complexities in the subsequent appellate process. Under the present proposed method of implementing the HRA in the immigration context, access to competent advice at the relevant time will become even more critical. A failure to argue article 3 grounds alongside an ordinary asylum appeal may preclude a subsequent human rights appeal and may lose the claimant an opportunity for a proper consideration of this broader form of protection. The consequences could be very serious as the Strasbourg Court has applied the concept of utilising and exhausting all prior domestic remedies even to cases under article 3 of the Convention[7]. Domestic timetables for the filing of evidence, the making of claims, and the marshalling of arguments will be determinative in the absence of good reason for an exceptional course, the consideration of which will lie in the first instance with the Secretary of State. Immigration advisers will have to develop interviewing practices designed to elicit all relevant information from the client and be familiar with the

---

5   See Hansard HL, 3 December 1998, WA 57 for a written answer to the effect that the public are entitled to expect that Ministers and civil servants will comply with the obligations imposed by the European Convention on Human Rights and the International Covenant on Civil and Political Rights, see Judicial Review [1999] vol 41, p 31.
6   See Report of the Legal Aid Board 18 May 1999.
7   *Bahddar v Netherlands* (1998) 26 EHHR 278.

evidential requirements of human rights claims at the earliest opportunity so that potential claims are not lost or discredited by delay in presenting them.

It is important to note that present Strasbourg jurisprudence does not suggest that the fair trial standards of article 6 of the Convention that apply to criminal cases and cases of civil rights and obligations import substantive requirements of procedural fairness into immigration claims. Notwithstanding some broad *dicta* in the European Court of Justice in Luxembourg[8], the Human Rights Court has held that public law decisions fall outside the scope of civil rights and obligations[9]. It remains to be seen whether domestic incorporation of the HRA means that every person within the jurisdiction now has a civil right not to be treated inconsistently with the Convention and that civil right is required to be enforced by every court and tribunal vested with jurisdiction over the subject matter. It would, however, appear on a narrow textual reading that neither the Refugee Convention nor the ECHR require there to be a right of appeal or public funding for accessible and competent legal representation, even though asylum and human rights claims may require greater legal skills in the identification and preparation of claims than discrimination or employment cases where article 6 clearly applies.

There are, however, implicit requirements in both Conventions that should shape policy and may give rise to legal argument. First, it is apparent that article 3 prohibits a result: a broad class of expulsions, leaving it up to national law to decide how this absolute injunction is to be achieved. Modern practice recognises that a single administrative decision conducted without a hearing, and often by officials who have never met the claimants, questioned them or posed the relevant questions to them, is completely inadequate to achieve this result. Where there are serious grounds to challenge a Home Office rejection, therefore, the Convention requires a standard of scrutiny that in practice is only likely to be achieved by an independent appeal. In article 3 cases this standard of scrutiny has been identified by the Court as requiring[10] 'independent scrutiny of the claim that there exist substantial grounds for fearing a risk of ill treatment'. Procedure rules, or other executive action that prevented an independent appellate body from performing a function of scrutiny of the facts to determine whether there were substantial grounds for the appellant's fears of inhuman or degrading treatment or punishment would not be consistent with the state's obligations under article 3. This may not require the state to provide legal aid, but it would prevent the state commenting on the absence of supporting evidence at an appropriate moment if there was no access to advisers who could reasonably be expected to produce the material.

The IAA will be the authority most concerned with the application of the HRA in the immigration context. It will be able to declare that immigration decisions are inconsistent with the duties of the public authority concerned – whether entry clearance officer, immigration officer or Secretary of State for the Home Department – and grant such relief as is presently available to it to give effect to its decisions. Where necessary this will include the grant of entry clearance, leave to enter or remain and the such like[11]. Where a family has been separated as a result of an immigration

8 *Pecastaing* [1980] ECR 691.
9 See Harris *et al* op cit, p 192.
10 *Chahal v United Kingdom* (1996) 23 EHHR 413 at para 153.
11 Immigration Act 1971, s 19(3).

decision, the IAA has no power to order pecuniary compensation, but there is no reason why it should not make a recommendation[12] to this effect that would save a need for judicial review to obtain just satisfaction[13].

4. The Asylum and Immigration Bill 1999[14]

The delay in implementing the HRA has profound consequences for immigration law in the light of the changes to the immigration appeal system proposed under the Immigration and Asylum Bill (IAB) published in February 1999. The government's target date for implementation of the IAB is 1 April 2000, a number of months before the HRA is likely to come into effect. The target for the IAB may itself slip in the light of concern about the ability of the Home Office to run the new system of benefit support for refugees envisaged by the Bill. However, there is likely to be a significant period during which immigration law is reformed but the HRA is not yet in force. I shall now examine some of the principal provisions of the IAB as it affects incorporated rights and the HRA.

4.1 Ministerial statements of compatibility

The IAB has been one of the first occasions for the use of the requirement of a Ministerial certification of compatibility. The Bill contains on its front page Mr Jack Straw's pronouncement 'in my view the provisions of the Immigration and Asylum Bill are compatible with the Convention rights'. This is a somewhat bland and sweeping statement unaccompanied by any indication of an internal audit of compliance. In the light of the very real concerns of many at the shift in power towards the executive in this Bill, attempts were made to discover how the conclusion had been reached. It is understood that legal advice was obtained to enforce the conclusion of compatibility, but we do not know from whom that advice was obtained, what issues it addressed or was asked to address, and how it reached its conclusion in the light of many Draconian provisions relating to carrier sanctions, confiscation of vehicles, denial of benefit to asylum seekers and the like. As a dry run of the added benefits of the HRA to parliamentary democracy, a claim of legal privilege in an area of such importance is regrettable and debatable. It is also self defeating. Part of the British way was to restore to Parliament the leading role in ensuring respect for human rights. If ministers make bland assertions to committees packed with their party members, an educational experience for the legislature will be lost. There is little room for debate and engagement and once more it will turn on the non-governmental organisations, the victims and the courts to show Parliament and the executive what human rights mean. Reasoned and fair laws are better for the public interest than expensive and contentious litigation.

---

12 Ibid.
13 HRA, s 8(1) and (2).
14 Clause references are to the Bill as amended in Committee in the House of Lords and printed on 28 July 1999.

4.2   Removal directions

By clause 8 of the Bill a person who is not a British citizen may be removed from the United Kingdom in accordance with removal directions given by an immigration officer if, having only a limited leave to remain, he or she fails to observe a condition of the leave, or remains beyond the period limited by the leave, or has obtained leave to remain by deception. Directions may also be given to family members of such a person.

The Bill proposes to abolish the concept of deportation for breach of conditions and overstaying and replace it with the administrative discretion to remove. There is no right of appeal against the making of removal directions and the full deportation appeal will also disappear with the concept of deportation[15]. This will mean the loss of the one opportunity that presently exists in immigration law where at present 'all relevant considerations' are required to be taken into account by the appellate authorities[16]. The ambit of relevant circumstances is broad and certainly permits account to be taken of the welfare of the child, and aspects of private and family life that would require specific consideration under the ECHR[17]. At present, adjudicators can substitute their own view of where the balance between the public interest in maintaining immigration control and the compassionate factors of the particular case lies[18] and this has been a significant safeguard against unreasonable and oppressive decisions by the Secretary of State and the immigration service.

It is to be doubted whether the new human rights appeal proposed by clause 59 of the Bill will be as effective as the present deportation appeal in restraining such decisions by immigration officers in the future. The threshold for violations of the right to family and private life has been a high one. Further, there is no transitional scheme proposed for those who have breached their conditions of entry before the new Bill takes effect but are only faced with removal after its coming into force. Transitional protection of appellate rights will not be implied[19]. Thus those who have been resident in the UK for some 12 years hoping to make an application for settlement under the 14 year policy, or who are awaiting the outcome of representations on family life claims, may suddenly find themselves without any right of appeal after the Bill has come into force.

4.3   HRA appeal

Instead of a general power to review the legality of removal decisions, of which the HRA would form a part, the Bill proposes a specific right of appeal on human rights grounds. By clause 59(1) a person who alleges that an immigration officer or the Secretary of State has, in taking any decision relating to that person's entitlement to remain in the United Kingdom, acted in breach of his or her human rights may appeal to an adjudicator against that decision. The HRA would provide some kind of substitute appeal right for overstayers who have married or have relationships akin to marriage or have strong connections with children resident here and clearly adds important protection to those who may suffer ill treatment but not persecution within the meaning of the Refugee Convention.

15 IAB Explanatory Notes, paras 10-11.
16 Immigration Rules HC 395, para 364.
17 See *Macdonald's Immigration Law and Practice*, 4th edn, para 15.60 *et seq.*
18 See, eg, *Idrish* [1985] Imm AR 155, IAT.
19 See IAB, Sch 4, para 4; Sch 5.

It would be peculiar to introduce a right of appeal based on the HRA before the HRA is itself brought into force, and so implementation of this clause may be delayed beyond the general commencement date of the IAB. However, commencement of the Bill in its present form without a clause 59 appeal would be disastrous and lead to a significant increase in judicial review or hopeless asylum claims. Those who do not have a variation appeal and are temporarily denied a human rights appeal would have to join the ever-lengthening queue, created by a series of disastrous statutes limiting appeal rights, of those seeking judicial review of immigration decisions to compensate for the inadequacies of the present appellate system. One had been led to believe that this was precisely what the present government had intended to avoid.

4.4 One stop procedure: clauses 68–73

The Bill introduces a procedure where a person in the United Kingdom who is refused further leave to remain must also respond to a notice served by the Secretary of State requiring details of any other claim the person may have to remain in the United Kingdom to be made at this point. This includes a claim under the HRA or an asylum claim (as originally drafted it also included a claim under a prescribed concession)[20]. It is also unclear how the government proposes to take into account compassionate factors that are not included in the immigration rules: for example claims by same sex partners.

This is a confused and an inadequate substitute for the present judicial discretion in deportation appeals. Prescribed concessions, even if includable, are as tightly drafted as immigration rules and incapable of accommodating all categories of deserving case. Concessions of course are just that and can be withdrawn without even the feeble measures of Parliamentary scrutiny permitted for immigration rule changes.

A review of compassionate circumstances, it now appears, will at best be restricted to the examination of whether on the true facts the appellant was entitled to the benefit of a prescribed policy. Whatever shape this procedure will take, the intention is that the appeal is delayed while these other claims are considered and then all issues are resolved in a single appeal by an adjudicator[21].

4.5 Certification of human rights appeals

Further alarm as to the scope and efficacy of the human rights appeal is generated by clause 67(2) of the IAB that enables the Secretary of State to certify that the sole purpose of a human rights appeal is to delay the removal of the applicant or any member of the family from the United Kingdom. In such circumstances there is no right of appeal. This again seems an unnecessarily cumbersome consequence of the decision to abandon deportation or removal appeals. Where there has been an effective right of appeal against expulsion in which all material circumstances could have been considered and no human rights claim was raised, it might be reasonable to curtail repeated claims made in respect of the same material[1]. This power does not

20 Clause 55(5)(c) of the original Bill, but this was later dropped. The scope now, if any, for a claim under a concession being included in the one stop procedure is unclear.
21 Clauses 71–72.
1   Under the Asylum and Immigration Act 1993, Sch 2, para 5 there was power to certify an appeal as frivolous and vexatious, and there has been debate over when a fresh claim was considered to have arisen: *R v Secretary of State for the Home Department, ex p Manvinder Singh* [1996] Imm AR 41; *R v Secretary of State for the Home Department, ex p Onibiyo* [1996] QB 768.

depend on there having been one effective appeal, however, and could be used to impose an effective first instance leave to appeal requirement. In practice, the minister would be ill advised to issue such certificates where there has been no appeal and gathering of material evidence, as there will be collateral judicial review of the certificate. A further disincentive to unmeritorious appeals is contained in clause 74 of the IAB, which enables the Immigration Appeal Tribunal (IAT) to award a financial penalty against appellants or their advisers who proceed with appeals after a warning notice has been given.

The danger in both cases is for the Secretary of State and the IAA to subordinate international obligations to domestic pre-occupations. There is evidence of such a tendency even in respect of the Refugee Convention where the IAT has decided that the good faith requirement needs to be read into the wording of article 1A(2) – the definition of refugee – so as to exclude those whose risk of persecution derives from their abusive self-exposure to harm[2]. The concept of abusive claims has given rise to differences in judicial opinion[3]. In *Ex p B*[4] the court was referred to a report of an admissibility decision by the Commission[5] as some support for a requirement to act reasonably in article 3 cases. In fact, the text of that decision makes plain that the application was rejected merely because, on the facts, there were no substantial grounds for fears of ill-treatment on expulsion and no duty to act reasonably was imposed. Since then the *Chahal* decision of the Strasbourg Court has also made plain that the focus is on the treatment that the applicant fears in the place of proposed expulsion, and that has to be ascertained and protection afforded without any regard to what the claimant has done in the host country to merit expulsion. Such an approach is inconsistent with a requirement of good faith or any other technique to limit examination of issues where there are sound reasons to fear prohibited consequences. If a person is at risk of ill treatment because they have infringed religious laws or social mores and may have behaved immorally by any standards, an expulsion giving rise to prohibited treatment cannot proceed. Again prior immigration history or poor credibility may not matter if there is objective evidence of risk[6].

4.6 Detention and bail: IAB Part III

The detention of asylum seekers has long given rise to concern that many were held in custody unnecessarily. There was no limit to the period of custodial detention under the Immigration Acts (in marked contrast to the regime where people are accused of crime) and no requirement on the immigration service to produce a detained person before an adjudicator. There was merely a power for such a person to apply for bail after seven days from arrival[7]. Mistakes could occur in the absence of judicial scrutiny[8]. There was a risk that detention was adopted as a policy to deter asylum

---

2 *Danian* [1998] Imm AR 462, now pending appeal to the Court of Appeal.
3 *R v Immigration Appeal Tribunal, ex p B* [1989] Imm AR 166; *Gilgam v Secretary of State for the Home Department* [1995] Imm AR 129; *Mbanza v Secretary of State for the Home Department* [1996] Imm AR 136.
4 See previous footnote.
5 Application 11933/86 *A v Switzerland.*
6 See Report of the Commission in *Matumbo v Switzerland* (1994) 15 HRLJ 164.
7 Immigration Act 1971, Sch 2, para 22.
8 *W v Home Office* [1997] Imm AR 302.

seekers arriving and making claims. During the passage of the HRA JUSTICE commissioned an opinion as to the requirements of article 5 of the Convention in respect of immigration detention. This opinion is attached at the end of this chapter as it gives a fuller outline of the requirements of effective judicial scrutiny of the detention of asylum seekers.

For present purposes, the opinion and the applicable principles can be summarised in the light of the decision of the Strasbourg Court in *Amuur v France*[9] and the comments of the UN Human Rights Committee in its opinion in *A v Australia*[10]. Article 5(1) of the ECHR only permits detention of immigrants or asylum seekers whose claims are still under consideration to *prevent* illegal entry. Arriving in the UK without a visa in order to seek asylum cannot be equated with illegal entry in this context, and so a blanket policy of detaining undocumented asylum seekers would not be lawful. A similar conclusion has been reached by the UN Committee Against Torture in its recent report to the UK on an inspection of immigration detention. If a blanket policy cannot be lawful, careful individual scrutiny of the likelihood of an asylum seeker absconding to effect an unlawful entry is required. Further, a detained person must be brought before a competent judicial authority as soon as practical after detention to ensure that the detention is lawful and to review whether it should be continued. A right to apply for bail after seven days is not sufficient to achieve this scrutiny even in cases where an effective bail application is not precluded by security grounds. Legality in this context extends to a greater degree of scrutiny than a formal jurisdiction to detain. It requires the independent body to determine whether the detention is for a purpose recognised by the Convention, and whether on all the evidence it is necessary and proportionate. The very Convention notion of justifying detention implicitly proceeds from a presumption of liberty even in aliens' cases. Finally, where a court concludes that detention is not lawful according to Convention criteria, a person is entitled to receive compensation for loss occasioned by the illegality. Again illegality is not confined to its domestic meaning of absence of authority to detain, but embraces any detention inconsistent with the principles of article 5.

In the IAB, clause 38(4) provision is now made for the Secretary of State for the Home Department to secure a reference to the court of the case of a person detained under immigration and asylum legislation no later than the eighth day following the day of detention, or in a security case, in accordance with the rules of the Special Immigration Appeal Commission. Under the original clause 31 the court was simply empowered to release the detainee on a recognisance with prescribed conditions. This was more like a grant of conventional bail on the merits than scrutiny of whether detention is lawful and in accordance with the Convention. However, by the time the Bill emerged from Committee in the House of Lords a general right to be released on bail was included (clause 40(1)) and this was immediately followed by the Court of Appeal decision in *R v Uxbridge Magistrates' Court, ex p Adimi*[11] in which it was held that article 31 of the Refugee Convention can be relied upon in English law to quash a prosecution in false document cases (weakening further the scope for legitimate detentions). Still, detention without production does not result in automatic release but merely a duty on the Secretary of State for the Home Department to inform the court of the breach (clause 38(10)).

9   (1996) 22 EHRR 533.
10   (1997) 4 BHRC 210.
11   (1999) Times, 12 August.

According to article 5(4) of the Convention any bail hearing will need to embrace the legality of the detention, and a conclusion that detention is incompatible with the Convention would not be consistent with a requirement that a recognisance be entered into. As the requirement of a recognisance under (original) clause 31(1) has been replaced by a discretion to make such a requirement (clause 41(1)(a)), a potential incompatibility has been avoided.

In respect of persons who have not entered appeals (and this will include the large category of those awaiting decision) the bail court will be the magistrates court (clause 38(12)(c); clause 47) who have presently little understanding of the difference between asylum seekers and criminals, and the special considerations that will apply in the case of the former. The bail court can sit in the detention centre or prison (clause 39(2)) and it is even contemplated that hearings can be conducted by video link (clause 46). There is no reference to a requirement of legal representation of detainees in the Bill and the indication in clause 49 is that the Secretary of State for the Home Department intends to proceed by way of grants to voluntary organisations rather than legal aid for lawyers. It is in the context of the challenge to the legality of detention that the Convention may require re-examination of the provisions of legal aid. While denial of entry to the territory may not breach a civil right, an interference with liberty will. Certainly, where the detained person seeks compensation for unlawful detention, Strasbourg has suggested that legal aid must be provided to ensure that the right is effective and accessible[12]. It would seem that similar reasoning lay behind the suggestions in *Amuur v France*, that access to a lawyer was a central need in order to exercise the article 5(4) rights of coming before a court to examine the necessity of future detention.

If this is so, then the Bill will require either a duty solicitor or public defender scheme or a significant extension of legal aid to cover detention hearings at the outset of the period. As the detention of asylum seekers is likely to raise immigration-related experience about the necessity of illegal departure, country of origin conditions, the prospects of success in a claim, the effects of trauma and the like, rather than the knowledge of an ordinary criminal court solicitor it would seem absurd that public provision of a specialist service at the front end of the process is limited to the appearance to review detention but does not at the same time embrace the substantive grounds for asylum that could not be realistically divorced from it. Early access to newly arrived clients by experienced and competent asylum practitioners will ensure that on interview the relevant considerations are taken into account and irrelevant ones excluded. The decision taker and the claimant could then focus on the real basis for claims for protection and take substantive and procedural decisions consistent with those issues[13].

4.7   Other human rights issues

This essay does not purport to provide a comprehensive human rights audit of the Bill in respect to the HRA. There is potential for conflict in many of its parts. Part VI

---

12   *Aerts v Belgium* (1998) 5 BHRC 383 at 403, para 59 where the Court concluded that a right to liberty was a civil right within the meaning of art 6(1) and that the legal aid authority was bound to grant legal aid to enable the applicant to appear before the Court. See also p 68.

13   See JUSTICE/ILPA Providing Protection Report 1996.

seeks to provide a very strict benefit regime in the hands of the Home Office for those seeking asylum and appealing against adverse decisions. There is potential for violations of articles 3, 5, and 8 by such a regime if it results in disproportionate interference with family or private life, exposes people to degrading circumstances or inhibits proper exercise of appeal rights. Part IX reviews civil marriage ceremony procedures and requires an investigation to be made into potentially abusive immigration marriages. No such requirement is imposed on church marriages, and this would seem to have a discriminatory impact on non-Christian communities. Part II increases the regime of carrier sanctions rendering vehicle owners liable to a penalty for carrying a concealed asylum seeker even if that person presents himself or herself on arrival. The procedures for confiscation of property may well engage Protocol 1 of the Convention. The considerable increase in immigration officer powers of search, entry, arrest and detention is not accompanied by an independent complaints authority. Absence of independent accountability may well lead to greater litigation as to abuse of discretion that interferes with liberty.

5. Conclusions

The enactment of the HRA and the commitment to effective implementation of international obligations is to be welcomed as a long overdue addition to our system of public law. It is unfortunate that in the immigration context, the minimum standards of human rights obligations are intended to replace a significant aspect of the appeal system designed to give appellate scrutiny of the compassionate merits of individual cases involving proposed removal. A leveling down to core obligations seems to be an aspect of European Union migration policy at present. The real concern is that this will lead to hard decisions of compassionate cases receiving inadequate judicial protection. As against this, there is at least a direct opportunity to restrain public officials acting in breach of their obligations that will be particularly important in cases of claims to protection from harm or ill treatment abroad.

Annex 1

IN THE MATTER OF
THE
INTERNATIONAL
HUMAN RIGHTS
PRINCIPLES
GOVERNING
DETENTION OF
ASYLUM SEEKERS

ADVICE

Nicholas Blake QC
2 Garden Court
Temple
London EC4
Tel 0171 353 1633
Fax 0171 353 4621

Solicitors:
JUSTICE

THE INTERNATIONAL PRINCIPLES GOVERNING DETENTION OF ASYLUM SEEKERS

ADVICE

Introduction

1.   I am asked to consider:-

i)   the principles governing the detention of asylum seekers under Article 5 of the European Convention on Human Rights and related human rights instruments consistent with that Article that would be taken into account by the Strasbourg Court;

ii)   the measures needed to be adopted in the United Kingdom to ensure compliance with these principles in the carrying out of immigration control.

2.   Discussion of the issue is considerably assisted by the decision of the European Court of Human Rights in *Amuur v France* (1996) 22 EHRR 533 and the decision of the UN Human Rights Committee in *A v Australia* (1997) applying the equivalent provisions of the International Covenant on Civil and Political Rights. Despite differences in wording between Article 5 of the ECHR and Article 9 of the ICCPR, these decisions demonstrate that the approach to the problems raised under both instruments is, in essential respects, the same, and I am confident that decisions of one body could be cited to the other with a view to a harmony on interpretation. The UK has ratified both instruments but at present only permits an individual right of access to the European Court of Human Rights. Relevant to the application of both instruments is the UN Body of Principles on All Forms of Detention (1988) that has been cited by both the European Court and the Human Rights Committee in resolving particular cases.

International Principles

3.   In my opinion, an analysis of these decisions and texts reveals the following principles:-

i)   Article 5(1) is engaged whenever a restraint on the liberty of free movement justified under Article 2.3 of Protocol 4 of the Convention becomes sufficiently prolonged in duration or repressive in character as to amount to a deprivation of liberty (*Amuur* para 43).

ii)   Article 5(1) is designed to prevent arbitrary detention (*Amuur* para 42) and therefore reflects the terms of Article 9 of the ICCPR where this concern is expressed directly.

iii) The concept of "in accordance with the law" in Article 5.1 is wider than merely accordance with national provisions and embraces the requirements of legality set down in the Convention (*Amuur* para 50).

iv)   A detention does not cease to be arbitrary because it is lawful under national law (*A v Australia* para 9.2).

v)   A detention of an asylum seeker can be considered arbitrary:

"if it is not necessary in all the circumstances of the case, for example to prevent flight or interference with evidence: the element of proportionality becomes relevant in this context" (*A v Australia* ibid).

vi) Detention is only justified under Article 5 (1)(f) to prevent "unauthorized entry into the country" or of those asylum seekers "against whom action is being taken with a view to deportation or extradition". Excessive restriction of liberty on those exercising their rights under international treaties would be incompatible with Article 5(1):

> "Holding aliens in the international zone does indeed involve a restriction on liberty, but one which is not in every respect comparable to that which obtains in centres for the detention of aliens pending deportation. Such confinement, accompanied by suitable safeguards for the person concerned, is acceptable only in order to enable States to prevent unlawful immigration while complying with their international obligations, particularly under the 1951 Geneva Convention and the European Convention on Human Rights. States' legitimate concerns to foil the increasingly frequent attempts to get round immigration restrictions must not deprive asylum seekers of the protection afforded by these Conventions" (*Amuur* para 43).

vii) The concept of detention in accordance with the law, requires a legal regime governing detention, as opposed to mere executive discretion to detain. The quality of all applicable measures relating to the detention is to be assessed:

> "Quality in this sense implies that where a national law authorises deprivation of liberty-especially in respect of a foreign asylum seeker-it must be sufficiently accessible and precise, in order to avoid all risk of arbitrariness. These characteristics are of fundamental importance with regard to asylum seekers at airports particularly in view of the need to reconcile the protection of fundamental rights with the requirements of State's immigration policies" (*Amuur* para 50).

viii) The applicable principles cannot be evaded by declaring that:-
   a) an airport is an international zone and so a person is deemed not to be in the territory of the Contracting state;
   b) the deprivation of liberty to be voluntary as the applicant is always free to leave the territory voluntarily and go elsewhere;
   (*Amuur* para 43, para 46 and para 52).

ix) A person deprived of liberty under Article 5(1) must have the right of access to a court for the purpose of a speedy decision determining the legality of the detention (Article 5(4); *Amuur* para 43).

x) Although the Convention lays no time limits on detention for the purpose of preventing unlawful entry, and imposes no duty to be brought before a court in a specified time (contrast Article 5(3) in respect of criminal detainees), the Convention requirements of legality impose a requirement of review by a court within a reasonable time. In the *Amuur* case the Court observed (para 43):

> "although by the force of circumstances the decision to order holding must necessarily be taken by the administrative or police authorities, the prolongation requires speedy review by the courts, the traditional guardians of personal liberties."

xi) The national court conducting such a review must not be confined to the restricted question of whether there is jurisdiction to detain according to national criteria but must also deal with the requirements for legality laid down by the international instrument (*Amuur* para 50 and 53; *A v Australia* para 9.5).

xii) In *Amuur* the detention was incompatible with Article 5(1) because (para 53):

> "At the material time none of these texts (administrative circulars) allowed the ordinary courts to review the conditions under which aliens were held or, if necessary, to impose a limit on the administrative authorities as regards the length of time for which they were held. They did not provide for legal, humanitarian and social assistance, nor did they lay down procedures and time limits for access to such assistance so that asylum seekers … could take the necessary steps".

xiii) The importance of effective control of the detention by the Courts is also emphasised by principle 4 and principle 11(3) of the UN Body of Principles. Those principles in addition require:-
a)   the detained person has an effective opportunity to be heard promptly by a judicial or other authority whether in person or by counsel;
b)   prompt receipt by the detained person of the order of detention together with the reasons therefore.
xiv) Detained asylum seekers are entitled to legal advice and assistance if they request it (*A v Australia* para 9.5; Principle 17(1)).
xv) Where detention is not lawful in the sense ascribed to it by any of the provisions of Article 5 of the Convention, there must be an enforceable right to compensation (Article 5(5)).

Application to the United Kingdom

4.   The United Kingdom has a code for regulating the examination and admission of non-nationals to its territory in the form of the Immigration Acts 1971 to 1996. Incidental to the process of examination of a passenger who is not a citizen in order to determine whether they should be admitted to the territory of the state, there is an ancillary power to detain pending conclusion of the examination and any removal thereafter. Such incidental restriction of liberty is consistent with international law and the principles of Protocol 4 of the Convention as explained in *Amuur*. However such incidental powers were not drafted with the problems of asylum seekers in mind, where a far longer process of examination and removal may occur. This gives rise to a potential conflict with international obligations.

5.   Under Immigration Act 1971, Schedule 2, an immigration officer is entitled to detain a person seeking leave to enter the United Kingdom whose examination is not complete or a person facing removal as an illegal entrant or pursuant to deportation powers. Under the Immigration (Places of Detention) Direction 1996, after five consecutive days detention, such detention must be at either a prison, remand centre, approved hospital, place of safety in respect of children or one of four authorised detention centres in England or Wales or an authorised police cell in Scotland. There is no time limit set to the length of the period of examination[1]. A right to apply to a special adjudicator for bail only arises 7 days after arrival[2].

6.   An immigration officer may, instead of detaining such a person temporarily, admit him or her at an approved address and may require a surety for such admission. Since 1991 there have been departmental instructions to immigration officers concerning the use of these powers in asylum cases. These were revised in 1994 and a copy

1   See *R v Secretary of State for the Home Department, ex p Thirukumar* (1991) Imm AR.
2   Immigration Act 1971, Schedule 2, para 22(1) and (1B) amended by Asylum Act 1996.

provided to Amnesty International following which they became known to practitioners in 1996[3]. It is said that the policy is:

> "to grant temporary admission/release whenever possible and to authorise detention only where there is no alternative. The aim is to free detention space for all those who have shown a real disregard for the immigration laws and whom we expect to remove within a realistic timetable".

7.   Eight factors relevant to the exercise of discretion are set out in the instructions. They are:

i)   previous absconding;
ii)   previous failure to comply with conditions of release;
iii) blatant disregard for immigration control (entry in breach of deportation order or clandestine entry);
iv)   attempted entry on falsified documents;
v)   likelihood of removal within a reasonable time scale;
vi)   previous history of compliance with immigration control;
vii) ties with the UK;
viii) the individual's expectations of success, and any continuing incentive to keep in contact with the department.

8.   A decision not to exercise temporary admission can be the subject of challenge:

i)   in a bail application to an adjudicator whose jurisdiction to hear such applications has been enlarged by the 1996 Asylum and Immigration Act to cover any case where a person is held pending removal directions[4];
ii)   in judicial review of a failure to exercise discretion lawfully and rationally and with regard to any directions or guidance issued to officers by the Home Office[5].

9.   In addition a detained person could challenge the jurisdiction to detain him by means of *habeas corpus* proceedings. However in *habeas corpus* proceedings the Court is limited to the question of whether there is power in law to detain the person and is not a means of reviewing the exercise of discretion to detain. As *habeas* proceedings are limited to an examination of the jurisdiction to detain[6], such a limited review would not by itself satisfy the requirements of Article 5(4) of the Convention as interpreted above. They could not engage the wider concept of legality[7]. There may, however, come a time when excessive duration of detention

---

3   For the disclosure of these instructions see CO 4251/95 *ex p Brezinski and Elowacka* Kay J QBD 19 July 1996 unreported
4   Immigration Act 1971, Schedule 2, para 22(1A).
5   See *R v Secretary of State for the Home Department, ex p AKB* CO 2053-96 McCullough J granting leave to move (unreported) 1996 where the question was whether the officers had properly applied the instructions; leave was also granted to challenge the Special Adjudicator's refusal of bail on the basis that "I do not believe that I have to give reasons. I think there is a chance that the appellant will not attend court".
6   *R v Secretary of State for the Home Department, ex p Muboyayi* (1992) QB 244. For the protection against an action for damages that an apparently valid detention order provides see also *Ullah v Home Office* (1995).
7   See the above principles and the decision of the ECtHR in the case of *Chahal v United Kingdom* where a violation of Article 5(4) was found.

pending removal makes the detention unlawful and amenable to intervention by *habeas corpus* [8]. Such an argument is founded on the proposition that the jurisdiction to detain pending removal is strictly limited to detentions where the possibility of removal to a third country is reasonably possible in the foreseeable future. Where removal is not a practical possibility for a variety of reasons such as: no transport connections, local unrest, no travel documents, refusal of admission, then the power to detain will cease to exist.

10.   Legal aid is available for applicants to challenge their detention in the High Court but there is no legal aid for representation before adjudicators including representation on bail applications.   Free legal assistance is however available to those in detention either for advice on making a bail application under the Green Form or assistance given by voluntary and charitable agencies concerned with the detention of asylum seekers, some of whom are in receipt of central government funds to provide this service.

Discussion

11.   In my opinion, there is clearly a statutory regime for the exercise of the power of detention in the United Kingdom; some limitation to its duration and purpose and some scope for effective access to challenge to the courts. There is consequently broad compliance with the terms of Article 5(1) of the Convention. Access to the statutory scheme will remain reasonably effective only for so long as funding arrangements are in place to ensure that every detained and impecunious asylum seeker has a right to representation for the purpose of bail proceedings. Further it is not sufficient that there is access to a court merely at the outset of the detention. Continued judicial supervision of the detention is necessary to ensure that it is necessary for one of the permitted reasons and proportionate in the light of all relevant circumstances.

12.   It is important to note that detention of those *arriving* in the UK is only permitted under Article 5 (1)(f) of the Convention in order to prevent *unlawful* entry to the territory of a Contracting State. A person who claims asylum at the port of entry is not acting unlawfully whatever incidental ruses have been adopted in order for the claim to be made. In terms of the domestic law code s/he is simply seeking admission. A person who arrives without a visa or has left his country on a forged passport or travel document is attempting to enter legally if s/he presents himself to the national authorities on arrival. This has been accepted by the House of Lords in *R v Naillie* [9]. A person who is a visa national may face refusal of admission if they did not have a current visa, but there is no requirement for refugees to have to obtain a prior visa in national law. No party to the 1951 Convention could impose such a requirement as a condition of applying the overriding duty of non-refoulement in Article 33(1) of the Convention. A policy of detention of asylum seekers by reference to support for a general visa regime for aliens would be incompatible with the Convention.

---

8   *R v Governor of Durham Prison, ex p Hardial Singh* (1984) 1 WLR 704; approved *Tan Le Lam v Tai A Chau Detention Centre* (1997) AC 97.

9   (1993) AC 694.

13.   In the case of admissions, therefore, following the passage of the Human Rights Bill, once detention is shown to exist within the meaning of Article 5 (1) the burden of justification of the detention should fall on the government in any proceedings to examine the compatibility of the detention with the law including the Convention. The government will need to demonstrate it falls within one of the purposes approved by the Convention. The principle of proportionality would require a fair examination and balance of the competing factors disclosed on the evidence.

14.   This does not mean that no asylum seeker seeking admission can be detained. Where there are strong grounds to conclude that the Convention claim is known by the applicant to be spurious and all the circumstances point to a real possibility that faced with refusal of the claim the applicant would abscond and go to ground and thereby illegally enter the UK, detention would not be inconsistent with Article 5(1)(f). General castigation of certain claims as "abusive" tends to obfuscate the issues unless a very tight definition of abusive is adopted that is consistent with international protection claims. Following incorporation, this will mean that *bona fide* claimants will include those facing return to inhuman or degrading treatment or punishment in their own countries as well as those who meet the definition in the 1951 Convention.

15.   Detention pending removal from the United Kingdom is also catered for in Article 5(1)(f) and in these cases the most material question is likely to be whether removal is such a remote and impractical prospect for the foreseeable future that it can no longer be said that the detention is for the purpose of the removal[10]. The fact that removal will necessarily be deferred whist an asylum claim is determined does not necessarily make it too remote to justify continued detention[11] but the kinds of delays that sometimes occur in asylum cases pending determination and appeal are clearly much longer than the initial than the ordinary immigration case originally envisaged by the Immigration Act and the Convention.

16.   At present the instructions issued to staff (which I understand still to be current practice) provide some material by which the exercise of the detention power is subject to supervision. However, it should be noted first that the instructions were not made publicly available as a circular to practitioners and adjudicators, and like so many other documents relating to the immigration system, came out by chance. In my opinion, such a random approach to an important text that may make the difference between liberty and custody in an individual case is unsatisfactory and not in accordance with the requirements of transparency and certainty as required by the Convention. Transparency, proportionality, consistency and effective judicial review all form part of the legality of the decision in the heightened sense used by the international instruments. Lawyers, judges and detainees must know what the criteria for detention are if bail applications and judicial review challenges are to be meaningful. The Convention concept of legality and certainty requires all such policies to be published and circulated to relevant authorities and bodies.

---

10   See *Hardial Singh* supra fn 8.
11   See *R v Secretary of State for the Home Department, ex p Chahal (No 2)* (1996) Imm AR 205 QBD and the European Court of Human Rights' decision in the same case commented on in para 17 below; see also *Secretary of State for the Home Department v Khan* (1995) 348 CA; *Re Samateh* (1996) Imm AR 1.

17.   Secondly, the present presumption in favour of liberty contained in those instructions and in the general law is not as clear as it should be. Certain parts of the circular suggest that the existing presumption of liberty if possible is dictated more by administrative concerns: (priority use of detention facilities and to effect speed of removal) rather than Convention principles of respect for human rights. It is uncertain whether domestic law of itself creates a presumption of liberty in the case of administrative detention. Despite the modern influence of human rights legislation there is a long history of administrative detention at the discretion of the state. Some argue that the presumption of liberty only applies to those who have the right of abode within the meaning of section 1 of the Immigration Act 1971[12]. As long as there is evidence that a person is seeking vindication of his /her international rights to seek protection from persecution or inhuman or degrading treatment abroad, then the international principles of legality as identified in paragraph 3 above would preclude detention that was not proportionate or necessary having regard to its impact on the right to seek asylum. In my opinion, therefore both the legislation and the published circulars should re-state the presumption of liberty in asylum cases and affirm that justification of detention rests with the state in the particular circumstances of the individual case. Compliance with Convention principles requires that asylum seekers are not treated worse than suspected criminals in this respect. As the Court noted in *Amuur* (para 43):

> "account should be taken of the fact the measure is applicable not to those who have committed criminal offences but to aliens who, often fearing for their lives, have fled from their own country".

18.   Further, the present arrangements for review of a decision to detain are inadequate. There is no duty to bring a detained person before an adjudicator or magistrate. There is no duty to explain the reasons for detention in the particular case. There is no legal limit to the numbers of days of detention in total or at any one stage of the process: consideration, appeal, removal. Clearly many asylum cases are complex, require careful consideration, examination of further evidence and judicial review and if good reason to detain exists throughout this process, substantial periods of detention pending removal may be compatible with the Convention. On the other hand the decision taker must keep under continuous evaluation whether admission should be granted on the broad range of humanitarian criteria, or that removal cannot be effected, or that past objections no longer apply and speedy release is required. A voluntary duty of internal review is insufficient and an independent judicial body needs to ensure that such evaluation has been undertaken and there has been no change of relevant circumstances. Insufficient reasons are given at present and errors consequently occur. In the case of *W v Home Office*[13] a Liberian asylum seeker was detained for a further 14 days beyond 28 days already suffered because a questionnaire completed by another asylum seeker designed to elicit whether he was indeed Liberian had been wrongly placed on his file. If the immigrant and his lawyers had been aware of the reason for detention they could have readily pointed out that no questionnaire had been completed. Whilst the ECtHR did not consider that the four

---

12   See Defendants arguments in *W v Home Office* fn 12 below. The Court of Appeal were not persuaded by this limb of the argument and concluded that unnecessary prolongation of the detention of an alien could amount to damage for the purpose of the law of negligence.

13   (1997) Imm AR 302.

years of domestic consideration engaged in the *Chahal* case represented a breach of Article 5(1) on the grounds of undue delay or overall excess. *Chahal* was nevertheless an exceptional case where considerations of national security dominated both the decision to expel and the decision to detain pending expulsion. Even in such cases, the Court found a violation of 5(4) because there was no adequate effective judicial remedy able to review and control the detention process demonstrating the point made in *Amuur* that it is not the formal legality of the detention but its necessity and proportionality to the human rights issues engaged that must be addressed.

19. In "normal" asylum cases the principles derived from *Amuur* above are applicable. It is to be noted in that case, the French Government was only seeking to detain in the international zone pending consideration of whether the asylum claim was manifestly ill founded rather than its substantive determination (although it may be that the French Government gives a rather over generous interpretation to the term "manifestly ill founded", the scope of the term being a matter of controversy).

20. In my opinion, once restriction on liberty by the requirement of examination at the ports lasts more than a few hours it becomes an interference of liberty that requires justification and judicial supervision. The present seven day bar on bail applications and production before a court equates asylum seekers who are not (or not necessarily) entering in breach of the laws with terrorists held under the Prevention of Terrorism Act. There should be a duty to bring detainees before a court after 48 hours and regular periods of remand pending decision or appeal thereafter.

21. Whatever the maximum period of unsupervised detention, it should enable proper reasons for the decision to detain to be drafted and served on the immigrant and the judicial authority. It should be wholly exceptional to refuse temporary admission or release to an asylum seeker whose claim is prima facie admissible and requires detailed investigation. Reasons must relate to the individual in hand rather than recite bland formulas.

22. Bail applications must be heard speedily. Conditions for admission to bail must not be excessive or inappropriate and the presumption of liberty and that exceptional nature of restriction of liberty of an asylum seeker should be respected and enforced by the decision taker and the courts. The fact that travel documents may have been destroyed pre-entry as part of the means of escape is not a sufficient reason to refuse bail. It may be that special duty adjudicators should be established to review these cases, or that bail jurisdiction could pass to stipendiary magistrates; in either case proper guidance as to the Convention principles needs to be given. I have already noted that access to legal representation and publication of relevant detention instructions are also necessary to ensure that judicial scrutiny is effective.

23. There should be better limits on the maximum periods of detention. The depressing and purposeless nature of the detention regime has been the subject of recent informed comment by the Chief Inspector of Prisons. Custody time limits in the criminal sphere have had the effect of focusing the minds on all concerned with the effective preparation and disposal of litigation and ancillary inquiries. There is little jurisprudence to define the limits of the power to detain in terms of precise length, each case depending on the particular problems presented by its own facts. Nevertheless, in my opinion, it should be the very rare and exceptional case that

would justify detention of an asylum seeker for longer than a few weeks. Those facing removal following refusal of their claims should not be detained for longer than six months and really substantial reasons would have to apply for this period of detention. After such a period the applicant should be released or at least brought before the court for the state to explain why exceptional measures are required that make continued detention unavoidable.

Nicholas Blake QC
April 27, 1998

Annex 2

PARLIAMENTARY UNDER
SECRETARY OF STATE

HOME OFFICE
QUEEN ANNE'S GATE
LONDON SW1H 9AT

Mr Murray Hunt
Mr Rabinder Singh
4-5 Gray's Inn Square
Gray's Inn
London WC1R 5AY

12 May 1998

Dear Murray + Rabinder,

Thank you for your letter of 13 March about clause 7(13) of the Human Rights Bill. I am sorry for not replying before now.

It is, of course, our intention that tribunals should be able to take account of Convention points where they are relevant to the cases before them. For the very good reasons you set out in your letter, we decided that it would be wholly inappropriate for the Convention rights to remain the preserve of the courts.

We agree that the aim of clause 7(13) is to deal with those very rare cases - the special adjudicator hearing certain asylum appeals under the Asylum and Immigration Appeals Act 1993 is the only one we are currently aware of - where the grounds on which proceedings may be brought before a tribunal are extremely narrowly defined, either by statute or by restrictive judicial interpretation of statutory provisions. In your letter you make the point that the current wording of clause 7(13) might be misleading. In particular, you explain that, contrary to the intentions of the Bill, tribunals might read it as preventing them from taking account of the Convention rights unless and until a Minister expressly confers power on them to do so under the clause 7(13) provision.

We accept that, notwithstanding the general terms in which other clauses of the Bill are cast, there is some danger that clause 7(13) might be read in this restrictive fashion. We want to remove any risk of such an interpretation, and we have been reflecting on how the potential problem you have identified can be addressed.

As you note, we have rejected the option of simply doing nothing in the Human Rights Bill and instead dealing with these rare cases by amending the relevant legislation restricting the tribunal's jurisdiction. The use of the order-making power is intended to be only a short-term solution until a suitable opportunity arises to amend the primary legislation in question. But we have concluded that it is important to have such a stop-gap provision in the Bill.

Like you, we also see the limitations of relying on Ministerial statements as a means of clarifying the intention behind clause 7(13). We do not see that as a satisfactory solution.

We have therefore decided to revise the wording of clause 7(13). The revised subsection will differ somewhat from the version you proposed, but I hope you will agree that it addresses the concerns in your letter. The phrase "to determine such questions arising in connection with the Convention rights", which you considered to be too wide in its scope, will be deleted. The subsection will be framed in terms of a power to give certain relief. It will relate back to unlawful acts under clause 6(1), and hence to the wording in clause 7(1). In addition, the revised version will make it clear that the power to make an order applies only where it is "necessary" to ensure that the tribunal in question can provide an appropriate remedy in respect of an unlawful act. And the word "jurisdiction" will be removed because its exact meaning in this subsection might not be entirely clear.

The revised subsection (13) will read as follows:

> (13) The Minister who has power to make rules in relation to a particular tribunal may, to the extent he considers it necessary to ensure that the tribunal can provide an appropriate remedy in relation to an act (or proposed act) of a public authority which is (or would be) unlawful as a result of section 6(1), by order add to -
> (a) the relief or remedies which the tribunal may grant; or
> (b) the grounds on which it may grant any of them.

We will be tabling an amendment to this effect at Commons Committee.

Thank you for drawing this issue to our attention.

I am copying this letter to Earl Russell, Nicholas Blake QC and Anne Owers. I am also copying it to Lord Lester, who wrote in support of your letter, and to the Lord Chancellor to whom Lord Lester copied his.

Regards,

THE LORD WILLIAMS OF MOSTYN

CHAPTER 3

The Human Rights Act: how to use it in Immigration and nationality cases

Raza Husain and Frances Webber

1. Introduction

This section explores procedural issues which are likely to arise in using the Human Rights Act 1998 ('HRA') to plead breaches of the Convention. It looks at the forum in which the Convention can be used, jurisdictional issues, standing, potential respondents, the courts' and tribunals' criteria for assessment in cases under the HRA, and the powers and remedies available to the courts and the appellate authorities.

The effect of the HRA will not be limited to cases in which an allegation of a breach of the Convention is made. The interpretive obligation in section 3(1), modelled on the approach to the domestic effect of Community law provisions laid down in *Marleasing Special Adjudicator v La Commercial Internacional de Alimentacion SA* C-106/89 [1990] ECR I-4135, requires all legislation to be interpreted so as to give effect to Convention obligations unless such an interpretation is impossible. This is revolutionary and will have a profound impact on principles of statutory interpretation in cases even where no breaches of Convention rights are pleaded. The approach to legislation required by section 3(1) was prevented in *R v Secretary of State for the Home Department, ex p Brind* [1991] 1 AC 696, but had been preferred by Lord Diplock in *Garland v British Rail Engineering* [1983] 2 AC 751. Recent cases have marked a trend to afford the ECHR more significance in domestic law (see reference below to *R v Secretary of State for the Home Department, ex p Ahmed and Patel* [1998] INLR 570 and *R v Secretary of State for the Home Department, ex p Thompson and Venables* [1998] AC 407). A presumption of conformity will apply henceforth not just to ambiguous statutory words, but to neutral ones, such as those contained in section 22(1) of the Immigration Act 1971 ('The Lord Chancellor may make rules (of procedure) for regulating the exercise of rights of appeal ...'). The presumption applies to all legislation, whenever enacted (section 3(2)(a)). It applies to primary and subordinate legislation. Immigration rules are subordinate legislation for the purposes of the HRA (section 21(1)). The importance of the interpretive obligation is revisited below.

Convention rights, defined in section 1 of the HRA, can be used as a shield: section 7(1)(a), or a sword: sections 7(1)(a) and 7(2).

2. Forum

The Convention can be relied on in every court or tribunal (including immigration adjudicators). Most breaches will be adjudicated on in the normal appellate process, or in proceedings for judicial review or habeas corpus.

It will also be possible to assert breaches of Convention rights in private law actions against the Home Office. For example, a false imprisonment case involving the illegal detention of an immigrant, asylum-seeker or British citizen, brought in the County Court or the High Court, might involve a breach of article 5(1); an unlawful removal from the country might be pleaded as a breach of article 3 or article 8 as well as (for example) misfeasance or negligence.

3.   Victim

Only those who would be victims under the Convention are able to bring proceedings under the HRA or rely on Convention rights in other proceedings: section 7(6). Article 34 ECHR defines this as persons actually and directly affected. In *Klass v Germany* ((1978) 2 EHRR 214) and *Marckx v Belgium* ((1979) 2 EHRR 330) the EctHR included those running the risk of being directly affected. The fact that a State has granted short-term status does not prevent the person from continuing to be a 'victim of a violation' for ECHR purposes: *Ahmed v Austria* ((1996) 24 EHRR 278, ECtHR). In article 8 cases where the applicant is overseas, the UK sponsor will be able to claim 'victim' status as someone actually and directly affected.

This class is much narrower than those who currently have standing for judicial review (see *R v Secretary of State for Foreign and Commonwealth Affairs, ex p World Development Movement Ltd* ([1995] 1 WLR 386 at 392G-396C and 403E)), where the High Court has become used to allowing public interest organisations (JCWI, ILPA) to bring proceedings. Often a 'representative' case such as JCWI's on withdrawal of benefits from asylum-seekers, ILPA's on mandatory application forms, or the Medical Foundation's on shipping asylum-seekers out of London, will save a multiplicity of proceedings and public funds. The inability of such organisations to take cases, in particular to challenge primary legislation, eg section 11 of the Asylum and Immigration Act 1996, or the seven-day delay before immigrants detained pending further examination can apply for bail (Sch 2, para 22 of the Immigration Act 1971) could be problematic, if a ready 'victim' cannot be found.

One solution, however, may be found in the growing practice in both domestic courts and the ECtHR of allowing intervention by public interest organisations in proceedings. In the House of Lords provision is made to allow appropriate intervention (Practice Directions and Standing Orders, Directions 34 and 29) and interventions were permitted in cases such as *R v Bow Street Metropolitan Stipendiary Magistrate, ex p Pinochet Ugarte* ([1998] 4 All ER 897), *(No 2)* ([1999] 1 All ER 577) and *R v Secretary of State for the Home Department, ex p Sivakumaran* ([1988] AC 958, 992D), *R v Bournewood Community and Mental Health NHS Trust, ex p Mr Liu Wei Ping* ([1998] 3 WLR 107, 112E-F), and *R v Secretary of State for the Home Department, ex p Thompson and Venables* ([1998] AC 407).   In the Court of Appeal, Lord Woolf MR commented in *R v Chief Constable of the North Wales Police, ex p AB* ([1998] 3 WLR 57, 66G-H) on the value of the interventions from both the SSHD and NACRO. Lord Woolf endorsed the conclusions of the Justice/Public Law Project Report on Public Interest Interventions (1996: chairman Sir John Laws), which had concluded that the disadvantages of such interventions are generally outweighed by the advantages. In the Divisional Court, interventions have been permitted in *R v Secretary of State for the Home Department, ex p Manjit Kaur and Cheung Hung* (CO/985/98, CO/444/99) pursuant to the Court's inherent jurisdiction to control its own process. An intervention by a private body was allowed in *R v Ministry of Agriculture Fisheries and Food, ex p Anastasiou* ([1994] ECR I-3087). Moreover an intervention was permitted by the ECtHR in *HLR v France* (29.4.97 (24573/94)(1997) 26 EHRR 29), while Lord Irvine of Lairg LC in the Second Reading of the Human Rights Bill in the House of Lords on 24 November 1997, recognised the 'development – that is to say, allowing third parties to intervene and be heard – which has already begun' and envisaged that 'our courts will be ready to permit' such interventions (HL Debs, cols 832-834).

Furthermore, it is arguable that there will also be scope for public interest litigation using Convention rights tangentially. ILPA, for example, may be able to bring an 'ordinary' judicial review of, eg, mandatory application forms for those seeking exceptional leave to remain on article 3 grounds as a *Wednesbury* unreasonable exercise of a rule-making power under the Act which has to be exercised in conformity with the Convention. The counter argument would be that such litigation falls within section 7(1)(b) and that ILPA lacks standing.

4. Respondents

The definition of 'public authority' includes courts and tribunals (section 6(3)(a)). Thus a ground of appeal to the Tribunal from a first-instance case would be the Adjudicator's failure to give effect to a Convention right.

'Public authority' also includes Group 4 and private agencies responsible for carrying out deportations, who may be liable in private law under article 3 for conditions in detention facilities or for inhuman or degrading treatment during removal such as resulted in the death of Joy Gardner. The definition would also encompass Eurostar and British Airways, and other carriers insofar as refusing tickets to passengers without visas or carrying deportees are public functions. The private acts of private bodies which carry out some public functions and are therefore public authorities for the purposes of section 6(3)(b) are excluded by section 6(5).

The definition focuses on the (public) nature of the functions being discharged rather than the (private) character of the body, and accordingly appears to be wider than the EU law 'emanation of a state' test and at least as wide as that in judicial review (eg *R v Panel on Take overs and Mergers, ex p Datafin plc* ([1987] QD 815)). This is consistent with the position under ECHR, where a private body is nevertheless liable if it performs functions which are the ultimate responsibility of the State (*Foti v Italy* (1982) 5 EHRR 313) or where the State controls its activities through, eg majority shareholding (*Loizidou v Turkey*).

5. Jurisdiction of appellate authority

By virtue of section 7(1) of the HRA, the Convention rights set out in Sch 1 of the Act can be relied upon in all appeals[1] before the appellate authority to allege that the decision or action complained of, whether of the entry clearance officer, immigration officer or of the Secretary of State, is unlawful as incompatible with a Convention right (section 6(1)). This will be regardless of whether a decision is or is not in accordance with any immigration rules applicable to the case. Thus, in cases where

---

1   At least all those governed by the Immigration Act 1971, ss 19, 20. For other appeals and appeals under the Immigration and Asylum Bill 1999, see below (and chapter 2 at p 35)

appeal rights exist but are currently hollow – such as refugee family reunion appeals, cases under Home Office concessions, refusals of exceptional leave to in-country applicants – the appellate authority will no longer be entitled or obliged to dismiss an appeal on jurisdictional grounds. Similarly, it is arguable that bail hearings under Schedule 2 of the 1971 Act or under the proposals for routine hearings under the 1999 Bill will be able to be used to determine the lawfulness of the detention with reference to article 5.

There are a number of situations, however, where no appeal right exists at all. Port applicants or illegal entrants who seek exceptional leave to enter have no right of appeal against refusal. Appeal rights were removed under the 1993 Act from people not holding particular documents (work permit, entry clearance) or who are the wrong age or nationality, or want to remain longer than the maximum period permitted under the immigration rules. In others, although a right of appeal exists, the normal jurisdiction under sections 19 and 20 of the Immigration Act 1971 is restricted and the appellate authority has no jurisdiction to consider whether a decision is in accordance with the law. In a restricted deportation appeal (Immigration Act 1988, section 5) the appellate authority's jurisdiction is limited to considering whether there is power in law to make the order *for the reasons stated in the notice*. The Court of Appeal held in *R v Secretary of State for the Home Department, ex p Malhi* [1990] Imm AR 275 that this did not empower adjudicators on appeal to decide the general legality of the decision (ie, whether it was in accordance with general principles of administrative law). Similarly, the appellate authority's jurisdiction on an asylum appeal under section 8 of the Asylum and Immigration Appeals Act 1993 is restricted to considering whether removal would be in breach of the UK's obligations under the 1951 Refugee Convention; it cannot consider whether removal would breach article 3 of the ECHR.

In the case of the restricted appeal right against deportation, the interpretive obligation under section 3(1) of the HRA, which requires primary and subordinate legislation to be read and given effect in a way compatible with Convention rights, means adjudicators may be able to interpret 'no power in law' as embracing rights under the HRA and to refuse deportation as breaching Convention rights. But it would not be possible to read section 8 of the Asylum and Immigration Act 1993 to extend protection beyond the 1951 Convention. After representations on this potential gap in protection, section 7(11) of the HRA was added by amendment, which gives the minister a rule-making power to widen the jurisdiction of the appellate authority by adding to the grounds on which it may grant relief as well as adding to the forms of relief or remedies a tribunal may grant.

In fact, the Immigration and Asylum Bill currently before Parliament purports to deal with these problems by the introduction of a free-standing 'human rights appeal'[2], which will be exercisable against any decision of an immigration officer or the Secretary of State 'relating to that person's entitlement to enter or remain in the UK'. This is clearly intended to provide an effective remedy against all breaches of the Human Rights Act so as to comply with article 13 (which has not been included in the incorporated rights in the Schedule to the Act). It would provide an appeal right against a refusal of leave to enter or remain, refusal of exceptional leave or decision to remove an overstayer or to deport on conducive or family grounds.

As drafted, however, the clause refers to past breaches of human rights by an IO or the Secretary of State, unlike section 7 of the HRA which explicitly covers proposals

2   Clause 59 (of the Bill as published on 28 July 1999 after amendment in Committee in the House of Lords).

to act in violation (such as decisions to deport or to remove). There is no indication in the Bill that an appeal under clause 59 would lead to suspension of any deportation or removal as long as that appeal is pending. Since other parts of the Bill abolish the suspensive effect of deportation appeals for overstayers, it is feared that the clause 59 appeal is not intended to be suspensive save perhaps in exceptional circumstances. (Such circumstances would need to be set out in rules, and would necessitate a stay on removal, equivalent to the European Court of Human Right's Rule 39 procedure[3], being granted by the adjudicator – a power currently not available but one which could be provided by rules made under section 7(11).)

6. Restrictions on appeal rights, procedural hurdles and article 6

The proposed human rights appeal in the 1999 Bill is not available against decisions of entry clearance officers, and is subject to strict procedural requirements of advance notice which will reduce its availability. It might be possible to argue that procedural bars and restrictions on appeal rights offend against article 6(1) (fair trial in the determination of civil rights and obligations). There is fierce debate as to how far article 6 ECHR (right to a fair trial) can be used in immigration and asylum appeals and applications. Although the jurisprudence equating civil rights with private law rights has been weakened considerably in recent years, immigration and nationality rights, and rights to asylum, have consistently been held to be outside the formula. 'The right of an alien to reside in a country is a matter of public law': *Agee v United Kingdom* (1977 7 DR 164); *P v United Kingdom* (13162/87, 54 DR 211).

However, it is now established that both social security and social assistance (means-tested benefits) are 'civil rights' attracting the due process guarantees of article 6§1 (*Feldbrugge v Netherlands* (29.5.86, Series A No 99 (1986) 8 EHRR 425) – right to social security; *Salesi v Italy* (26.2.93, Series A No 257-E); and *Schuler-Zgraggen v Switzerland*, 24.6.93, Series A, No 264 (1993) 16 EHRR 405 – right to social assistance). And rights to respect for family life (mostly cases involving the welfare of children) have been held to require fair trial guarantees under article 6 (Harris, O'Boyle and Warbrick, pp 180-181, and cases cited there).

What this means is that procedural bars or restrictions to appeal rights would be challengeable by reference to article 6 if they impacted on family life or on welfare rights. Thus, the denial of an appeal under clause 59 to a deportee who had failed to indicate in advance that he intended to raise human rights issues would engage article 6(1) if family life issues were raised. Restriction of appeal rights in cases of refusal or removal affecting rights to occupy property in the UK, would similarly offend against article 6 because the right vindicated is not a right to residence in the country but the 'civil right' of peaceful enjoyment of property. Free movement rights, involving rights to exercise professions or to engage in or continue employment, would engage article 6, again not through the right to residence aspect but through the rights to exercise a profession or to work in a particular job.

Article 6 would be available, too, to challenge refusal of support to destitute asylum-seekers during the period while they were appealing the decision that they are not entitled to support, since access to a court must be effective (*Golder v United*

3   Rule 39, that is, of the Strasbourg Rules of Court (formerly r 36).

Kingdom (1975) 1 EHRR 524; *Airey v United Kingdom* 9.10.79, Series A No 32) and will not be effective if they cannot survive to pursue it (*R v Secretary of State for Social Security, ex p Joint Council for the Welfare of Immigrants* [1997] 1 WLR 275). Since the right to a fair trial applies par excellence to criminal cases and to the imposition of quasi-criminal penalties (see eg *Lauko v Slovakia* (4/1998/907/1119)), article 6 will be available to challenge the lack of a court hearing and the reverse burden of proof on carriers of clandestine entrants who are to be penalised under the 1999 Bill. These challenges (in common with all challenges to gaps in the structures of protection) would have to be by way of judicial review, since they are predicated on absent appeal rights.

Unless, however, the right to asylum itself can be claimed as a civil right the determination of which requires fair trial guarantees, it will be impossible to argue that such devices as the reduction of appeal rights because of failure to produce a valid passport (under the accelerated procedures for 'manifestly unfounded' applications, Sch 2, para 5 of the Asylum and Immigration Appeals Act 1993 as amended, to be duplicated by the 1999 Bill provisions), engage article 6.

Of course, in cases where there is no appeal right or no effective appeal right, judicial review will, as before, be available. But the importance of retaining full appeal rights in all cases where human rights are engaged lies in the appellate authority's fact-finding role, which distinguishes it from the supervisory jurisdiction of judicial review.

7.   Judicial review and article 13

The High Court has become familiar with the Convention albeit to some extent at second hand, through cases on the Home Office policy on marriage and deportation (eg *Amankwah* [1994] Imm AR 240), where the issues were treated more as policy ones than engaging international obligations or fundamental rights. Sedley J has been prepared to speak the language of fundamental rights in cases such as *R v Secretary of State for the Home Department, ex p McQuillan* [1995] 4 All ER 400. It is in freedom of speech cases such as *Derbyshire County Council v Times Newpapers Ltd* [1993] AC 534 that the courts have been most prepared to look at the merits of particular restrictions and more or less apply a full-blown proportionality test. In immigration, however, the High Court has been on the whole very reluctant to look at the merits or to move away from a *Wednesbury* review.

In *Chahal v United Kingdom* (1996) 23 EHRR 413 the ECtHR said that article 13 (an effective remedy) required:

'... the provision of a domestic remedy allowing the competent authority both to deal with **the substance** of the relevant Convention complaint and to grant appropriate relief ...'

In an article 3 case:

'... the notion of an effective remedy ... requires **independent scrutiny** of the claim that there exist substantial grounds for fearing a real risk of treatment contrary to Art 3...'

The court held that judicial review was not an effective remedy for a Sikh who faced deportation on national security grounds, because the domestic court was precluded from reviewing the factual basis underlying the national security considerations invoked by the Secretary of State to justify deportation. However, in *D v United*

Kingdom ((1997) 24 EHRR 423) judicial review was held to be an effective remedy and *Chahal* was distinguished. The judgment that judicial review was effective in that case was predicated on the absence there of any dispute of fact.

The independent scrutiny required for an effective remedy will now be provided by the appellate authority in most cases (including those involving national security, by virtue of the Special Immigration Appeals Commission Act 1997). In an article 3 case, where the protection afforded is wider than that provided by article 33 of the 1951 Refugee Convention since the activities of the individual however undesirable or dangerous cannot be a material consideration, it is arguable that the requirements of article 13 would not be satisfied by a judicial review of an expulsion which afforded only a *Wednesbury* review of determinations of factual disputes. The Secretary of State's proposed power to deny appeal rights to those certified as timewasting (clause 70(5) of the 1999 Bill) would itself be challengeable on the basis that there was no effective remedy (article 13) without an independent factual review, but it appears that such a challenge to primary legislation would have to be mounted in the European Court of Human Rights, since article 13 has been expressly excluded from the Convention rights incorporated under Schedule 1. The High Court would have no jurisdiction to issue a declaration of incompatibility in relation to the provisions. It is likely that as time goes by, the omission of article 13 from the incorporated rights will result in further gaps in protection necessitating recourse to the Strasbourg court.

8. Criteria for assessment

Deciding the facts is not the same as looking at the merits of a decision. The High Court is not as used to this function as the appellate authority is, but will have to get used to it. In cases where rights are derogable (eg family and private life, freedom of expression, assembly and association, liberty and security of person) the process the court will have to go through is a five-stage one[4] (although some of the stages involve very little):

(1) Does the case engage a Convention right?
(2) Is there an interference with that right?
(3) Is that interference prescribed by law?
(4) Does it pursue a legitimate aim?
(5) Is the interference proportionate to the legitimate aim pursued?

In practice, this means that an adjudicator dealing with a case involving a deportation or removal which impacts on family life will have to ask:

(1) Is there family life here? Is there a real relationship or merely a biological one?
(2) Are there serious obstacles to family life being conducted elsewhere? If not, the measure does not constitute an interference with it.
(3) Is the measure in accordance with domestic law (ie Immigration Acts)?
(4) Is immigration control a legitimate aim? (There is ample Strasbourg Court jurisprudence to say that it is.)
(5) Is the interference, if any, proportionate to the requirements of immigration control?

---

4   Analysed in more detail in Chapter 1 in terms of <u>six</u> stages: see pp 11-16.

Whether an interference with a Convention right is 'prescribed by law' does not mean merely checking it against a domestic statute, since this would result in a lack of protection where a measure complied with domestic law because domestic law was itself badly drawn. The phrase 'prescribed by law' relates to the quality of the law, requiring it to be compatible with the rule of law, a concept inherent in all the Articles of the Convention (see eg *Amuur v France*, 17/1995/523/609 (1996) 22 EHRR 533). Thus a law authorising interference with human rights, whether it regulates detention or telephone-tapping, must be sufficiently accessible and precise, to avoid all risk of arbitrariness. Detention of asylum-seekers arguably falls foul of this requirement for lack of any statutory criteria or time limits, and the 1999 Bill does not remedy this.

It is, however, normally the last stage, that of proportionality to the legitimate aim pursued, which will involve weighing the merits of the case against immigration control requirements, and it is here that conservative judges draw back, tending to become excessively deferential to the executive. There have already been pre-emptive moves by some judges (in journal articles and in pre-Act judgments) to try to revert to a quasi-*Wednesbury* test by abuse of the doctrine of 'margin of appreciation' as if it referred to a minister's range of reasonable responses. In fact it refers to a State's freedom in international law as to how it ensures enjoyment of Convention rights: see eg *D v United Kingdom*, supra, at para 69. The principle of proportionality is applied in a less deferential way than a *Wednesbury* test. In the ECJ, administrative action interfering with free movement rights is scrutinised to see whether there was a less restrictive way of achieving the same aim (see eg Case 33/74 *Van Binsbergen* [1974] ECR 1299).

In cases involving non-derogable rights (life, freedom from torture, inhuman or degrading treatment, freedom from slavery, freedom of thought, conscience and religion) only the first two stages are conducted since interference with the right is never justified. (There are exceptions of course: the right to life is not sacrosanct in time of war, and the right to *manifest* beliefs is qualified.)

Practitioners will of course need to refer the adjudicator or court to relevant ECHR jurisprudence, which the court is obliged to take into account (section 2). Jurisprudence does not merely extend to the European Court of Human Rights (ECtHR) judgments, but also to the court's advisory opinions, declarations and decisions, and more importantly to decisions and opinions of the Commission. This will enable cases such as the *East African Asians* cases (4403/70 et seq)(Commission report that immigration laws denying the Applicants entry to the UK on racially discriminatory grounds put the UK in breach of articles 3 and 14, followed by friendly settlement) and *Fadele v United Kingdom* (13078/87 (1990) 1 CD 15 – admissibility ruling on complaint that prevention of entry to Nigerian father of UK-resident children whose mother had died breached article 8 and Protocol 1, article 2, followed by friendly settlement) must be taken into account in appropriate cases.

The jurisprudence of the ECHR institutions must be taken into account but is not binding on the court. This could lead to a divergence between UK and European Court jurisprudence on the Convention. If UK courts' interpretation of Convention rights provides less protection than the Strasbourg Court, the remedy will remain to go there. Public authorities have no right of recourse to Strasbourg to complain about overly generous interpretations of Convention rights.

It is to be hoped and expected that increasing familiarity with ECHR will create a more favourable climate for the use of other Conventions. But strictly, notwithstanding arguments about the meaning and effect in UK law of article 53, and Murray Hunt's argument about the long title of the Act ('to give *further* effect to rights and freedoms guaranteed under ECHR...', which implies that some effect is already given to them in domestic law, leaving the door open for the others), other Conventions are not necessarily affected. Their status will probably remain similar to that of the ECHR before incorporation; a reflection of common values informing the common law; customary international law perhaps, relevant on a *Wednesbury* challenge. It may be possible however to argue that the interpretive obligation of section 3 should apply across the board, alone or in conjunction with section 11 (safeguard for existing human rights). Recently the courts have been more sympathetic to the argument that a general presumption exists that the UK intends to act in conformity with international obligations in the absence of a clear indication to the contrary. This has been reflected in cases such as *R v Secretary of State for the Home Department, ex p Ahmed and Patel* ([1998] INLR 570), where Lord Woolf accepted that 'the entering into a Treaty by the Secretary of State could give rise to a legitimate expectation on which the public in general are entitled to rely', and in *R v Home Secretary, ex p Thompson and Venables* ([1998] AC 407), where Lord Browne-Wilkinson said (of the UN Convention on the Rights of the Child):

> 'The Convention has not been incorporated into English law. But it is legitimate in considering the nature of detention during Her Majesty's Pleasure ... to assume that Parliament has not maintained on the statute book a power capable of being exercised in a manner inconsistent with the Treaty obligations of this country.'

9. Temporal jurisdiction

Sections 7(5) and 22(4) sets out the courts' temporal jurisdiction in human rights cases. Section 7(5) provides that proceedings against the public authority for an act which is incompatible with the Convention must be brought within a year (with power to extend the time limit), subject to rules imposing stricter time limits. The time limits under the immigration laws are likely to remain comparatively strict, although it may be arguable that the unrealistically short time limits for some asylum appeals have the consequence of depriving meritorious claims of a proper chance to be heard.

Section 22(4) provides that the courts will not apply the Convention to acts by the public authority performed before the coming into force of the Act, except in proceedings brought by the public authority itself. This would allow someone against whom extradition proceedings were brought before the Act came into force to use section 7 to challenge the extradition, because extradition proceedings are legal proceedings brought by the CPS under an authority of the Secretary of State (both public authorities). It would also allow Convention points to be taken in proceedings on a criminal charge brought before the Act comes into force such as facilitating entry to the UK, or against a court's recommendation for deportation. But an administrative decision to deport or remove taken before the coming into force of the Act is not vulnerable to Convention challenge under the Act in an appeal after the Act is in force, according to section 22(4). This is patently absurd, since an adjudicator or tribunal failing to give effect to Convention rights in a hearing once the Act is in force (whether or not it related to a decision taken before or after the Act came into force) would itself be acting unlawfully under section 6(3)(a) of the Act. In *R v DPP, ex p Kebilene* [1999] 3 WLR 175, the Court of Appeal struck down the DPP's decision to continue with a prosecution under sections of the Prevention of Terrorism Act which the trial judge had held to contravene article 6(2) by imposing a reverse burden of proof. The Court said that the DPP should take account of the probable consequences of any incompatibility with ECHR because after the Human Rights Act is passed those convicted under these provisions of the PTA will have their appeals allowed. Courts and tribunals are thus on notice that they should be having regard now to their future responsibility to give effect to Convention rights.

10.   Legal Aid

ECHR jurisprudence emphasises that States may have positive obligations under the Convention, (eg the provision of effective remedies) and that rights must be real and effective. In *Airey v United Kingdom* (supra) the Strasbourg Court held that the right to legal representation was ineffective without legal aid because of its prohibitive cost. Article 6 provides for legal aid for those on criminal charges. It is probable that the failure of the 1999 Bill to provide legal aid for bail applications before adjudicators would be held in breach of the right to effective judicial supervision of detention under article 5(4), particularly if it can be shown that the resources of the government-funded representation bodies, RLC and IAS, are utterly inadequate to cover all those who might want to apply for bail or who will be eligible under the proposed routine bail application provisions. At present, a very small proportion of those detained pending a decision or appeal on their asylum claims apply for bail and it is likely that the absence of legal aid is a real deterrent. Similarly, it may be possible to argue that legal aid should be available for other immigration hearings invoking Convention rights before the appellate authority, in particular article 3 (which would cover most asylum appeals), if it can be shown (a) that the statutory bodies cannot cover all appellants and (b) potential appellants are deterred from exercising appeal rights because of the cost of private representation. See also Chapter 2, p 44.

11.   Powers

The appellate authority will generally be able to allow appeals in its 'not in accordance with the law' jurisdiction under section 19(1)(a)(i) of the Immigration Act 1971 or the equivalent provision of the 1999 Bill, or directly under a clause 59 appeal, on the basis that a particular decision or action of the Secretary of State for the Home Department (SSHD) (or immigration officer or entry clearance officer) was incompatible with a Convention right (section 6(1)). This jurisdiction will cover cases which fall inside the rules and those which are governed by policy, falling outside the rules. Furthermore, the requirement to act in an ECHR-compatible manner will impact considerably on cases which involve the exercise of intra- and extra-rule discretion.

The authority will be able to allow an appeal on the basis that particular provisions of the rules were in breach of Convention rights, so long as the parent Act does not prevent compliance. Thus the appellate authority might say that para 317 or para 246 of HC 395, preventing the entry of certain relatives except in the most exceptional circumstances, violated article 8 as imposing disproportionate obstacles on the enjoyment of family life for parents trying to maintain contact with UK-settled children or for under-21s, and (in conjunction with article 14) that it discriminated vis-à-vis European nationals in doing so (comparing the much more generous family reunion provisions in EEC Regulation 68/1612, for example). This would be within its power since the parent Act (Immigration Act 1971, section 3(2)) does not prevent immigration rules on dependent family members from complying with ECHR. Such power would be particularly useful in respect of the Asylum Appeals (Procedure) Rules 1996, SI 1996/2070, made under the authority of section 22 of the Immigration Act 1971 (eg rule 42(1) – deemed receipt of documents irrespective of actual receipt) if UK jurisprudence extends the determination of 'civil rights and obligations' for the purposes of article 6 to determination of refugee status (see discussion above).

Further, where the appeal falls outside the rules and the decision is taken under the policy, in reviewing the legality of the decision, the authority will be able, and indeed obliged, to review the ECHR-compatibility of the policy. Thus the restrictions in application of the Somali Family Reunion Policy to various classes of sponsors (distinguishing between dependants of refugees and dependants of those on exceptional leave, for example) where a breach of article 8 could be shown will not prevent the appeal being successful.

In the cases where the appellate authority is permitted to review the exercise of discretion on appeal (sections 19(1)(a)(ii) and 19(2), new clause 59), the appellate authority must exercise discretion in line with ECHR since the prohibition on acting incompatibly with Convention rights falls upon the appellate authority as well as the SSHD. The merits jurisdiction under clause 59 will also apply where at present the appellate authority is precluded from reviewing discretion because the application involved a request of the SSHD to depart from the rules (section 19(2)); the issue will be whether the decision breaches Convention rights.

12. Remedies

Having found the particular requirements of a rule incompatible with the ECHR, the appellate authority will not be able to direct the SSHD to substitute a rule which complies with ECHR. This is because the jurisdiction under section19(3) is limited to the issuing of 'such directions for giving effect to the determination as the adjudicator thinks requisite'.

The appellate authority will however be able to issue directions to give effect to ECHR rights after a finding of breach (sections 8(1) and19(3) of the Immigration Act 1971, or equivalent under 1999 Bill). So, for example, in a Somali family reunion case where a breach is found the Adjudicator will not, having allowed the appeal, be limited to remitting the case back to the SSHD to decide according to law, as currently, but will be able to direct the issue of entry clearance. Similarly in a deportation or removal case, a successful article 8 argument may result in a requirement for a direction for leave to be granted (on the basis that remaining in limbo, with no status and in particular no access to work because of section 8 of the 1996 Act, and no access to any welfare benefits, itself potentially engages articles 2, 3 and 8 of the ECHR).

The appellate authority could direct the release of an immigration detainee who had not been lawfully detained under article 5(1) (*Amuur v France* (1996) 22 EHRR 533), but could it direct the release of a person not given written reasons for the detention, or who had not been able to come to court promptly to determine the lawfulness of detention? (In the latter case no direction would be possible where the delay of seven days in applying for bail was rooted in statute (Schedule 2, para 22 of the Immigration Act 1971), and so would need a declaration of incompatibility and consequential remedial action.)

13.   Declarations of incompatibility

The appellate authority cannot make declarations of incompatibility. In immigration cases, it is the higher courts alone that will be able to make such a declaration (section 4(5)). A declaration may be made in any case where a court determines whether a legislative provision is compatible with a Convention right (section 4(1), (3)). Thus, declarations are not limited to cases where the ground of complaint is section 6(1) and there is a ready victim under section 7(1). A declaration may issue following an 'ordinary' judicial review action which engages the general interpretive obligation in section 3.

The precondition for the issue of a declaration is either that a provision of primary legislation is in breach of Convention rights, or that a provision of subordinate legislation is in breach provided that primary legislation prevents removal of incompatibility. Thus it is unlikely that declarations would be issued in respect of provisions of the immigration rules or appeal procedure rules under the Immigration Act 1971 because the relevant primary legislation (sections 3(2) and 22 of the Immigration Act 1971) does not prevent removal of the incompatibility. The position may well be different for rules made under powers presently proposed in the 1999 Bill.

Where a Court is considering making a declaration, the Crown is entitled to be given notice and joined as a party (section 5).

A declaration is not binding and does not affect the validity or continuing operation of the provision declared incompatible, thus preserving Parliamentary sovereignty (section 4(6)). The Minister may take remedial action where a declaration under section 4 has been made or where after the coming into force of section 10, the European Court of Human Rights (ECtHR) has found a provision of UK legislation incompatible with its international ECHR obligations. Such action may also be taken where a provision of subordinate legislation is quashed or declared invalid (section 10(4))

A remedial order must be approved in draft form by resolution of each House of Parliament (Schedule 2, para 2(a)). Where urgency prevents such approval, the order must contain a declaration to that effect (Schedule 2, para 2(b)), be laid before Parliament after it is made, and if 120 days after it was made, a resolution has not been passed by each House the order ceases to have effect (Schedule 2, para 4).

14.   Suspensory effect

The ECHR provisions suspending potentially violative acts are weak. The ECtHR has no power to make binding interim orders under rule 39 of its Rules of Procedure, which merely provides that it may indicate an interim measure the adoption of which seems desirable in the parties' interest or the proper conduct of proceedings. Nor does the individual right to petition the Commission under article 25 contain a right to interim protection (eg *Cruz Varas* A 201 (1991) 14 EHRR 1, para 102). States normally comply with a rule 39 request, but the power is only exceptionally used, classically in cases involving a prospective breach of article 3.

However, in the new UK domestic law section 7(1) extends the power to grant a stay and/or injunction where a breach of Convention rights is the sole ground of a judicial review application. Further, domestic practice is consolidated through section 7(1) by enabling the grant of injunctive or quasi-injunctive relief, so that a proposed deportation can be litigated fully before removal.

It is arguable that in cases where judicial review is not available owing to the existence of an appellate remedy exercisable only from abroad, injunctive relief preventing removal could be sought under section 8(1). Thus a student returning on section 3(3)(b) leave who has no in-country right of appeal because s/he has no visa and therefore cannot at present judicially review a refusal of leave to enter because there is a statutory appeal right would be able to argue that the exclusion breached his/her education rights under article 2 Protocol 1 and that interim relief under section 8(1) should issue.

15. Damages and just satisfaction

The appellate authority cannot award damages, since that is not within its normal powers: section 8(2). The higher courts can, but in an application for judicial review, damages must be expressly pleaded: CPR, Sch 1 RSC Ord 53, rule 7.

Damages may only be awarded in respect of acts of public authorities which are unlawful under section 6(1) (section 8(6)). Thus where Convention rights were being relied on through the medium of section 3 (because, for example, there was no ready victim), no damages may be awarded under the HRA. Further, damages may not be awarded against the Court or the appellate authority for judicial acts done in good faith, except where the award is for compensation for breaches of articles 5(1)-(4) and thus required by article 5(5) (section 9(3)).

The principles for awarding damages are those employed by the ECtHR in assessing just satisfaction for the purposes of article 50 (section 8(3), (4)). The ECtHR has been reluctant in some immigration cases to award compensation in just satisfaction (cf *Chahal* (1996) 23 EHRR 413).

Article 5(5) provides for an enforceable right to compensation. This entails procedural guarantees (the decision must be binding on the respondent) as well as providing for a substantive award. Thus damages may issue against an adjudicator for denial of bail in circumstances where the detention breached article 5(1), in the context of a judicial review action for prolongation of unlawful detention.

CHAPTER 4

Asylum and people at risk

Rick Scannell

1. Introduction

The right to enjoy 'asylum from persecution' is embodied in article 14 of the Universal Declaration of Human Rights. It is in this broad sense that the phrase 'asylum and people at risk' is used in this paper as a reference to those in need of international protection. Those who need such asylum are by no means limited to 'refugees' as defined by the 1951 Convention and the 1967 Protocol Relating to the Status of Refugees ('the 1951 Convention') and yet it has hitherto in practice largely only been when the removal of an asylum seeker would breach the United Kingdom's obligations under the 1951 Convention that resort has been had to the Courts. Such primacy given to the 1951 Convention was reflected by the requirement in the immigration rules that claims for asylum were to be considered in accordance with the provisions of the 1951 Convention. In 1993 express statutory provision for such 'primacy of the (1951) Convention' was provided by section 2 of the Asylum and Immigration Appeals Act 1993 ('the 1993 Act'). The absence of reference in the immigration legislative framework to other international human rights instruments is by contrast stark. *Subject to incorporation* the present position remains that it is only by reference to the 1951 Convention that the removal of an asylum seeker is *substantially* justiciable before the immigration appellate authorities on a section 8 appeal[1].

Seen in this context the casual observer could be forgiven for thinking that the 1951 Convention provides the only source of the United Kingdom's international asylum obligations. This is of course manifestly not the case and the ECHR provides but one, albeit significant, source of international asylum obligations. Although seldom acknowledged it is no doubt such wider international obligations that have – in part at least – founded the Home Office's approach to 'exceptional leave to remain' (ELR). Historically ELR was granted to significant numbers of persons seeking

---

1 Section 8 of the Asylum and Immigration Appeals Act 1993 ('1993 Act'). See *R v Secretary of State for the Home Department, ex p Mehari* [1994] QB 474, [1994] Imm AR 1514. As to the means of the implementation of the Human Rights Act, see clause 45 of the Immigration and Asylum Bill 1999. For an excellent pre-HRA booklet on asylum and the Convention see Nuala Mole's *Problems raised by certain aspects of the present situation of refugees from the standpoint of the European Convention on Human Rights*, Council of Europe publishing, Human rights files No 9, rev ISBN 92-871-3385-9 (1997).

asylum. In the first half of 1993, prior to the coming into force of the 1993 Act, decisions on 76% of asylum applications were to grant ELR; in the second half of 1993 the figure was 22%, while outright refusals rose. By 1996 only 14% of asylum decisions were to grant ELR and in recent years the figure has dropped to just 9%.

Statistics rarely tell the whole story, although it is a source of grave concern that the coming into force of the 1993 Act is reflected by so dramatic a decrease in the rate of 'protection' afforded to asylum seekers. Doubtless a contributory – if not causal – factor in such decrease is the cynicism routinely applied to 'refugees' and 'asylum seekers', itself in turn no doubt a reflection of the increase in the numbers of persons seeking asylum. Such cynicism about asylum seekers is plain to see: indeed, the Labour government has inherited the language of the last in its description of 'bogus' refugees and asylum seekers - a cry adopted with customary zeal by the press. Such Europe wide increase in numbers seeking asylum during the last decade has been met with both national and Europe wide measures to prevent persons from even making claims[2].

Such 'climate' is reflected also by an increasingly 'strict' approach by the Courts to the interpretation of the 1951 Convention which has resulted in an ever increasing 'gap' between the number of applicants and the number of persons falling within the article 1A definition of 'refugee', not to mention the over frequent use of 'credibility' in the rejection of claims both by the Home Office and on appeal, even where persons come from countries whose human rights records are abysmal.

These factors would appear to have caused an alarming 'protection gap'. In this chapter I consider in turn:

- 'protection gaps' under the 1951 Convention;
- the Home Office's approach to the grant of 'exceptional leave to remain' (ELR) in purported vindication of its wider international obligations; and
- article 3 of the ECHR insofar as it is potentially relevant to 'protection' issues.

In conclusion I will consider the likely impact of the incorporation of ECHR rights into British law on the protection gap identified.

2. Protection 'gaps' under the 1951 Refugee Convention

2.1 'Convention' reasons

The most obvious scope for such a gap lies in the fact that the 1951 Convention is expressly limited (both in the article 1A 'refugee' definition and the article 33 'refoulement' prohibition) to persecution for reasons of 'race, religion, nationality, membership of a particular social group or political opinion'. The enumeration of particular reasons contrasts (for example) with the generality of article 14 of the Universal Declaration of Human Rights 1948 (UDHR) already referred to. While plainly necessary to give effect to the convention reasons enumerated, the preamble

---

2   For example Asylum Carriers Liability Act 1987 (in 1997 the Home Office collected £10.7 million in its recovery of charges, bringing the total to over £63 million); the imposition of mandatory visas for all likely refugee producing states; 'third country' measures, including the Dublin Convention.

to the 1951 Convention, with its reference to the 1948 UN declaration and the affirmation of the principle affirmed by the General Assembly that 'human beings shall enjoy fundamental rights and freedoms without discrimination', would be consistent with a broad approach to the interpretation of such 'convention' reasons.

Thus for example in respect of the meaning to be ascribed to membership of a 'particular social group' there is much to commend an approach which sees the 1951 convention as 'a living thing, adopted by civilised countries for a humanitarian end which is constant in motive but mutable in form' lest the 1951 Convention 'will eventually become an anachronism' (per Sedley J in *R v Immigration Appeal Tribunal and Secretary of State for the Home Department, ex p Shah* [1997] Imm AR 145). Regrettably there are times when the 1951 Convention as applied by our national courts already seems anachronistic.

Until recently (see further below) it was unable to provide protection to Pakistani women accused of transgressing social mores who were at risk of severe violence and death, popular retribution and severe discrimination in circumstances where the state is both unable and unwilling to offer protection (see decision of the Court of Appeal in *Shah and Islam* [1997] Imm AR 584); nor even to Algerian midwives at risk from the fundamentalists (from whom the authorities are unable to provide protection) on account of their role in giving advice about contraception – a role which the Tribunal had found they ought not to be required to give up (*Secretary of State for the Home Department v Hafsa Ouanes* [1998] Imm AR 76, Court of Appeal)[3]. That women in these circumstances should create such a protection gap was surely not within the contemplation of the framers of the 1951 Convention – in spite of the absence of 'sex' or 'gender' as express convention reasons[4].

The decision of the House of Lords in *Shah and Islam*[4a], however, marks a very welcome exception to such observation. By a majority (Lord Millet dissenting) their Lordships held that women in Pakistan were members of a particular social group. The broad proposition was put forward during argument by Lord Hoffman whose speech (in particular) draws heavily on anti-discrimination principles ('the concept of discrimination in matters affecting fundamental rights and freedoms is central to an understanding of the Convention').

2.2 The meaning of 'persecution'

Hathaway defines 'persecution' as the sustained or systemic violation of basic human rights resulting from a failure of state protection[5]. He identifies four categories of rights – the first three of which if breached are able to found a claim to have been *persecuted*: first, those which permit no derogation whatsoever (rights to life, protection against torture, inhuman or degrading punishment or treatment etc); second, those from which states may derogate in times of 'public emergency which

---

3   See also the decision of the Australian High Court in *A v Minister for Immigration and Ethnic Affairs* [1998] INLR 1 where the majority rejected the contention that parents facing compulsory sterilisation and abortion for breaching China's one child policy were not members of a particular social group.

4   Contrast the 1979 Convention on the Elimination of All Forms of Discrimination Against Women. See generally *Women as asylum seekers: a legal handbook* by Heaven Crawley, 1997.

4a   Judgment 25 March 1999. Lords Steyn, Hoffman, Hope, Hutton and Millett.

5   See James C Hathaway's *The Law of refugee Status* (1991, Butterworths Canada) at 101-112.

threatens the life of the nation and the existence of which is officially proclaimed' (freedom from arbitrary arrest and detention, fair trial etc); and third, those rights which states are required to take progressive steps to realise (rights to work, education etc). This approach – together with a similar analysis contained in a submission of the UNHCR has found favour with the Tribunal in *Gashi and Nikshiqi v Secretary of State for the Home Department*[6].

There has been some judicial endorsement of Professor Hathaway's approach. In *Ravichandran v Secretary of State for the Home Department*[7] Simon Brown LJ referred to his first two categories whilst apparently approving his broader approach. And Professor Hathaway's analysis found clear favour with the Court of Appeal in *Adan v Secretary of State for the Home Department* [1997] Imm AR 251 where Hutchison LJ confirmed that the denial of re-entry could be 'persecution'. Of particular importance *Adan* confirmed also that the *non refoulement* provision of article 33 was intended to apply to all persons determined to be refugees under article 1A, including those who would face persecution short of threats to 'life or freedom' provided only that it involved serious harm. Such dicta would seem to provide resounding endorsement of a definition which would include denial of Professor Hathaway's 'third category' rights.

By the same token, however, many special adjudicators often fail to 'recognise' persecution falling outside danger to life or deprivation of liberty. And it is precisely when this occurs that there is a tendency to treat the definition of persecution as a 'question of fact'. Thus for example in *Kagema* [1997] Imm AR 137 the Court of Appeal stated the definition of the term to be a matter of fact and not law - subject to challenge only on *Wednesbury* principles[8]. In *Kagema* a special adjudicator had equated persecution with danger to life or deprivation of liberty; whilst accepting that 'persecution can include violations of human rights other than life and liberty' the applicant – a Kikuyu from the Rift valley who had been forcibly displaced from his home and camp by government agents three times – was found by the special adjudicator not to have been persecuted in the broader sense. Thus asylum seekers can face the prospect of being denied protection simply on the basis of the personality of the tribunal hearing any appeal – hardly conducive to either legal certainty or consistent decision making. Indeed, the truth of such observation is plainly shown by the fact that in *Kagema* both Aldous and Ward LLJ seemed firmly of the view that the applicant *had* been persecuted!

2.3 Civil war and 'differential impact'

The recent decision of the House of Lords in *R v Secretary of State for the Home Department, ex p Adan*[9] has undeniably widened the 'protection gap'. Leaving entirely to one side the first issue considered as to the meaning to be ascribed to article 1A[10],

6   [1997] INLR 96.
7   [1996] Imm AR 97. But contrast the judgment of Staughton LJ who defined persecution as 'at least persistent and serious ill-treatment without just cause by the state, or from which the state can provide protection but chooses not to do so' (at 114).
8   *Kagema v Secretary of State for the Home Department* [1997] Imm AR 137.
9   [1998] INLR 325.
10 The first issue considered was whether absent a current well founded fear of persecution the respondent was nevertheless a refugee if he fled his country of nationality as a result of a well founded fear of Convention persecution and has been unable to return to that country or avail himself of protection subsequently. The Court of Appeal had decided the issue in Adan's favour; the House of Lords allowed the Secretary of State's appeal holding that a current well founded fear *is* required.

the House of Lords considered whether a state of civil war whose incidents are 'widespread clan and sub-clan based killing and torture' could give rise to a Refugee Convention fear of persecution where the individual asylum seeker was at no greater risk than others similarly at risk for reasons of their clan and sub-clan membership. It might have been thought that to be at risk of death and torture simply on account of clan membership would suffice for the purposes of the 1951 Convention: indeed, as Simon Brown LJ had noted in the Court of Appeal[11] virtually all civil wars are by their nature 'Convention based' with opposing factions divided by issues of 'race, politics or the like'.

Yet the House of Lords disagreed. The leading judgement was given by Lord Lloyd. So long as a state of civil war continues it is necessary for such asylum seeker 'to show fear of persecution for Convention reasons over and above the ordinary risks of clan warfare'. Lord Lloyd continues:

> Once the civil war is over, and the victors have restored order, then the picture changes back again. There is no longer any question of both sides claiming refugee status. If the vanquished are oppressed or ill-treated by the victors, they may well be able to establish a present fear of persecution for a Convention reason, and in most cases they would be unable to avail themselves of their country's protection.

Adan is in many respects an alarming decision. The 'accepted' facts upon which the second question was premised ('widespread clan and sub-clan based killing') undeniably amounted to 'persecution' for the Refugee Convention reason of 'race' of membership of a 'particular social group' (ie clan membership) – and in any other circumstances would plainly have made the asylum seeker a refugee. It is perhaps difficult to avoid the conclusion that the House of Lords was fundamentally concerned by the prospect of 'numbers' such as are caused by 'both sides claiming asylum'. Whilst Simon Brown LJ acknowledged such 'unappealing' aspect of Adan's case he concluded that the submissions on his behalf 'more faithfully reflect the evident intentions of those responsible for the Convention and give better effect to its broad humanitarian purpose'[12] – sentiments lacking from the judgment of the House of Lords.

2.4 The permissible 'range of tolerance' as between different Convention signatories

Section 2 of the Asylum and Immigration Act 1996 enables the Home Secretary to remove an asylum applicant to a 'safe third country' without substantive consideration of his or her claim if satisfied that the applicant's life and liberty would not be threatened there for Refugee Convention reasons and that the government of the third country would not send the applicant to another country or territory otherwise than in accordance with the (Refugee) Convention.

Section 2 has been considered in a number of recent decisions of the Court of Appeal. See *R v Secretary of State for the Home Department and Immigration Officer, Waterloo International, ex p Canbolat* [1997] INLR 198 and *R v Special Adjudicator, ex p Kerrouche* [1998] INLR 88 (both of which concerned return to France). What is

11 [1997] Imm AR 251 at 264.
12 Ibid, at page 265.

required is that there should be 'no real risk that the asylum seeker would be sent to another country otherwise than in accordance with the Convention' (*Canbolat* 207A). More is required than a difference in emphasis in interpretation: the difference must be of such significance that it can be said that in making the decision affecting the position of the particular applicant for asylum the third country would not be applying the principles of the Convention. The approach of the third country must be 'outside the range of tolerance which one signatory country, as a matter of comity, is expected to extend to another' (*Kerrouche* 92G-93C).

Both these decisions were considered by the Court of Appeal in *R v Secretary of State for the Home Department, ex p Iyadurai* [1998] INLR 472 where counsel for the applicant criticised the court's approach in *Kerrouche*. Lord Woolf MR stated that the important question for the Secretary of State is whether 'on the material available to him' he regards the third country as 'properly giving effect to the Convention' (478A):

> This exercise involves examining the approach adopted in the third country against the proper international interpretation of the provisions of the Convention. It remains the situation that the Secretary of State is not required 'to become deeply involved in a comparative analysis of the law of different signatories of the Convention (*Kerrouche* at 93D) and the third country can be complying with the Convention although it expresses its approach in different language to that which would be used in this country. If the Secretary of State has formed the opinion required by s 2 then the court's role is limited to one of supervision. The court can do no more than inquire whether the Secretary of State has (i) taken adequate steps to inform himself of the position of the third country, (ii) properly considered the information which is available to him, and (iii) come to an opinion which is consistent with that information, recognising that it is his responsibility to evaluate the material which is available to him. (478A-C)

If the court comes to the conclusion that the approach of the other country is 'clearly inconsistent' with the Convention this will strongly suggest that the opinion of SSHD is flawed (479B-C).

The issue *Kerrouche* was whether France applied a narrower interpretation to what is a political crime under article 1F(b) of the 1951 Convention than would be applied by the United Kingdom. On the facts the Court had concluded that the evidence did not establish there to be 'any significant difference' in the approach of the French authorities from that in English law.

But this would seem to produce the anomalous result that a person who the United Kingdom would recognise as a refugee could be 'safely' returned to a third country and risk refoulement from that country in breach of article 33 (*as interpreted by English courts*) on the basis of such third country's narrower interpretation of the convention. If there is 'a real risk' (ie the *Sivakumaran* standard) of this happening then as far as the United Kingdom is concerned the third country's approach is surely outside 'the range of tolerance' or 'margin of appreciation' accorded to the other signatory since the return to the third country would give rise to a real risk of refoulement. It is somewhat artificial to construct a test which potentially redefines refugees into different categories – in effect as between those considered substantively and third country cases. On the one hand there will be those in respect of whom breach of article 33 would not be contemplated and on the other those who on the United Kingdom's interpretation of refugee law could also be recognised as refugees (were their claims considered substantively), but in respect of whom breach of article 33 is contemplated.

In such a situation it is difficult to understand how from the United Kingdom's perspective any such third country could be regarded as one which adheres to the principles of the Convention and Protocol since *on the UK's interpretation* of refugee law such third country would be 'refouling' refugees in breach of article 33. Whilst the facts of *Kerrouche* perhaps fell short of this possibility given the Court's finding that there was no significant difference in approach to article 1F in any event other 'differences' are likely to prove more difficult.

An obvious example is the failure of some signatory states to recognise 'persecution' by 'non state agents'. UNHCR has expressed the view that the approach of France, Germany, Italy and Sweden to this issue 'is contrary to the text and to the spirit of the 1951 Convention'. In one of the few successful challenges to a third country removal the applicant in *Aitseguer*[13] argued successfully that the approach of France to non state agents was indeed outwith the permissible range of tolerance. The applicant Algerian asylum seeker feared persecution at the hands of the GIA which could found a successful claim for asylum in the UK based on the Government's inability to provide protection. In France by contrast he would be required to show complicity ('encouragement or toleration') on the part of the Algerian authorities with the GIA. 'Mere incapacity' to provide effective protection could not lead to recognition of refugee status. The contrast in the case of *Lul Adan*[14] was no less stark. The Somali asylum seeker would have satisfied the UK's (strict) interpretation of article 1A(2) if her claim was considered substantively in the UK; in Germany however she could not be a 'refugee' because of the absence of any state authority. Yet in this case the Divisional Court held that Germany's approach was *within* the permissible range of tolerance required. Both cases are pending consideration on appeal to the Court of Appeal.

It is not difficult to see how the protection gap is widened where removal is permissible to a third country which is unlikely to give refugee status, but, on the UK's interpretation of the 1951 Convention the same claim would be likely to succeed. THis point was appreciated, none too soon, by the Court of Appeal in the landmark decision of *ex p Adan, Subaskaran and Aitseguer* (1999) Times 28 July).

2.5   Exclusion under article 1F

Unlike the position in respect of certain articles of the ECHR (see further below) permitting no derogations the 1951 Refugee Convention does not give an absolute right to non-refoulement unless a person meets the definition of 'refugee'. Thus article 1F provides that the Convention 'shall not apply' where there are 'serious reasons' for considering that the person has committed a crime against peace, a war crime or a crime against humanity (sub-paragraph (a) refers); a 'serious non-political crime outside the country of refuge prior to admission' (sub-paragraph (b) refers) or that s/he 'has been guilty of acts contrary to the purposes and principles of the Convention' (sub-paragraph (c) refers)[15].

13   *R v Secretary of State for the Home Department, ex p Hamid Aitseguer* (1998) 18 December (CO/1765/98) Sullivan J.
14   *R v Secretary of State for the Home Department, ex p Lul Omar Adan* [1999] Imm AR 114, DC, Rose LJ and Mitchell J.
15   For analysis of the meaning of 'serious non-political crime' under article 1F(b) see *T v Immigration Officer* [1996] AC 742.

2.6   National security, public order and the commission of 'particularly serious crimes'

An assertion by the Secretary of State that a case involves 'national security' highlights the manifest shortcomings of the 1951 Convention – in particular given the historical reluctance of the English Courts to seek to go behind such assertions[16]. The prohibition against the expulsion of refugees lawfully in a contracting state's territory may be disapplied where expulsion is 'on grounds of national security or public order' under article 32.1 of the 1951 Convention. And the prohibition on refoulement in article 33.1 is similarly disapplied in respect of a refugee 'whom there are reasonable grounds for regarding as a danger to the security of the country in which he is, or who, having been convicted by a final judgement of a particularly serious crime, constitutes a danger to the community of that country'.

2.7   'Punishment' in contradistinction to 'persecution'

The UNHCR handbook makes clear that convention persecution is to be distinguished from 'punishment for a common law offence'[17]. Whilst this is plainly an important distinction, cases undoubtedly arise where persons detained in respect of common crimes risk (for example) torture or other serious human rights violations without any element of persecution for a Convention reason.

3.   The Home Office's approach to ELR

The Home Office's use of ELR for asylum applicants is a long standing one. In its December 1984 memorandum submitted to the Race Relations and Immigration Sub Committee of the Home Affairs Committee the Home Office said that the grant was given in two discrete sets of circumstances. First, to individuals in the light of the particular circumstances of their cases; second, and on a more general basis, to nationals of certain countries said to be experiencing 'particular disruption whose return against their will it is adjudged to be unreasonable to enforce'[18]. Amongst those to benefit from this policy have been nationals of Afghanistan, Iran, Lebanon, Poland, Uganda and El Salvador. A similar policy has been applied to, *inter alia*, Sri Lankan Tamils and nationals of China, Liberia, Somalia, Bosnia and the FRY. More recently 'upheaval declarations' (in respect of for example Sierra Leone and (former) Zaire) have created temporary 'stays' on removals of failed asylum seekers.

Perhaps conscious of the lack of any apparent legitimate justification for the recent dramatic decrease in the grant of ELR, the Home Office has sought to justify the large numbers of persons previously granted such status by reference solely to 'large backlogs'. In a letter dated 23 February 1994 to the Refugee Council, the Home Office

---

16   See *inter alia R v Secretary of State for the Home Department, ex p Chahal* [1994] Imm AR 107. The contrast between the approach of the national authorities as reflected by the decision of the Court of Appeal there reported is contrasted by that of the European Court.

17   Paragraph 56 of the UNHCR handbook on procedures and criteria for determining refugee status. See also para 57-60.

18   Memorandum at para 44.

explained how on account of such backlogs 'a number of unsuccessful asylum seekers were granted exceptional leave to remain because it was not possible for practical or other reasons to remove or to seek to remove them'. The intended inference would seem to be that such persons were not deserving of international protection – although in terms of the human rights records of the countries generating asylum applications this would seem inadequate justification. Indeed, it is plain that events in asylum producing countries during the 1990s would have amply justified a similar approach to the use of the ELR as was evidenced statistically prior to 1993. Nor can the change be justified by reference merely to the increase in *numbers* of asylum seekers since that date because in fact numbers have fallen since 1991, the year when most applications were recorded as having been made (44,800 excluding dependents). Such fall is attributed by the Home Office in its 1998 annual report to 'various measures introduced to deter multiple and fraudulent applications' – a plain attempt to suggest that there is a direct link between numbers and credibility. While plainly such view is reflected by the Home Office's use of 'credibility' in its rejection of applications, such analysis is likely to be flawed, if and insofar as the objective situation in asylum producing countries remains at least as bad as it was when grants of asylum were high.

The Asylum Directorate's March 1998 instructions on ELR provide that ELR should normally be granted only after substantive consideration and rejection of the asylum claim under the 1951 Convention. ELR will only be granted if asylum applicants fall into one of the following criteria:

- s/he is a national of a country to which 'a general country policy' applies (presently only Liberia);
- where there are '*substantial* grounds for believing that a person would be tortured or otherwise subjected to inhuman or degrading treatment', even though this would not amount to persecution within the terms of the 1951 Convention (for instance because the persecution was not for a Convention reason);
- where there are '*substantial* grounds for believing that someone will suffer a disproportionate punishment for a criminal offence eg execution for draft evasion';
- where credible medical evidence shows that return would result in substantial damage to the 'physical or psychological health of the applicant or his dependants'; or
- where no decision on an application has been made for seven years (presently under Ministerial review).

It is plain that the UK's ECHR obligations – as interpreted recently by the European Court – have provided the 'focus' of these instructions.

4. ECHR article 3

Article 3 provides that 'no one shall be subjected to torture or inhuman or degrading treatment or punishment'. It is unqualified and permits no derogation. Ill treatment must attain a minimum level of severity in order to fall within the article – but such threshold is *relative* depending on all the circumstances of a case, including 'the duration of the treatment, its physical or mental effects and in some cases the sex, age and state of health of the victim, etc'[19].

19 *Ireland v United Kingdom* (1978) A 25, para 162, 2 EHRR 25.

4.1   Torture

Torture means 'deliberate inhuman treatment causing very serious suffering'[20]. In the *Greek* case[1] the Commission described torture as an aggravated form of inhuman treatment which has a *purpose*, such as the obtaining of information or confession, or the infliction of punishment. Torture was held to have occurred in the *Greek* case (falanga /severe beating of all parts of the body with a view to obtaining information as to the political activities of subversive individuals) – although not in *Ireland v United Kingdom* in respect of the five techniques (wall standing, hooding, subjection to noise, sleep deprivation and food and drink deprivation) because the intensity of such suffering had been insufficient. Such treatment need not be physical: mental anguish would suffice, provided that the suffering caused is sufficiently serious.

In *Aydin v Turkey*[2] the European Court of Human Rights considered the treatment of the applicant by the Turkish security forces. She had been stripped, beaten, sprayed with cold water and raped. She argued that she had been subjected to physical ill treatment and rape amounting to torture contrary to article 3. The Court upheld her complaint. The accumulation of acts of physical and mental violence to which the applicant had been subjected, which included the especially cruel act of rape, itself rendered particularly grave and abhorrent by being carried out by a state official, 'clearly amounted to torture'.

4.2   Inhuman treatment

Inhuman treatment requires less intense suffering than in the case of torture, nor need it be deliberate. A threat of torture if 'sufficiently real and immediate' may give rise to sufficient mental suffering to constitute inhuman treatment[3]. In *Ireland v United Kingdom* the five techniques were found to constitute inhuman treatment: the methods were applied in combination with premeditation and for hours at a stretch; they caused, if not actual bodily injury, at least intense physical and mental suffering and led to acute psychological disturbance during interrogation. The physical assaults in both the *Greek* and *Ireland* cases constituted inhuman treatment. In the former case these included the application of electric shocks, squeezing of the head in a vice, pulling out of hair from head or pubic region, kicking in the male genital organs, dripping water on the head and the use of noise to prevent sleep. In the latter the detainees were severely beaten by the security forces such as to cause contusions and bruising.

The conditions or treatment of persons in a place of detention may also amount to inhuman treatment. In the *Greek* case the conditions in which many political detainees were kept were held to be inhuman treatment by reference to overcrowding and to inadequate heating, toilets, sleeping arrangements, food, recreation and provision for contact with the outside world. Such deficiencies were found in different

---

20   Ibid at para 167.
1   (1969) 12 YB 1 at 186.
2   [1997] 3 BHRC 300. Case 57/1996/676/866. Contrast the decision of Collins J in *R v Special Adjudicator, ex p Okonkwo* [1998] Imm AR 502 upholding a decision of a special adjudicator that the asylum seeker's rape did not amount to torture. The contrast of the cases further illustrates the 'protection gap' identified.
3   *Campbell and Cosans v United Kingdom* (1982) A 48, para 26, 4 EHRR 293.

combinations and were not all present in each of the places of detention where breaches of article 3 were found. In *Cyprus v Turkey*[4] the withholding of food and water and medical treatment was inhuman treatment. Generally a state will not be responsible for self imposed conditions[5]. Conditions of detention in mental hospitals have been the subject of consideration by the Commission[6]. Solitary confinement or segregation of itself will not breach article 3 and is permissible for reasons of security or discipline or to protection. But in each case regard must be had to 'the surrounding circumstances, including the particular conditions, the stringency of the measure, its duration, the objective pursued and its effects on the person concerned'[7]. Solitary confinement arrangements for remand or convicted prisoners have not founded a successful article 3 challenge in Strasbourg – although it was recognised in *Ensslin*[8] that 'complete sensory isolation coupled with complete social isolation can ... destroy the personality' at which point article 3 would be infringed however strong the justification for segregation. There is a wide margin of appreciation given to national authorities in this area[9]. Medical treatment is required to be given to persons detained – and the denial of it may amount to inhuman treatment contrary to article 3 where the result is to cause serious injury to health.

4.3 Inhuman punishment

Inhuman punishment must reach a minimum relative level of severity (in terms of the applicant's age, sex, health etc). Birching was not inhuman punishment in *Tyrer v United Kingdom*[10] since the threshold level was not reached. Account must be taken of both the nature and context of the punishment as well as the manner and method of its execution.

4.4 Degrading treatment

Degrading treatment is conduct that 'grossly humiliates' although causing less suffering than torture[11]. Would a person of the applicant's age, sex health etc of normal sensibilities be grossly humiliated? In *Abdulaziz, Cabales and Balkandali v United Kingdom*[12] the Court appeared to require an intention to humiliate: the immigration rules distinguishing between spouses of husbands and wives did not amount to degrading treatment because 'it was not designed to, and did not, humiliate or debase but was intended solely to achieve specified non discriminatory aims'. As Harris, O'Boyle and Warbrick note[13] such requirement runs counter to the Court's general

---

4 (1984) 4 EHRR 482 at 541.
5 *McFeeley v United Kingdom, No 8317/78* (1980) 20 DR 44 – the 'dirty protest' whereby cells were defiled with urine, faeces and waste food. Such conditions would have been inhuman treatment if attributable to the state.
6 See *B v United Kingdom No 6870/75* (1981) 32 DR 5 and *A v United Kingdom No 6840/74* (1980) 3 EHRR 131.
7 *Ensslin, Baader and Raspe v Germany No 7572/76* (1979) 14 DR 64 at 109.
8 Ibid.
9 See *Kröcher and Müller v Switzerland No 8463/78* (1982) 34 DR 25.
10 (1978) A 26; 2 EHRR 1.
11 The *Greek* case (1969) 12 YB 1 at 186.
12 (1985) A 94, para 91; 7 EHRR 471.
13 *Law of the European Convention on Human Rights* (1995, Butterworths) at p 81.

reading of article 3 'by which, other than in cases of torture, the test of liability is solely in terms of the suffering caused'. Note that the same treatment may be both degrading and inhuman (for example the five techniques). Racial discrimination can be degrading treatment[14]: see again Harris, O'Boyle and Warbrick[15] discussing the Commission's reasoning in the *East African Asians* cases and expressing the view that 'ordinary' incidents of direct or indirect racial discrimination could be degrading treatment. Further, the Commission's statement in that case that a 'special importance' was attached to discrimination on grounds of race was not to be taken to mean that other forms of discrimination could not found a claim under article 3. While in *Marckx v Belgium*[16] legislation discriminating against illegitimate children and their parents was held not to be degrading treatment under article 3 on its own, discrimination against illegitimate children was held to be contrary to article 14 read together with article 3 in *Inze v Austria*[17], as was discrimination on grounds of sex in *Abdulaziz*[18].

The treatment of persons in detention has also founded allegations of degrading treatment. In *Hurtado v Switzerland*[19] the Commission found degrading treatment where an applicant who had defecated in his trousers was not permitted to change his clothing until the next day. The conditions of the IRA prisoners in the 'dirty protest' was also degrading – although there was no liability because they were self imposed[20]. In *Gurdogan, Mustak, Mustak and Mustak v Turkey*[1] the lips of the applicant Kurdish villagers were smeared with human excrement by Turkish security forces: their claims were admitted for consideration on the merits.

4.5 Degrading punishment

Degrading punishment must be more than the usual element of humiliation following the very fact of conviction and punishment by a court. A sentence of three strokes of the birch imposed by an Isle of Man juvenile court on a 15-year-old boy for assault and carried out by a police constable at a police station was held to be a degrading punishment in *Tyrer v United Kingdom*[2]. Whilst a punishment carried out in public might have been more humiliating the absence of publicity would not necessarily prevent a punishment being sufficiently humiliating to be degrading. The Court was particularly influenced by the fact that the punishment was state 'institutionalised violence' with the applicant 'an object in the power of the authorities'. It was irrelevant that such form of punishment was widely supported by Manx public opinion – which itself was not reflective of 'commonly accepted standards in the penal policy' in a Council of Europe state. Thus the Court's examination of the nature and context of the punishment was mots influential in the result.

---

14 *East African Asians cases* (1973) 3 EHHR 76.
15 *Law of the European Convention on Human Rights*, op cit, at p 82.
16 (1979) A 31, para 66; 2 EHRR 330.
17 (1987) A 126, para 41; 10 EHRR 394.
18 (1985) A 94, para 91; 7 EHRR 471.
19 (1994) A 280-A.
20 (1980) 20 DR 44.
1   *Nos 15202-5/89* (1989) 76A DR 9.
2   (1978) A 26; 2 EHRR 1.

4.6 Applicability to 'removal' cases

Prior to the landmark decision of the Strasbourg Court in *Soering v United Kingdom*[3] there might have been little confidence in the ability of the Convention to deal effectively with 'removal' cases. The Convention after all provides no rights against deportation or extradition; nothing is remotely reflective of article 14 UDHR. In *Soering* the applicant German national faced extradition to the USA to face trial on a capital murder charge. It was argued that if his extradition was implemented it would give rise to a breach of article 3 from his exposure to the 'death row phenomenon'. The UK had argued that it was not responsible for the arrangements made by the Virginia authorities which gave rise to his complaint and that other international instrument[4] dealt specifically with the problems of removal to another jurisdiction. But such considerations could not 'absolve Contracting Parties from responsibility under Article 3 for all and any foreseeable consequences of extradition suffered outside their jurisdiction'[5]. In reaching its decision the Court stated:

87. In interpreting the Convention regard must be had to its special character as a treaty for the collective enforcement of human rights and fundamental freedoms. Thus the object and purpose of the Convention as an instrument for the protection of individual human beings require that its provisions be interpreted and applied so as to make its safeguards practical and effective. In addition, any interpretation of the rights and freedoms guaranteed has to be consistent with 'the general spirit of the Convention, an instrument designed to maintain and promote the ideals and values of a democratic society.
88. Article 3 makes no provision for exceptions and no derogation from it is permissible under Article 15 in time of war or other national emergency. This absolute prohibition on torture and on inhuman or degrading treatment or punishment ... shows that Article 3 enshrines one of the fundamental values of the democratic societies making up the Council of Europe. .... It would hardly be compatible with the underlying values of the Convention, that 'common heritage of political traditions, ideals, freedom and the rule of law' to which the Preamble refers, were a contracting state knowingly to surrender a fugitive to another state where there are substantial grounds for believing that he would be in danger of being subjected to torture, however heinous the crime allegedly committed. Extradition in such circumstances, while not explicitly referred to in Article 3, would plainly be contrary to the spirit and intendment of the Article, and ... this inherent obligation not to extradite extends to cases in which the fugitive would be faced in the receiving State by a real risk of exposure to inhuman or degrading treatment or punishment.
.....
90. It is not normally for the Convention institutions to pronounce on the existence or otherwise of potential violations of the Convention. However, where an applicant claims that a decision to extradite him would, if implemented, be contrary to Article 3 by reason of its foreseeable consequences in the requesting country a departure from this principle is necessary in view of the serious and irreparable nature of the alleged suffering risked, in order to ensure the effectiveness of the safeguard provided by that Article.
91. In sum, the decision ... to extradite a fugitive may give rise to an issue under Article 3, and hence engage the responsibility of that State ... where substantial grounds have been shown for believing that the person concerned, if extradited, faces a real risk of

3   (1989) A 161; 11 EHRR 439.
4   1951 Convention, the 1957 European Convention on Extradition and the 1984 UN Convention Against Torture and Other Cruel, Inhuman and Degrading Treatment.
5   Para 86.

being subjected to torture or to inhuman or degrading treatment or punishment in the requesting country. ...

In *Cruz Varas v Sweden*[6] the Court applied the *Soering* approach to the deportation of a refused asylum seeker, albeit concluding that on the facts there were no substantial grounds for believing there to be a real risk of prohibited ill treatment if the applicant was returned to Chile. Subsequent case law (see below) makes clear that all removals can potentially engage article 3 obligations.

4.7   Standard of proof

The 'real risk' test is higher than that of 'mere possibility'. This was shown by the facts of *Vilvarajah v United Kingdom*[7]. Despite the fact that three of the five returnees had in fact been ill treated on return the Court held that 'there existed no special distinguishing features in their cases that could or ought to have enabled the Secretary of State to foresee that they would be treated in this way'. Large numbers of Tamils had in fact been returning voluntarily; while there remained the 'possibility' that the Tamil applicants might be detained and ill-treated, this was not sufficient to establish a breach. In the prevailing situation the applicants were not especially at risk. 'General risk' will only suffice if sufficient to establish a real risk for all persons.

4.8   *Chahal v United Kingdom*[8]

This is a case of profound importance. Its history is summarised at footnote 9 below. The Court held *inter alia* as follows:

(By twelve votes to seven) that the implementation of Mr Chahal's deportation to India would violate article 3[9]

The UK Government had argued that the article 3 guarantees were not *absolute* and that in a national security case such factor could be taken into account (proving an

---

6   (1991) A 201; 14 EHRR 1.
7   (1991) A 215, para 111; 14 EHRR 248.
8   *70/1995/576/662* (1996) 23 EHRR 413.
9   On 14 August 1990 the Secretary of State decided to deport Mr Chahal to India on national security grounds and on 16 August 1990 Mr Chahal was detained. On 16 August 1990 Mr Chahal applied for asylum on the grounds that he would be subjected to torture and persecution if returned to India (on the basis *inter alia* of his previous detention and torture in Punjab in 1984; his political activities identifying him with Sikh separatism; the detention, torture and questioning of relatives in India and the interest shown by the Indian national press in his alleged Sikh militancy). The application was refused on 27 March 1991. On 10 June 1991 Mr Chahal's case was considered by the national security advisory panel. The Secretary of State's case setting out his views of the national security elements of his deportation decision – although neither the sources of nor the evidence for such views – were provided to Mr Chahal's solicitors who responded by letter dated 7 June 1991 setting out his case to be put before the advisory panel. Mr Chahal appeared before the panel in person – although was not permitted to call witnesses on his behalf, be represented by a lawyer nor be informed of the advice given by the panel to the Home Secretary. On 25 July 1991 the (then) Home Secretary Kenneth Baker signed the deportation order.

implied limitation on the scope of article 3). In rejecting this argument the Court stated that it was 'well aware of the immense difficulties faced by States in modern times in protecting their communities' (para 79). However, as the Court went on to state:

> The prohibition provided by Article 3 against ill-treatment is .. absolute in expulsion cases. Thus, whenever substantial grounds have been shown for believing that an individual would face a real risk of being subjected to treatment contrary to Article 3 if removed to another State, the responsibility of the Contracting State to safeguard him or her against such treatment is engaged in the event of expulsion. In these circumstances, the activities of the individual in question, *however undesirable or dangerous, cannot be a material consideration. The protection afforded by Article 3 is thus wider than that provided by Articles 32 and 33 of the United Nations 1951 Convention on the Status of refugees* [Emphasis added].

The Court stated that the relevant time for the assessment of risk was 'that of the Court's consideration of the case' (para 86 refers). On the facts the risk to Mr Chahal was substantiated (para 107).

On 9 August 1991 Mr Chahal applied for judicial review of the refusal of his asylum claim and the signing of the deportation order. The asylum refusal was quashed by Popplewell J on 2 December 1991: the Secretary of State's reasoning had been inadequate, principally since he had neglected to explain whether he believed the evidence of Amnesty International relating to the situation in the Punjab – and if not, the reasons for such disbelief.

On 1 June 1992 a further decision was made refusing asylum. The Home Secretary reasoned that the breakdown of law and order in the Punjab was the result of Sikh terrorists and not evidence of persecution; furthermore, relying on articles 32 and 33 of the 1951 Refugee Convention, even if Mr Chahal were at risk of persecution, he would not be entitled to protection because of the threat he posed to national security. On 2 July 1992 The Home Secretary declined to withdraw the deportation proceedings, relying *inter alia*, on an assurance received from the Indian Government that Mr Chahal would 'enjoy the same legal protection as any other Indian citizen' and would not 'suffer mistreatment of any kind at the hands of the Indian authorities'. A further application was made for judicial review. Leave was granted on 16 July 1992 in respect of both decisions. On 23 July 1992 bail was refused.

On 12 February 1993 the application for judicial review was dismissed by Potts J, (as was a further bail application). Mr Chahal appealed. On 22 October 1993 the Court of Appeal dismissed the appeal. It held that the combined effect of the Immigration Rules and the 1951 Convention in national security cases was that a balance *was* required between the threat to Mr Chahal's life or freedom if deported and the danger to national security if permitted to stay (see [1994] Imm AR 107). However, it had not been shown that the Home Secretary had failed to carry out such balance, nor was it possible to categorise the decision to deport Mr Chahal as *Wednesbury* unreasonable. In March 1994 the House of Lords refused leave to appeal.

On 27 July 1993 Mr Chahal had made an application to the European Commission of Human Rights alleging violations of articles 3 (real risk of torture or inhuman or degrading treatment if returned to India); 5(1) and (4) (his detention had been too long and judicial control thereof had been ineffective and slow); 8 (deportation would breach right to respect for family life) and 13 (lack of effective remedy (*inter alia*) in respect of Convention claims because of national security elements in case). On 1 September 1994 the European Commission of Human Rights declared the application admissible. In its report of 27 June 1995 it expressed the unanimous opinions that there would be violations of article 3 and 8 if he were deported to India; that there had been violation of article 5(1) because of the length of his detention and that there had been violation of article 13.

In the light of the Commission's report Mr Chahal applied for habeas corpus and judicial review of the Home Secretary's decision to continue detain him. This was refused by Macpherson J on 10 November 1995.

(Unanimously) there was violation of Article 5(4)

Article 5(4) does not guarantee a right to judicial review of such breadth as to empower the court, on all aspects of the case including questions of pure expediency, to substitute its own discretion for that of the decision making authority (para 127). Nor, does it demand that domestic courts have the power to review whether the underlying decision to expel could be justified under national or Convention law (para 128). But the question arose 'whether the available proceedings to challenge the lawfulness of Mr Chahal's detention and to seek bail provide an adequate control by the domestic courts' (para 129). Because national security was involved the domestic courts were not in a position to review whether the decisions to detain Mr Chahal and keep him in detention were justified on national security grounds. 'Furthermore, ... bearing in mind that Mr Chahal was not entitled to legal representation before the panel, that he was only given an outline of the grounds of the notice of intention to deport, that the panel had no power of decision and that its advice to the Home Secretary was not binding and was not disclosed ... the panel could not be considered as a "court" within the meaning of article 5(4)' (para 130).

The mere fact that the use of confidential material may be unavoidable in national security cases could not enable national authorities to be free from effective control by domestic courts whenever they choose to assert that national security and terrorism are involved. The Court concludes its judgement on article 5(4) as follows:

> The Court considers that neither the proceedings for habeas corpus and for judicial review of the decision to detain Mr Chahal before the domestic courts, nor the advisory panel procedure, satisfied the requirements of Article 5(4). This shortcoming is all the more significant given that Mr Chahal has undoubtedly been deprived of his liberty for a length of time which is bound to give rise to serious concern (para 132).

(Unanimously) that judicial review and the advisory panel procedure were inadequate remedies for the Article 3 complaint since there could be no review of the decision to deport with reference solely to the question of risk to Mr Chahal, leaving aside national security considerations

The effect of Article 13 is to require the provision of a domestic remedy allowing the competent national authority both to deal with the substance of the relevant Convention complaint and to grant appropriate relief (paragraph 145). The Court had previously held in *Vilvarajah* (1991) 14 EHRR 248 that judicial review proceedings were an effective remedy in respect of a complaint under article 3. In respect of complaints under articles 8 and 10 the Court had also held (in *Klass* A 28 (1978) 2 EHRR 214 and *Leander* A 116 (1987) 9 EHRR 433) that article 13 only required that a remedy be 'effective as can be' in circumstances where national security considerations did not permit the divulging of certain sensitive information. But such limitation is not appropriate in respect of a complaint under article 3, where issues concerning national security are immaterial (para 150):

> In such cases, given the irreversible nature of the harm that might occur if the risk of ill-treatment materialised and the importance the Court attaches to Article 3, the notion of an effective remedy under Article 13 requires independent scrutiny of the claim that there exist substantial grounds for fearing a real risk of treatment contrary to Article 3. This scrutiny must be carried out without regard to what the person may

have done to warrant expulsion or to any perceived threat to the national security of the expelling state (para 151).

In *Chahal* neither the Courts nor the advisory panel could review the decision to deport with reference solely to the question of risk (leaving aside national security). The Court was concerned with assessing whether the Home Secretary had carried out a balance. Before the advisory panel Mr Chahal was not entitled to legal representation, he was only given an outline of the grounds for the notice of intention to deport, the panel itself had no power of decision and its advice was not binding: in the circumstances the panel did not offer sufficient procedural safeguards for the purposes of article 13. The extent of the deficiencies of both judicial review and the advisory panel were such that 'the Court (could not) consider that the remedies taken together satisfy the requirements of Article 13 in conjunction with Article 3'.

In *Ahmed v Austria*[10] the applicant Somali national lost his refugee status following his criminal conviction. He was under threat of deportation to Somalia on the grounds that he had committed a 'particularly serious crime' within the meaning of article 33.2 of the Refugee Convention and had lost the protection against 'non refoulement'. The Commission had expressed the unanimous opinion that there would be violation of article 3 if the applicant were to be deported to Somalia. The Court reached the same view. It attached 'particular weight' to the fact that the Austrian Minister of the Interior had granted the applicant refugee status in May 1992. The Court reiterated the position adopted in *Chahal* that the material point in time for assessment of risk was that of its consideration of the case. But circumstances in Somalia had changed little since 1992; there was no indication that the danger to which the applicant would have been exposed in 1992 had ceased to exist or that any public authority would be able to protect him. Again as the Court had done in *Chahal*, the Court reiterated the absolute prohibition of expulsion in breach of article 3. 'The activities of the individual in question, however undesirable or dangerous, cannot be a material consideration' (para 41). Following the decision of the House of Lords in *Adan* it is noteworthy that *Ahmed* would not even have been recognised as a refugee!

The potential breadth of the use of article 3 in removal cases is well shown by *D v United Kingdom*[11]. The applicant suffering from AIDS faced removal to St Kitts. His terminal and incurable illness was at a critical stage; his limited quality of life enjoyed in UK resulted from the availability to him of sophisticated treatment and medication in the UK and the care and kindness of a charitable organisation. The abrupt withdrawal of such facilities by his removal would entail the most dramatic consequences for him and would hasten his death; the conditions in St Kitts would subject him to acute mental and physical suffering. In these exceptional circumstances the Court held that D's removal would amount to inhuman treatment

---

10 *71/1995/577663* (1996) 24 EHRR 278. See also *MAR v United Kingdom* (28038/95)(1996) 23 EHRR CD 120 where the applicant refugee faced return to Iran following a number of drugs convictions as a result of which the Secretary of State had decided to make a deportation order on 'conducive to public good' grounds (a decision upheld by the IAT which had held also that his crimes were particularly serious and that he constituted a danger to the community within the meaning of article 33.2 of the Refugee Convention). The European Commission held the application (alleging violations if expelled under articles 2, 3, 5 and 6 of the European Convention) to be admissible. The case subsequently reached a friendly settlement.

11 *146/1996/767/964* (1997) 24 EHRR 423.

in violation of article 3. Although the conditions in St Kitts would not themselves breach article 3, his removal would expose him to a real risk of dying under most distressing circumstances which would amount to inhuman treatment.

Again the 'absolute' nature of article 3 is emphasised by this case. *D* was a convicted drugs smuggler whose case under article 3 did not depend on any allegation whatsoever of harm to him attributable to the authorities in St Kitts.

5. Some conclusions

It is plain that the protection provided by the European Convention is much wider than that provided by the 1951 Refugee Convention. The most obvious differences are the absence of a need to identify a convention reason for persecution and the absolute nature of the protection afforded by article 3. Nowhere is the latter point more clearly made than in the *Chahal* decision which quickly led to the release of persons hitherto detained on 'national security' grounds, including the appellant in *T v Immigration Officer*[12]. Whether a person is said to pose a threat to national security, whether s/he is said to have been involved in terrorist outrages (or even acts contrary to the purposes and principles of the UN) or whether on account of the commission of a particularly serious crime s/he is said to constitute a danger to the community, removal will breach article 3 if there are substantial grounds for believing that there is a real risk of treatment contrary to article 3. In many cases this risk will be obvious. Perhaps less obvious is the potential use that might be made of the conditions in places of detention: such conditions are often appalling in refugee producing countries.

Following incorporation it is expected that of the 'protection gaps' identified in section 2 above all will be filled. Assuming that treatment reaches a minimum level of severity the 'relative' threshold of article 3 (dependent *inter alia* on the sex, age and state of health of the victim), the inclusion of discriminatory treatment as the basis for a claim of degrading treatment and the breadth of approach shown by (for example) the decision in *D v United Kingdom* will hopefully render the possible treatment of 'persecution' as a question of fact and not law less relevant. Of course depending on the meaning ascribed to 'persecution' in the Refugee Convention many cases in which breaches of Hathaway's first and second category rights are alleged would plainly fall within article 3 in any event. The concern that third category rights might not reach the article 3 threshold would seem likely to be unfounded in view of the decision in *D v United Kingdom*. Further, as Harris, O'Boyle and Warbrick argue, discrimination prohibited by article 14 of the ECHR ought to be able to found a claim under article 3. But as shown by cases such as *Kagema* much, if not all, depends on the view of the particular tribunal considering a case in any event. Certainly the analysis of the developing case law on the meaning ascribed to the various forms of prohibited treatment reflect no such similar tendency to treat the meaning to be ascribed to such terms as matters of fact and not law.

It is undeniably the case that *Adan* would be irremovable under article 3 ECHR. As already observed there could be no question of removal in article 1F cases, national security cases or 'criminal' cases.

Although not (yet) a casualty of a court ruling in the UK some may feel unsure of the approach in future to persecution by non-state agents, particularly in view of the

House of Lords' decision in *Adan* and the approach to the same question of France and Germany (which only grant refugee status where the state is complicit in such treatment – see the Court of Appeal decision in *R v Secretary of State for the Home Department, ex p Adan, Subaskaran and Aitseguer* (1999) Times, 28 July). It is believed that no such problem would arise under article 3. As already observed, *D v United Kingdom* provides a good example of a case in which no allegation of harm was sought to be made against the country of proposed removal, its servants or agents.

Despite the potential to plug the protection gaps identified recognition as a refugee would plainly be preferable, given the extra rights and obligations that flow from such recognition (settlement after four years; family reunion; 'juridical status' (articles 12-16 of the 1951 Convention); 'gainful employment' rights (articles 17-19); 'welfare' rights (articles 20-24) etc). It remains to be seen whether the 'status' granted to someone whose removal is found to breach the European Convention will be any more 'formalised' than it is at present. It certainly should be; there is no logical reason why those who are irremovable under article 3 are any the less 'deserving' of the kinds of rights that flow from recognition as refugees, once an 'incorporated' human rights instrument is engaged.

Other concerns remain. Most important, that the illiberal attitudes which appear all too often in the decision-making of the Home Office and courts in 'refugee' cases might come to be reflected in the approach to 'protection' under the European Convention. In June 1985 Taylor J heard an application for judicial review by a Sri Lankan asylum seeker who risked ill treatment as a Tamil. He acknowledged the 'administrative problem of numbers seeking asylum' but stated that it could not be right 'to adopt artificial and inhuman criteria in an attempt to solve it'[13]. There is ample cause for concern that (albeit with a number of notable exceptions) such robust sentiments rarely feature in refugee decision-making any longer. While the 'incorporation' of the 1951 Refugee Convention and the provision of in-country appeal rights (sections 2 and 8 of the 1993 Act) were plainly positive steps, the consequential 'hardening' has been all too plain to see. The culture of disbelief into which asylum seekers step when making claims, and the cries of Government and press about the number of fraudulent claims has without doubt had an adverse affect on the development of refugee case law. This must not be allowed to happen as a result of incorporation of the European Convention. It is to be hoped that – at least arguably in contrast to the position following 'incorporation' of the 1951 Refugee Convention – the integrity of the European Convention is able to withstand the demands of political expediency.

---

13 *R v Secretary of State for the Home Department, ex p Jeyakumaran* reported in [1994] Imm AR 45.

CHAPTER 5

Families, dependants, relationships

Duran Seddon

Cases in which persons who are subject to immigration control have an emotional and/ or dependant relationship with a person settled in the United Kingdom, have been at the forefront of attempts to invoke the Convention in immigration law prior to incorporation[1]. The relevance of rights under the Convention to immigration decisions in this area has also been reflected in an express policy intent on the part of the Home Office to operate with direct regard to the right to respect for family life under article 8[2].

This paper is concerned with the effect rights protected under the Convention will have upon immigration law in the area of families, dependants and relationships.

1. Rights under the Convention

1.1 Which rights are relevant?

The rights under the Convention which are of potential relevance in the context of families and dependants are articles 8 (right to respect for private and family life, home and correspondence) and article 12 (right to marry and to found a family). An immigration decision resulting in family separation may also raise an issue under article 3 (torture or inhuman and degrading treatment and punishment)[3] In certain circumstances, article 14 (right to be free from discrimination on any ground in the enjoyment of the rights and freedoms set

---

1   See for example *Gangadeen, Jurawan, Khan v Secretary of State for the Home Department* [1998] Imm AR 106 (attempt to demonstrate that, in applying enforcement policy, the Secretary of State should give primacy to interests of children effected by the deportation of parents and that such was consistent with the jurisprudence under article 8 ECHR); *Mirza v Secretary of State for the Home Department* [1996] Imm AR 314 (relevance of article 8 in construing enforcement policy statement in case of marriage contracted after knowledge of commencement of enforcement procedures) and also see *R v Secretary of State for the Home Department, ex p Amankwah* [1994] Imm AR 240; *R v Secretary of State for the Home Department, ex p Ozminnos* [1994] Imm AR 287, *R v Secretary of State for the Home Department, ex p Patel* [1995] Imm AR 223; *Hlodmodor* [1993] Imm AR 534.
2   See for example introductory section to Home Office instruction on enforcement DP/2/93 (now superseded but for transitionally protected cases).
3   See *Berrehab v Netherlands* (1985) D & R 41, p 196 where the Commission stated that where a decision raises an issue under article 8, an article 3 complaint on the same basis should not automatically be excluded.

out in the Convention) may also be relevant used in conjunction with the foregoing substantive rights[4].

1.2   The ingredients of article 8

Article 8 protects four discrete interests (private life, family life, home, correspondence). The interest of prime importance here is that of 'family life'. In order to demonstrate a violation of article 8 in relation to family life, it is necessary to satisfy the following (often interrelated) matters[5]:

(i) Is 'family life' established?

Although the most important 'family' relationships are those between husband and wife and parent and child, depending on the strength of the emotional ties, relationships between siblings, between grandparents and grandchildren[6] and even between uncle and nephew, are potentially within the scope of 'family life'[7]. Whether the relationship is sufficient to amount to 'family life' depends upon the substance rather the form of the relationship and so informal relationships of sufficient substance and stablility may fall within the ambit of family life[8] as may prospective relationships, for example between fiancées[9] and also relationships between parties to a formally invalid polygamous marriage[10]. Similarly, a relationship of form only, for example a 'sham' marriage, would be likely to fall outside the scope of article 8[11]. Nonetheless, form has a role in the establishment of family life; the adoption of a child for example gives rise to family life between adoptive parents and child[12]. Despite, however, this general emphasis upon substantive ties, the Commission has consistently rejected the proposition that same sex relationships are capable of falling within the ambit of 'family life' in article 8[13]. It has also been held that national

---

4   See *Abdulaziz* (1985) 7 EHRR 471 where the 1980 Statement of changes in immigration rules was held to be discriminatory as regards the differential provision for men and women to be admitted as spouses.

5   These elements are alternatively encompassed under the heads of 'Applicability' (the existence of effective family life) and 'Compliance' (interference and justification) in Hugo Storey's analysis of the case law of the Commission in '*The Right to Family Life and Immigration Case Law at Strasbourg*' International and Comparative Law Quarterly 1990, p 328. For the stages of consideration in an ECHR case generally, see p 11.

6   In *Marckx v Belgium* (1979) 2 EHRR 330 at para 45, the Court expressed the view that 'family life' included 'at least the ties between near relatives, for instance those between grandparents and grandchildren ...'

7   Application 3110/67 *Moustaquim v Belgium* (1991) 13 EHRR 802; *X v Germany* (1968) 9 YB 449; *Marckx* above.

8   *Johnston v Ireland* (1986) 9 EHRR 203; *Marckxl*

9   *Abdulaziz* (1985) 7 EHRR 471 paras 61-63; Application 15817/89 *Wakefield v United Kingdom* (1990) 66 DR 251 at 255.

10 Application 14501/89 *A and A v Netherlands* (1992) 72 DR 118 at 121–123, although it is permissible to preclude admission under article 8(2) where the consequence would be the estblishment of two wives residing together with their husband in a country which otherwise does not permit polygamy (Application 19628/92 *Bibi v United Kingdom* (1992) and see HC 395 at paras 278–279 to this effect).

11 *Moustaquim v Belgium* (1991) A 193 Com Rep para 511; 13 EHRR 802.

12 Application 9993/82 *X v France* (1992) 31 DR 241.

13 *S v United Kingdom* (1986) 47 DR 274 paragraph 2; *X v United Kingdom* (1983) 32 DR 220; Application 15666/89 *Kerkhoven v Netherlands* (19 May 1992, unreported).

provisions which, for the purposes of protecting the family, treat married couples and couples of opposite sex living together more favourably, are not contrary to the anti-discriminatory provisions of article 14[14].

A child born of a subsisting marital union forms part of the family relationship[15]. From the time of such child's birth and by the fact of it, there exists between child and parents a bond amounting to 'family life' which subsequent events cannot break save in 'exceptional circumstances'[16]. There is a general presumption in favour of family life between natural father and child[17]; but where the father retains no contact with or interest in the child or mother, the natural relationship may not be sufficient to give rise to family life between father and child.

(ii) Is there an 'interference' with the 'right to respect' for family life?

Not every decision which affects the interests protected by article 8 constitutes an interference with the right to 'respect' for that interest. Before one considers whether a breach of a particular right can be justified (article 8(2)), one needs to establish that there has been a breach[18]. In determining what is required in any particular context to maintain 'respect' for a particular interest, it is necessary to weigh the interest of the individual against the interest of the community[19]. In *Abdulaziz*[20], the Court indicated that there was a 'wide margin of appreciation' afforded to states in determination of the question of what is required in order for a state to demonstrate that it has maintained 'respect' for a particular interest. In that case, the Court recognized that the question of an applicants' family life had to be viewed in the context of the right of States to control the entry of non-nationals onto the territory. The Court then rejected the proposition that, commensurate with such 'respect', was the right of married couples to choose their country of matrimonial residence. Central to the question of whether the refusal of entry would constitute a denial of respect, was the question of whether there were 'obstacles' in the path of, or 'special reasons' why family life could not be established elsewhere[1]. There is therefore no general positive obligation to allow a family to establish itself in the country of its choice. Other relevant factors in determining the ambit of 'respect' in this context are the links between the family members and the proposed country of destination, the existence of relationships with other family members in that country, the prospect of joint residence in the respondent state at the time the family was founded and the economic consequences of removal[2].

14 *S v United Kingdom* (1986) 47 DR 274, para 7; *B v United Kingdom* (1990) 64 DR 278, para 2.
15 *Berrehab v Netherlands* (1988) 11 EHRR 322 at para 21.
16 *Gul v Switzerland* (1996) 22 EHRR 93 at para 32.
17 *Keegan v Ireland* (1994) 18 EHRR 342.
18 See Harris, O'Boyle & Warbrick *Law of the European Convention on Human Rights* (1995 Butterworths), p 328, commenting on cases involving excessive noise from aircraft and its effect on family and private life:'While it may not have influenced these applications, it does seem important generally that the two tests under articles 8(1) and 8(2) are not collapsed into a single one. For the government, the matter is simple: it ought not to be put to justifying that which it is not in breach of a duty anyway. For an applicant, the establishment of the positive duty will be of significance in his dealings with the government in "environmental" cases'.
19 *Cossey v United Kingdom* (1990) 13 EHRR 622.
20 *Abdulaziz, Cabales and Balkandali v United Kingdom* (1985) 7 EHRR 471 at pp 497-498.
1   The Court in *Abdulaziz* (paras 78-83) nevertheless determined that there was a violation of article 14 taken with article 8, namely that there was an unjustifiable difference in treatment as regards the admission of non-national husbands compared to wives in the operation of the immigration rules operative in 1980 (HC 394).
2   See, *inter alia*, Application 5445, 5446/72 *X and Y v United Kingdom* (1973).

Once it is established that a particular decision engages the right to respect for family life, it is often a short step to demonstrate an 'interference' with such right and indeed often the issue of 'interference' is conceded. Exceptions include cases where it is not apparent that the measure will or has materially affected the individual in question.

The close interface between the determination of the content of the right and the question of 'interference' with such right is exemplified by *Berrehab*[3] in which the complaint of a Moroccan national centred on an order expelling him from the Netherlands which would prevent him from continuing to exercise his rights of access to his four-year-old daughter from whose mother he was separated. The Court[4] had regard to the distance between the Netherlands and Morocco, the financial difficulties which would attend expulsion, the age of the child and the frequency of the pre-existing contact (four times per week) in order to determine that the exclusion constituted an interference with the protected article 8(1) right.

(iii) Is the interference 'in accordance with the law' and in pursuance of one of the aims set out in article 8(2)?

Any interference must, in order to preclude a violation, be 'in accordance with the law' and taken in pursuit of one of a number of specified legitimate aims. This requirement reflects a concern that any interference with a protected right should not be arbitrary and unregulated but must be underpinned by law. In a case involving the interference with a prisoner's mail, *Silver*[5], the Court set out the criteria for determining this question: there must be a basis for the interference in domestic law, the law must be adequately accessible, it must be sufficiently precise so that it's consequences are foreseeable and a law which confers a discretion must indicate the scope of that discretion[6]. Decisions made in the context of a framework of law including primary statutory provisions and published immigration rules of practice are unlikely to fail to comply with these requirements.

In more general terms, immigration control has consistently been held by the Court to relate to the prevention of disorder, the protection of the rights and freedoms of others and the preservation of the economic well-being of the country thus falling within those identified aims set out in article 8(2). An immigration decision which interferes with the right to respect for family life is therefore generally legitimate at least insofar as it may be said to have been taken in order to further a competing proper purpose.

(iv) Is the extent of the interference 'necessary in a democratic society'?

Again, in order to avoid a violation, a state must ensure that the extent of any interference with the protected interest can be justified by reference to the indentified competing policy aim. Put another way, any interference with the protected interest is only permitted under article 8(2), if the action is proportionate to the identified aim. Essentially, this question focuses on whether there is a 'pressing social need' for the implementation of the decision in the light of the purpose pursued.

---

3   *Berrehab v Netherlands* (1988) 11 EHRR 322.
4   Ibid, at paras 22-23.
5   *Silver v United Kingdom* (1983) 5 EHRR 347.
6   *Silver*, paras 86-88.

In answer to this question, similar to the determination of the content of the right (above), the Strasbourg Court has afforded states a 'wide margin of appreciation'. It is thought that while this doctrine may form an important part of the Strasbourg Court's determination of the international obligation of differing states in relation to one another, it has no place when the domestic Court comes to determine the scope of the UK's obligations when the provisions have been incorporated.

1.3 Other rights

(i) Respect for 'home'

Article 8 further protects the right to respect for the 'home'. It is suggested that reliance upon this discrete right in the immigration context will be possible only in limited circumstances. That this is the case is demonstrated by the case of *Gillow*[7]. In that case, the Court found a violation in respect of decisions of the Housing Authority of Guernsey refusing the applicants a permanent or temporary residence licence to allow them to return and reside in their house. The Court found that the legislation permitting the disqualification of persons in the position of the applicants was in accordance with the law and, in being directed to dealing with the problem of overcrowding on the island, was in pursuance of a legitimate aim. The Court went on to find that the particular decision was disproportionate having regard to the fact that the applicants had built the house for themselves and their family at a time when they possessed residence qualifications, that by letting it in their absence, they had contributed to the housing stock of the island and further that the house, needing repair, could not immediately be let out. Relevant also in relation to persons seeking admission to a country, is the Court's emphasis on the fact that the applicants had established no other 'home'.

This right may, therefore, be of use in cases of long residence where, in the absence of family ties, an applicant can demonstrate an ownership link with the UK with no commensurate link elsewhere.

(ii) Right to marry and found a family (article 12)

Article 12 has been used to re-inforce the proposition that within the scope of the right to respect for 'family life' in article 8, is the need of a family to cohabit[8]. Standing alone, the use of article 12 in the immigration context is limited. The wording of article 12 is even more susceptible to the approach that the right may be exercised elsewhere than the rights protected by article 8. A further limitation is that the Court has found that article 12 only applies to traditional marriages between two persons of opposite biological sex[9].

There may nevertheless be certain narrow circumstances in which the right may be of relevance in an immigration context. In *Sharara*[10], the Commission declared inadmissible a complaint that the arrest of an illegal entrant just prior to his marriage on

---

7   (1986) 11 EHRR 335.
8   See *Abdulaziz*, at para 62.
9   *Rees v United Kingdom* (1986) 9 EHRR 56 at para 49; *Cossey v United Kingdom* (1990) 13 EHRR 622 at para 43.
10   Application 10915/84 *Sharara and Rinia v Netherlands*.

the basis that a short delay (on the facts nine days) in contracting the marriage was not sufficiently substantial to constitute a breach of article 12. Conceivably, if an immigration measure was to substantially delay or prevent a person from marrying and founding a family, an infringement under the article 12 head could potentially be demonstrated.

In general terms, however, it is to be assumed that an immigration decision causing separation will more appropriately raise issues under article 8[11].

There may also be some scope for the use of article 12 in conjunction with article 14 in the context of being denied the opportunity to found a family dependent upon financial means. In one case[12] involving a refusal of a UK citizen of no independent financial means to bring to the UK his Philippine fiancée, the Commission recalled its jurisprudence to the effect that there was no right to choose the geographical location of the marriage and further indicated that the imposition of immigration controls in respect of those who would create an economic burden was acceptable. *However*, the Commission also indicated that 'family and humanitarian considerations [could not be] wholly subordinated to financial criteria' and determined the case essentially upon the less than compelling facts (the applicant had not even met his fiancée).

As the Commission further indicated, 'hard' cases falling into the latter category may well be catered for pursuant to the Home Office's discretion outside the immigration rules. A negative exercise of such discretion in a case of sufficient merit might nonetheless raise an issue under this head.

2. Effect on UK law and practice and common problems

2.1. Interference With Protected Rights

Marital relationships

Marriage will generally bring the two partners within the scope of 'family' even if 'family life' has not yet been fully established, ie even if the couple have not assumed cohabitation.

An extremely common circumstance facing immigration practitioners is that presented by a non-national married to a person settled in the UK, the marriage having been entered into either after the expiration of any leave enjoyed by the non-national or indeed after the commencement of enforcement action. Any application to remain on the basis of marriage is automatically outside the immigration rules and can only call for discretionary treatment[13]. Enforcement action against such a person potentially interferes with the right to *respect* for that family life depending on matters such as the length of the relationship, its stability, connections with the UK and the question of establishing family life elsewhere.

---

11 See *Beldjoudi v France* (1992) 14 EHRR 801 at para 81, the applicants had raised a complaint under article 12 as well as article 8 but it was unnecessary to go on to consider the application of article 12; the inference is that it is unlikely that an article 12 complaint will be made out in cases such as this where there is not a violation of article 8, see further however Application 11026/84 *Taspinar v Netherlands* where the Commission declared admissible complaints under both articles 8 and 12 in a case in which an applicant sought residence in the Netherlands with his son previously cared for, until her death, by the applicant's own mother in Turkey.

12 Application 9773/82 (1983) 5 EHRR 296.

13 Para 284(i) HC 395 imposing the requirement that the applicant 'has limited leave to remain in the UK'.

The present framework for considering such cases lies under the immigration rules in cases where enforcement is by way of deportation[14] and in both cases of deportation and other cases, policies set up outside the framework of the rules[15]. An over-rigid application of the requirement that a relationship commenced prior to any particular enforcement decision or that it had not existed for a particular prescribed qualifying period of time either at the date of the initial enforcement action or indeed by the time of the proposed removal[16], may, on the facts of an individual case, result in interferences with the right to respect for family life where there is no practical possibility of establishing family life elsewhere. Indeed interferences may arise were the Secretary of State to continue the practice of enforcement in a family case in reliance upon the fact of a marriage post-dating enforcement executed upon some unrelated *previous* occasion subsequent to which the person lawfully returns to the UK and, for the first time, establish family ties[17].

Although adherence by the Home Office to arbitrarily drawn but universally applied rules may result in interferences in certain cases, the circumstances in which this will be the case will inevitably be limited. By way of illustration, although *Abdulaziz* was a case where the applicants were settled spouses who were themselves (at least initially) non-nationals, the Court found, that the applicants' asserted obstacles/special reasons: closeness to family in the UK combined with sickness[18], age/difficulty in finding work in the other country[19] and strong ties in the UK combined with a risk of social rejection in the other country[20], did *not* constitute sufficient reasons preventing the establishment of family life elsewhere.

Further, the Court dealt with the issue of the applicants' foreknowledge of the threat that immigration measures might have upon their family life in terms of what the applicants knew or should have known of the requirements for admission and settlement[1] not simply the actual initiation of enforcement procedures. It seems unlikely therefore to be the case that a marriage prior to enforcement action could alone preclude enforcement action under article 8.

The stringency of the test relating to obstacles is further illustrated by the more recent case of *Gul*[2]. In that case the applicant, a Turkish Kurd who had been granted the equivalent of exceptional leave to remain in Switzerland (having not suffered

---

14 Paras 364-367, 374-375 HC 395.
15 Relevant to married partners are DP/2/93 (in cases where the marriage came to the attention of the Home Office prior to 13 March 1996), 'Marriage Policy' DP 3/96; these instructions are supplemented by DP/4/95, DP/4/96, DP/5/96 and a Parliamentary Written Answer of 1 March 1999 in cases involving children.
16 See para 2 DP/2/93 and para 5(b) DP 3/96 – the latter imposing the additional requirement that a marital and cohabitational relationship has *existed* for at least two years prior to enforcement action as there also defined.
17 For cases where the Secretary of State's application of the internal instructions adopting this approach has been upheld as being a consistet and rational interpretation of the policy, see *Zellouf* [1997] Imm AR 120 and *R v Secretary of State for the Home Department, ex p Resham Singh* (1 August 1996, unreported) QBD and see *Adebiyi v Secretary of State for the Home Department* [1997] Imm AR 57.
18 *Abdulaziz*, para 43.
19 *Cabales*, para 49.
20 *Balkandali*, para 54.
1 *Abdulaziz*, paras 68-69.
2 (1996) 22 EHRR 93 at para 42 and see Application 17229/90 *Akhtar v United Kingdom* (1992) where a wife's constant illness in Pakistan was held not to constitute serious obstacles given that she had lived there for may years previously; and see Application 24831/94 *Kamara v United Kingdom* where an illness which could not be properly treated in the country of proposed removal was known of prior to the marriage.

personal persecution in Turkey) attempted to bring his two sons also to Switzerland where his wife had been granted a residence permit on humanitarian grounds (ill-health requiring specialist medical treatment) and where the couple's daughter had been taken into state-run care as she could not satisfactorily be cared for at home. Despite the recognition that the 'Gul family situation is very difficult from the human point of view'[3], the Court maintained that there were still, strictly speaking, no obstacles preventing the development of family life in Turkey. The decision is perhaps best understood in the light of the fact that the applicant and his wife had in fact returned to visit Turkey.

Sufficient obstacles or special reasons in these circumstances may be legal ie the inability to obtain rights of residence for both parties in any other jurisdiction[4]. They may also be demonstrated by an inability to enjoy Convention rights in the alternative destination (for example if inhuman and degrading treatment would attend an attempt to establish the family elsewhere) or if the settled partner has a well-founded fear of persecution in the alternative destination. Obstacles will be more easily demonstrated where the settled family member has no other linkage with the country of proposed alternative residence[5].

One useful example, although involving children, is the case of *Fadele*[6]. In that case a non-national father was permitted to return to the UK where his children had enjoyed rights of residence following the substantial prejudice forced exile to Nigeria had *demonstrably* already caused them; in particular very severe health difficulties and an absence of schooling. The case was disposed of by way of friendly settlement following the decision of the Commission[7].

'De facto' relationships

Under this head are covered both relationships between men and women not 'legitimated' by marriage and relationships between those of the same sex.

(i) Relationships between men and women
There are presently no provisions in the immigration rules providing for admission or an extension of stay on the basis of relationships of this nature[8]. An important aspect of article 8 is that it essentially looks beyond formal relationships ie. sexual relationships legitimated by marriage and children born to such relationships, to the *substance* of the ties that have been established[9]. Further, in *Cabales*[10] the Court

---

3   At para 43.
4   See Application 8061/77 *X v Switzerland.*
5   Application 266998/95 *Adegbie v Austria* (1996).
6   Application 13078/87 *Fadele v United Kingdom* (1990) 70 DR 159.
7   For a discussion of the facts ramifications of this case and comparison with the similar earlier case of *Hasbudak*, see 'Second-generation immigrants and the right to family life' Jacqueline Bhabha, LAG, July 1991, pp 19-21.
8   Indeed, the immigration rules, from October 1994, implicitly provide negatively for such relationships (paras 320(8), 322(1) HC 395). Fiancées are accommodated but must of course intend to marry (paras 290-295 HC 395); and those seeking an *extension* of stay as such must have been admitted as a fiancées and show 'good cause' why the marriage did not take place within the currency of the earlier leave (para 293(i)(ii) HC 395).
9   See *Marckx v Belgium* (1979) 2 EHRR 330 at paragraph 31 concerning the effect of the Belgian laws relating to legitimacy: 'By guaranteeing the right to respect for family life, article 8 presupposes the existence of a family...article 8 makes no distinction between the "legitimate" and the "illegitimate" family. Such a distinction would not be consonant with the word "everyone"....'.
10 At para 63.

considered that it was not necessary for it to descend into the nuances of Philippine law in order to determine the validity of a marriage. The fact that the couple believed themselves to be married, lived together and wished to cohabit in a committed relationship was sufficient to attract the application of article 8. The immigration rules are of course very largely informed by criteria which specify requirements as to form as well as to substance (see marriage/fiancé rules[11] and the rules governing adoptive children[12])[13].

Insofar as *de facto* male/female relationships are concerned, where a committed and settled relationship can be demonstrated, certainly one which is akin to a marriage, family life will generally be established. The relevant factors in determining whether such a relationship has enough of substance to constitute 'family life' are the length and the stability of the relationship, the intentions of the parties, their commitment to one another and dependency between them[14]. There is no pre-requisite that the couple should cohabit although this is another material factor[15]. Again, there may be an interference with the right to respect for family life where persons are to be excluded from the UK or else removed in circumstances where it would not be possible for them to re-establish family life elsewhere.

A decision, therefore, the basis of which was to preclude admission or settlement of a person on the basis of such a relationship, because the nature of the relationship was one which, by choice, did not conform to particular formal conventional arrangements, would appear to entail an interference with the protected right. Such a decision could further be said to have a discriminatory effect in relation to the enjoyment of article 8 rights when taken with article 14.

In this context, it is of note that the practice presently operated by the Secretary of State outside the formal provisions of the immigration rules for those in common-law relationships[16], requires the satisfaction of the criterion that it is *not possible* to form a marriage relationship (ie the parties must be 'legally unable to marry under United Kingdom law, other than by reason of consanguinous relationships or age')[17].

(ii)   Same sex relationships
Despite the fact that same sex relationships have been held to be incapable of falling within the scope of 'family life', sexual relations may fall within the the scope of 'private life' in article 8. Immigration decisions which result in the separation of

---

11 HC 395 paras 277-296.
12 HC 395 paras 6, 310-316.
13 Following the grant of leave to move in *Ex p Glowacka* (1997), unreported), QBD, the Home Office agreed to treat the parties of an invalid customary (Roma) marriage in the same way as if validly married for the purposes of the immigration rules concerning dependants of refugees (part IX, HC 395); the applicants had submitted that the parties were 'spouses' for the purposes of such rules.
14 *Keegan v Ireland* (1994) 18 EHRR 342, paras 44-45; *X, Y, Z v United Kingdom* (1995) 20 EHRR CD 6, paras 50-51.
15 *Kroon v Netherlands* (1994) A 297-C para 30.
16 'Common-law and same sex relationships (unmarried partners)' Immigration Directorates Instructions, Chapter 8, Section 7.
17 See paras 1(iii), 2(v) and 4(iii) of the above-mentioned instructions; the onerous further requirement, under the same policy, in respect of those in common-law relationships is to have been living in a relationship which has existed for four years or more. The criteria are not tailored to the substance or to any investigation of the individual merits of a case but rather to strictly objectively ascertainable criteria (length of time) which, while plainly relevant, cannot be exhaustive of the matters relevant for the purposes of article 8.

such partners may therefore raise an issue under article 8 upon the application of similar criteria to those applied in considering heterosexual relationships[18] and the same comments may be made as above in relation to qualifying periods of cohabitation[19].

It is further of importance that the Court has held that the prohibition of homosexual conduct carried out in private between consenting adults constiutes an unjustifiable interference with the right to respect for such private life[20]. An issue may therefore be raised under article 8 where an immigration decision would result in a same sex couple facing the prospect of being able to continue their relationship only in a country in which their right to respect for private life would be interfered with by that country's law or otherwise contrary to the Convention. This may be the case even in circumstances where the state policy is not to prosecute such conduct but the existence of an offence relating to acts of homosexuality nevertheless creates interference in the form of fear and distress, investigation and even private prosecution[1].

There are further grave difficulties presented in attempting to rely on the Convention to protect the rights of those in same sex relationships in relation to their children which form part of the domestic unit. In *Kerkhoven*[2], the Commission held that the relationship of a woman with the child of her long term same sex partner did not fall within the scope of family life.

More recently[3], however, the Court accepted that these were 'de facto' family ties between a transsexual who had undergone gender reassignment surgery, her female partner and their child born following AIDS treatment. Although the Court held that the failure of the UK to allow legal recognition of the relationship between the transsexual and the child did not amount to a failure to respect family life[4], this would not preclude an interference with the protected right in a different context such as separation.

Children

The vulnerability and dependency of children clearly renders the child–parent relationship central to the meaning of 'family life' within article 8. The establishment and maintenance of 'family life' in cases involving children is often assumed or simple to demonstrate. For example, in *Boughanemi*[5], the Court accepted that the existence of family life as between father and child was not broken even though the

18 See Application 9369/81 5 EHRR 581 at 601 in which the Commission held inadmissible a complaint against the United Kingdom in respect of a decision of the immigration authorities to refuse to allow a Malaysian citizen to remain in the UK with his settled male partner on applying the same approach as in *Abdulaziz*.

19 Common Law and Same Sex Relationship (Unmarried Partners), Immigration Directorates Instructions, Chapter 8, Section 7, the current practice is to apply a 'four year' cohabitation qualifying period as with heterosexual common law relationships.

20 *Dudgeon v United Kingdom* (1981) 3 EHRR 40 at paras 96-97 and 115; *Modinos v Cyprus* (1993) 16 EHRR 485 at paras 20-25; and see *Laskey, Jaggard, Brown v United Kingdom* (1997) 24 EHRR 39.

1 See *Modinos* and *Dudgeon* above.

2 Application 15666/89 (19 May 1992, unreported).

3 *X, Y, Z v United Kingdom* (1997) 24 EHRR 143 at paras 50-70, the case in fact concerned the right of a female to male transsexual (the first applicant) to be registered as the father of a child born to the first applicant's female partner.

4 *X* at para 52.

5 *Boughanemi v France* (1996) 22 EHRR 228.

father was separated from his common-law spouse prior to the birth of the child in respect of which the asserted family life was based and in circumstances where the father had not formally recognised the child until ten months after his birth, had not provided for the child, contributed to the child's education or demonstrated that he enjoyed parental rights.

Similarly, it may be said that the parent-child relationship, particularly where young children are involved, is exceptionally susceptible to severe interference by way of separation.

The circumstances in which parent-child relationships may be found to give rise to an interference with article 8 rights where, for example, the relationship between the parents has broken down and it is proposed to enforce against the non-settled partner where such would inevitably involve separation between child and parent and/or where the child has rights of residence, will almost certainly be the focus of litigation.

The judgement of the Court of Appeal in *R v Secretary of State for the Home Department, ex p Gangadeen & Khan*[6] indicates the view of the domestic Court to the jurisprudence of the Strasbourg Court to be to the effect that the interests of the child in such circumstances are not to be seen as pre-eminent but rather that the scales start even with no preference given to the child's interest. Cases will inevitably turn upon their facts. So in a case referred to by the Court in the latter case[7], a minimal resultant effect was found to flow from enforcement against a child where the contact with his settled father had been by telephone only.

Certainly, in cases involving divorced and separated parents, it may not be sufficient for the Secretary of State to maintain, as in certain cases at present, that family life has 'broken down' as between the separated partner and the child as a result of their no longer residing together[8]. Careful enquiry is required in cases such as this in order to determine whether in fact and in the circumstances of the case, the prospect of periodic access visits from abroad[9] would be sufficient to prevent an unjustifiable interference with family life. The legality of the parents' stay in the UK, in particular at the time the relationship was initiated and the child was born will also be of importance.

Where it is suggested that a child with rights of residence may accompany a parent abroad, both the adaptability and age of the children must be considered and, although the child may have rights of residence and/or citizenship in the state concerned which they cannot enjoy for many years if their parent/s are excluded, the Commission has declined to accept this as being decisive[10].

The impact of the right to respect for family life may also be brought to bear in cases involving family relations between adult children and parents[11]. The relationship between parent and adult child retains little significance insofar as the immigration rules are concerned yet it requires careful examination of factors such

---

6 [1998] Imm AR 106 especially at pp 117-119 (the case is now understood to have been given provisional leave to appeal to the House of Lords).

7 *Poku v United Kingdom* (1996) 22 EHRR CD 94.

8 See para 6 Home Office instruction DP/4/96 which states 'in this type of case there is unlikely to be a breach of article 8 of the ECHR as "family life" has already broken down' – this would appear to be in conflict with cases such as *Berrehab*.

9 See paras 246-248 HC 395, designed to provide for precisely such visits.

10 Application 239938/93 *Sorabjee v United Kingdom* (1995); Application 25297/94 *PP v United Kingdom* (1996) 21 EHRR CD 81; Application 24865/94 *Jaramillo v United Kingdom* (1995).

11 Cf Statement of Immigration Rules HC 395, paras 297-319 providing generally for the admission of minor children.

as continued dependency in the context of article 8[12]. The applicant *Moustaquim*[13], in which the Court found an unjustifiable interference with the applicant's private and family life in circumstances where he had lived with his family (including parents and numerous brothers and sisters) in Belgium since he was one year old, was 21 years at time of the deportation proceedings.

2.2   Proportionate to the aim pursued

If an interference is made out, in order to preclude a violation of article 8, it is in all cases for the state to demonstrate that the interferences 'correspond to a pressing social need and, in particular, that [they are] proportionate to the legitimate aim pursued'[14].

It is necessary to consider the nature and severity of the interference and the corresponding prejudice caused to the affected persons which will often involve considerations such as length of residence, strength of family links and the circumstances which await the individual in the country of origin. The level of interference then requires to be weighed against the prejudice to the legitimate aim pursued in declining to implement the proposed measure.

The weight to be attached to either side of the balance will vary enormously from case to case. It will often be the case that it is the conducting of this balance which is determinative of the issue since, in many cases, it will be trite that family life is established or that there is at least *some* interference with that interest by the proposed action. At one extreme, the proposed action might preclude altogether the continuation of firmly established family life.

Similarly, the prejudice to the legitimate aim will be of lesser weight in the case of a person who has a good immigration history, long residence, proven working record or who would be highly likely to obtain admission for settlement under the normal immigration rules upon an application being made from overseas. On the other side of the scales are cases where the interest in maintaining immigration controls reaches beyond issues of resources or employment but into the realm of criminal activity. Such cases have not received the unsympathetic consideration of the Court at least where second generation non-nationals have been concerned, where such persons have maintained no links with the country of origin[15]. In *Moustaquim*[16], the Court found that an unjustifiable interference would be caused to the applicant's right to respect for family life by his deportation to his country of nationality (Morocco) in circumstances where the applicant had lived the vast majority of his life in Belgium where he enjoyed very substantial ties with the remainder of his family notwithstanding a quite extensive criminal record. A similar conclusion was reached in *Beldjoudi*[17]. In both cases, however, it should be remembered that there were very substantial periods of residence and, in *Beldjoudi*, the applicant's wife was found to face severe practical and legal obstacles in relation to joining her husband in Algeria.

---

12 *X*, above, at para 52.
13 (1991) 13 EHRR 802.
14 *Berrehab*, para 28 and judgments there cited.
15 Cf *Boughanemi* (above) where the applicant was found to have still had links with his country of origin.
16 (1991) 13 EHRR 802.
17 (1992) 14 EHRR 801.

This test of proportionality may have a role in moderating the approach of the Home Office and the immigration appellate authorities in cases of deportation deemed 'conducive to the public good'[18] and the criminal court in recommending deportation following conviction for an imprisonable offence[19]. This is particularly the case given that recidivism and a propensity to commit further offences are not necessary preconditions in relation to the power to deport upon 'conducive' grounds[20], whereas if the legitimate aim relied upon was the *prevention* of disorder or crime (under article 8(2)), matters of propensity would be key to the outcome.

There may also be matters of wider public policy relevant to the interests of the family which will be material to the assessment of proportionality. To take an example, the government's policy on care in the community might, in an appropriate case, bear positively for the individual on both sides of the scales. The 1990 community care legislation, in conjunction with a myriad of approvals, directions and guidance papers issued pursuant to the legislation, requires the social services departments of local authorities to carry out care assessments in relation to sick, elderly, disabled and otherwise vulnerable persons who appear to require assistance with a view to the provision of any of a wide range of services aimed at promoting their welfare[1].

Of particular relevance to the delivery of community care[2] are the Government White Paper *'Caring for people'*[3] and policy guidance also issued by the government[4]. Primary to the provision of care in both documents is the need to assist persons to 'achieve a maximum independence and control over their own lives'[5], a recognition that most care is provided by 'family, friends and neighbours' and the corresponding need to assist and support those carers' 'valuable contribution to the spectrum of care'[6], to enable people to 'live an independent and dignified life at home...'[7]. Respect is also to be paid to the cultural needs of the person requiring care.

Enforcement against a carer in circumstances where that person is providing services to a relative falling with the spirit of the above, prima facie engages three of the interests protected under article 8 ('family life', 'private life' and 'home')[8]. Seen in this context, the prejudice that would be caused to these relevant interests by a decision causing separation, is clearly exacerbated.

18 ΙΜΜΙΑΡΑΙΙΙΟΝ ΑCΤ 1971, s 3(5)(b).
19 Immigration Act 1971, s 3(6).
20 *R v Immigration Appeal Tribunal, ex p Florent* [1985] Imm AR 141, CA; *Said v Immigration Appeal Tribunal* [1989] Imm AR 372, CA.
1 National Health Service and Community Care Act 1990, s 46(3) defines 'community care services' by reference to various legislative provisions. The aspect of these services best known to immigration practitioners has been the provision of assistance in the form of accommodation and vouchers for food and necessities provided to asylum-seekers pursuant to s 21(1)(a) of the National Assistance Act 1948 (*R v Westminster City Council, ex p M* [1997] CCLR 85) but the importance of community care has also been raised in relation to issues of enforcement in immigration proceedings (see *R v Secretary of State for the Home Department, ex p Zakrocki* [1997] COD 304; *Ex p Green* (29 October 1996, unreported) per McCullough J, QBD; on appeal (31 January 1997, unreported), CA).
2 See *Community Care Assessments, A Practical and Legal Framework* 1996 FT Law & Tax, Richard Gordon QC and Nicola Mackintosh, para 1.7.
3 *Caring for People* Cmnd 849.
4 *Community Care in the next decade and Beyond: Policy Guidance.*
5 *Caring for people*, para 2.2.
6 *Caring for people*, para 2.3.
7 *Community care in the next decade and Beyond: Policy Guidance*, para 1.1.
8 There are likely therefore to be cases where the dogmatic application of the Home Office policy on 'carers' (BDI 2/95) which is heavily restricted by time, may be in violation of article 8.

3. Conclusions

The incorporation of the European Convention is highly likely to result in opportunities to challenge individual decisions in the context of family relationships. In addition to the potential areas of conflict which are disclosed by a comparison of the case law of the Strasbourg Commission and Court and existing UK law and practice examined above, there will of course be scope for exploring new approaches to the rights under the Convention beyond the existing case law. Much will inevitably depend upon the reaction of the judiciary to the application of human rights in this sensitive area of practice.

CHAPTER 6

The prohibition against discrimination in the exercise of rights and freedoms under the Convention

Stephanie Harrison

1. Introduction

1.1 Article 14

> 'Article 14
> The enjoyment of the rights and freedoms set forth in this Convention shall be secured without discrimination on any ground such as sex, race, colour, language, religion, political or other opinion, nationality or social origin, association with a national minority, property, birth or other status.'

Prominent in the formation of international human rights law is protection against discrimination particularly through the promotion of equality before the law in the exercise and enjoyment of the fundamental rights and the minimum guarantees contained in the various human rights instruments beginning with and drawing inspiration from the Charter of the United Nations and the Universal Declaration of Human Rights[1] through to the more comprehensive prohibition on discrimination in the International Covenant on Civil and Political Rights (ICCPR) article 26 and the Covenant on the Elimination of all forms of Discrimination Against Women 1979 (CEDAW)[2].

The relevance to the practice of immigration law of a prohibition against discrimination needs little introduction. Discrimination in many forms on the grounds of race, nationality, sex, marital status and sexual orientation to name the most obvious are the stuff of the daily experience of the administration of immigration control in the United Kingdom (UK).

Race discrimination is inherent and has been the underlying rational of much of the substantial developments in modern immigration law. Successive governments have implemented a policy since the 1960s of stopping and reversing the migration of black and Asian Commonwealth Citizens through primary legislation, through

---

1 Article 2 of the UN Declaration states that: 'Everyone is entitled to all the rights and freedoms set forth in this Declaration without distinction of any kind such as race,colour, sex, language, religion, political or other opinion, national or social origin, property, birth or other status'.
2 See also the Convention Relating to the Status of Refugees 1951 and the 1967 protocol as interpreted, *inter alia*, by the House of Lords in *R v Immigration Appeal Tribunal, ex p Shah and Islam* [1999] 2 All ER 545 as providing international protection to those exposed, through lack of domestic protection, to discriminatory denial of their fundamental human rights.

visa controls, and through increasingly restrictive rules and conditions notably the primary purpose rule and the requirements as to maintenance and accommodation extended to cover the spouse and minor children of Commonwealth Citizens in 1988[3].

Many of the rules that directly discriminated on the grounds of sex have been abolished over the years, however, the requirements as to maintenance and accommodation provide a formidable obstacle to women particularly as sponsors. In the context of female asylum seekers the application of the law and the inadequacies of the processing of such cases is increasingly being recognised as an institutionalised failure to address and to meet the protection needs of women, particularly those whose claims are based upon rape and other forms of gender specific violations[4].

Recent policy reviews have indicated a developing awareness of the differential impact on women of immigration control in the areas of domestic workers and the 12-month rule for the grant of indefinite leave to remain for spouses. Changes campaigned for over a number of years have now been adopted, by the Home Office, to reduce the opportunity for exploitation by, *inter alia*, employers and husbands of women who are made vulnerable to violence and intimidation because of their dependent and insecure immigration status[5].

The rights of gay and lesbians to reside with their non-British partners has been recognised but the policy on cohabitees introduced in October 1997[6] continues to deny equality with heterosexuals in the exercise of the right to private life and leaves many couples in committed relationships deprived of this right.

2. Domestic protection against discrimination

Whilst the immigration rules at HC 395, para 2 prohibits individual racism by Immigration Officers who are required to carry out their duties 'without regard to race, colour or religion' currently UK law (excluding European Community law dealt with below) provides no effective protection against discrimination in the application of the Immigration laws and practice. It may form part of a rationality challenge in judicial review but it is largely outside of the ambit of the Sex and Race Discrimination Acts since the Courts have held that immigration control does not constitute a provision of 'a service or facility' within the meaning of the Acts[7]. There is, therefore, currently no independent legal rights infringed by discriminatory acts occasioned and/ or sanctioned by executive decision making[8].

---

3   Section 1 of the Immigration Act 1988 abolishing s 1(5) of the Immigration Act 1971.
4   See for a more detailed analysis and a guide to non-discriminatory practice in *Gender Guidelines for the Determination of Asylum Claims in the UK*, Refugee Women's Legal Group July 1998.
5   See the Domestic Servants Concession within the IND's Instructions to Staff on the IND web site and see the Domestic Violence Concession announced in the form of a written answer to a parliamentary question (Hansard, House of Commons, 16 June 1999).
6   Concession announced on 10 October 1997 (see IND web site) as varied by a written answer to a parliamentary question (Hansard, House of Commons, 16 July 1999).
7   See *Re Amin* [1983] 2 AC 818 and *Kassam v Immigration Appeal Tribuinal* [1980] 2 All ER 330, although the Court of Appeal in an unreported case of *Anglin v Foreign and Commonwealth Office*, were prepared to accept as arguable that a distinction could be drawn between the decision making function of immigration officials which was not covered and the processing of an application in the instant case in the form of an interview for entry clearance in which the Plaintiff claimed he had been subjected to racial sterotyping and insults.
8   In the aftermath of the Lawrence Inquiry, extending the ambit of the Race Relations Act not only to police officers but to all public servants is now firmly on the political agenda.

2.1 EC Nationals and their Families

The exception to this rule is cases involving European Community nationals as article 6 of the Treaty of the European Union (TEU) prohibits 'any discrimination on the grounds of nationality' in the application of the Treaty. This naturally includes the rights to free movement within the Community for nationals of the Member States and their families[9]. The domestic courts have, however, adopted a restrictive interpretation of article 6, TEU, where domestic law provides a more favourable status for the spouses of British citizens than under EC provisions and have concluded that there is no requirement for conditions of entry and residence to be equivalent to national law which is distinct from and cannot benefit those electing to exercising Community rights[10].

3. Incorporation of the ECHR

The incorporation into domestic law of the European Convention on Human Rights (ECHR) through the introduction of the Human Rights Act 1998, therefore, creates for the first time through article 14 a specific legal mechanism for challenging discriminatory laws and decision making, as well as the discriminatory impact of the administration of immigration control for UK and non-EC nationals.

3.1 The ambit test

Article 14 does not provide a general comprehensive free standing protection since it is restricted to protecting persons against discrimination only with respect to the rights and freedoms contained in the Convention. Furthermore it is a negative obligation not to discriminate rather than to promote equality of treatment. To a great extent it is, therefore, a right parasitic upon the substantive obligations and the European Court of Human Rights (ECtHR) has developed a practice, further marginalising the role of article 14, of generally declining to decide separately an article 14 breach if a substantive right has been found to be violated although this is not always the case and will depend upon whether discrimination is a 'fundamental aspect' of the substantive breach[11].

However, establishing a breach of article 14 does not depend exclusively upon establishing a violation of one of the substantive articles. Indeed it is not necessary even to claim a substantive violation although this is likely to be the case. The test

---

9   EEC Regulation No 1612/68 and for an example of prohibited discriminatory practice see for example *Netherlands v Reed* [1986] ECR 1283.
10   See *Boukssid v Secretary of State for the Home Department* [1998] Imm AR 270 at 276-278: spouse of an EC national who sought entry under EC provisions and was issued with a family permit. A subsequent application for indefinite leave to remain was refused and a five-year residence permit issued contrasting with the position of spouse of British Citizens under the immigration rules. Also *Secretary of State for the Home Department v Sahota* [1997] Imm AR 429. It is difficult to reconcile the logic of the Court of Appeal with the plain terms of article 6 and it is understood that the House of Lords have granted leave to petition in *Boukssid*. See also p 112.
11. *Airey v Ireland* (1980) A 32 para 30 and *Dudgeon v United Kingdom* (1981) A 45 para 69; 4 EHRR 149.

is only that the claim falls within *the ambit* of one of the substantive Articles. *Inze v Austria* (1987) A 126 paras 43-45; 10 EHRR 394; *Abdulaziz Cables and Balkandali v United Kingdom* (1985) 7 EHRR 471. Even where a Convention obligation is not directly engaged but if a state confers a right eg to education, or to entry, if it is restricted on a discriminatory basis it is justiciable under the Convention (*Abdulaziz* (supra)). The 'ambit' test, therefore, provides a measure of flexibility and independence in pursuing article 14 violations and presents scope for the development of the use of the article in domestic proceedings.

If the ambit test is satisfied then the specific forms of prohibited discrimination are comprehensive, the list in article 14 itself being long and not exhaustive. They are examples only.

4.   Defining discrimination

Discrimination is not expressly defined but direct discrimination requires a difference in treatment of people in similar positions on the basis of a personal characteristic where there is no 'objective or reasonable justification' for the difference in treatment (*Rasmussen v Denmark* (1984) A 87; 7 EHRR 371). The Court has drawn a distinction between permissible differentiation and unlawful discrimination by adopting an approach which was set out in the early *Belgian Linguistics (No 2)* case (1968) 1 EHRR 252:

> '... the principle of equality of treatment is violated if the distinction has no reasonable and objective justification. The existence of such a justification must be assessed in relation to its aim and effects of the measure under consideration, regard being had to the principles which normally prevail in democratic societies. A difference in treatment in the exercise of a right laid down in the Convention must not only pursue a legitimate aim: Article 14 is likewise violated when it is clearly established that there is no reasonable relationship of proportionality between the means employed and the aim sought to be realised.'

The test is very similar to 'pressing social needs' in the substantive articles. This reflects the test in the Equal Treatment Directive 76/207 [ETD] for indirect discrimination and an article 2(2) derogation, and the jurisprudence as to interpretation and application of these provisions in from the European and domestic courts can assist.

To this extent the domestic Sex and Race Discrimination legislation would provide better protection against those specified forms of direct discrimination because they create absolute prohibitions and there is no 'defence' of objective justification. Nevertheless the state has the burden of establishing justification for discrimination which must be strictly and objectively construed and the justification must be independent of and unrelated to any discrimination (*Bilka Kaufhaus* [1986] ECR 1607). General statements or beliefs will not meet the objective standard of justification (*Rinner-Kühn* [1989] IRLR 493 and *London Underground v Edwards (No 2)* [1997] IRLR 157.

Indirect discrimination, ie where a general measure disproportionately advantages or disadvantages one particular group over another, may be covered by Article 14 since the Court is concerned with the 'aims and effects' of measures. There is, however, no direct statement to that effect, although it has been argued and not rejected by the Court. (The European Court of Justice embraced indirect discrimination without specific provision in interpreting the Equal Treatment provisions and it is expressly part of domestic discrimination law.) One example is the *Abdulaziz* case where consideration was given to the effect of the disqualifying requirement of the parties having met in the immigration rules and the differential impact on arranged marriages in the Indian sub-continent. In a dissenting opinion in the Commission these requirements of the rule were identified 'by their practical side effect, in the short term and their very real purpose [as] indirectly racist'. The Court did not specifically address the indirect discrimination claim since they accepted the government's stated legitimate aim of excluding entry on the basis of bogus marriages as being the reason for the adoption of the primary purpose requirement and not race discrimination but by the same token did not reject indirect discrimination as outside the ambit of article 14. The European Court of Justice embraced indirect discrimination without specific provision in interpreting the Equal Treatment provisions (*Bilka-Kaufhaus*) and it is expressly part of domestic discrimination law.

It is a live issue in the context of article 14 but even if covered the burden of establishing indirect discrimination is undoubtedly a high one and in *Abdulaziz* the Court gave the arguments short shrift. The case does illustrate the difficulties in establishing an ulterior discriminatory purpose behind government policy which is readily able to identify 'a legitimate aim' for the measure apparently independent of the discriminatory impact and the European Court generally accords a wide margin of appreciation in this area. This margin is not available in the domestic courts to the same extent and experience in the context of EC discrimination provisions in that the Courts have applied the rigorous approach required by EC law in testing the government's contentions. The best example of which is the litigation relating to part-time workers and qualifications for employment protection which has been found to be indirectly discriminatory against women notably in *R v Secretary of State for Employment, ex p Equal Opportunities Commission* [1995] AC 1.

In deciding these matters including whether the margin of appreciation has been exceeded the European Court has developed some useful general indicators:

(i) certain forms of discrimination are identified as particularly serious, ie race (*East African Asians* (1981) 3 EHRR 76), sex (*Abdulaziz*), and illegitimacy (*Marckx v Belgium* (1979) 2 EHRR 330). The three categories so far identified are marked by a consensus in the member states to eliminate such forms of discrimination backed by various international instruments prohibiting such discrimination. In these cases a heavier burden is placed upon the state to justify the difference in treatment;

(ii) where the applicant can point to a European standard and a developing consensus outside of the contracting state this is an important indicator of lack of objective justification;

(iii) if an Applicant can point to a non-discriminatory alternative to secure the stated aim this is evidence although not necessarily decisive evidence of disproportion.

4.1 Summary

The requirements to establish an article 14 breach are:
Upon the applicant:

(i) less favourable treatment on any ground identified or analogous to those identified in the article;

(ii) *effecting one* of the substantive obligations;

If so established the burden shifts to the State to show:

(iii) a legitimate aim which has a rational basis and an evidential foundation independent of discrimination (ie is objectively justified);
(iv) the measure is proportionate to the identified aim.

5. Possible application of article 14 after incorporation

5.1 General

The domestic court applying the incorporated provision of the ECHR can look behind the neutrality of the language of new statutes and the rules and look at both the policy intention and the impact of legislation to assess compatibility with article 14 where one of the substantive obligations are engaged. The Commission in the *East African Asians* case gives the lead in this respect with the finding of fact that the Commonwealth Immigrants Act 1968 was racially motivated and it covered a particular racial group in its impact.

Practice in the administration of the immigration control is now also open to be measured by the non-discrimination requirements of the ECHR.

Evidence as to the discriminatory impact of legislation and/or practice that engages the substantive obligations may be powerful evidence that a violation has taken place and/or that the government cannot justify its actions.

A finding of discriminatory treatment may also serve to enhance the seriousness of any violation and in particular take conduct over the 'minimum level of severity' to establish inhuman or degrading treatment (*East African Asians* case) or infringement of moral and physical integrity protected by article 8 since humiliation of the individual is intrinsic to the experience of discrimination[12].

Engaging Article 14 also opens up the possibilities of reliance upon the other more comprehensive international human rights instruments particularly the ICCPR and CEDAW at least as a guide to interpretation; see article 31(3) of the Vienna Convention and *Golder v United Kingdom* (1975) 1 EHRR 524.

5.2 Specific

Experience suggests that it is in the area of personal and family relationships that the Human Rights Act as it applies to immigration law will be most extensively engaged and thus would also appear to be true of article 14. While article 3 is of great importance in the area of asylum the absolute character of this obligation makes additional article 14 violations unlikely to be utilised unless discrimination is fundamental to the content of the prohibited treatment.

12. In the *East African Asians* case the Commission decided that a person is subjected to degrading treatment 'if it lowers him in rank, position, reputation or character, whether in his own eyes or in the eyes of other people' and described racial discrimination as a 'special form of affront to human dignity'. It is, of course, to be remembered that the consequences of the discriminatory treatment by the UK in denying entry left the East African Asians effectively stateless and in a country where they were denied a livelihood and subject to destitution.
12 See Immigration Rules HC 395, rule 6.

It is outside of the scope of this paper to provide a comprehensive description of the areas of immigration law in which article 14 claims will arise, not least because of its pervasive presence, never mind, whether such claims can be successfully pursued. The following consideration is by way of example only.

5.3   Personal and family relationships

Recourse to public funds

The abolition of the primary purpose rule and practice in general has increasingly focused attention upon recourse to public funds (the categories of which have been progressively extended) as the central excluding requirement to the admission of dependants and, the exercise of the rights under articles 8 and 12 of the ECHR[13]. There has also been an increasingly restrictive interpretation of the public funds provisions within the Immigration Appeal Tribunal (although decisions go both ways) appeals have even been rejected where there will be no actual recourse to public funds but financial support comes from parties other than the sponsor[14]. The incorporation of article 8 together with article 14 may, therefore, provide new possibilities for restating the purposive approach to these rules[15] if not challenging their application where they result, which is too often the case, in the permanent separation of families.

Whether discrimination on the grounds of financial status is itself a characteristic within the ambit of article 14 is not conclusively decided. Discrimination on the grounds of property is expressly within article 14. In *Airey v Ireland* the Court did not reject out of hand a claim that an applicant had been discriminated on the grounds of her poverty but chose instead to restrict consideration to the substantive violation.

The issue is difficult since it stands the unpalatable proposition that enjoyment of fundamental rights depends upon personal wealth against a State's interest in protecting scarce public resources.

In addition statistics and sociological research is very likely to show that the 'no recourse to public funds requirement' has an indirectly discriminatory impact upon both women and ethnic minorities given the unequal access to the labour market and the disproportionate numbers of such groups in receipt of welfare benefits.

5.4   Relationships outside of marriage

The absence of equivalent provision for married and non-married couples outside of the October 1997 policy which requires a four relationship and lawful residence before permission to remain is possible, generates a large number of potential article 8 cases. It also raises the issues of status discrimination and discrimination on the grounds of sexual orientation (categorised as either sex – *Toonan v Austria* (1994) 1-3 EHRR 97 – or status discrimination).

---

13 See for example Hussain (113372).
14 See *Baktar Singh v Immigration Appeal Tribunal* [1986] Imm AR 352, and *Alexander v Immigration Appeal Tribunal* [1982] 1 WLR 1076.
15 This was stated, *inter alia*, in judicial review proceedings in which leave is granted to challenge a refusal by the Home Office to follow such a recommendation: *R v Secretary of State for the Home Department, ex p McCubbin-Peake.*

In the context of relationships where children are concerned the anomalous positions arises where separated and divorced parents are, often in a better position than co-habiting parents see *Berrahab v Netherlands* (1988) 11 EHRR 322 because of the promotion of marriage as the pre-eminent social relationship underpinning family and private life.

The consequences for homosexual and lesbian couples is a significant and often insurmountable legal hurdle to establishing a right to reside in the UK and the experience of the implementation of the October 1997 policy is that strictly applied it permanently frustrates the possibility of residence on the basis of the relationship for those who do not yet have a four year relationship. The Home Office has made it plain, despite numerous recommendations in individual cases by Adjudicators that it has no intention of granting periods of limited leave to committed couples in order to satisfy the four year requirement[16].

The jurisprudence from the European Court in respect of same sex relationships to date is both conservative and cautious. Whilst recognising sexual relationships as 'the most intimate aspect' of private life it has not concluded that homosexual couples enjoy family life[17]. Furthermore a violation of private life in the context of immigration control will only be established if there are exceptional circumstances and the couple cannot migrate anywhere else in the world: *X and V v United Kingdom* (1983) 5 EHRR 601. In the case of *Grant v South West Trains* [1998] ECR I-621 the ECJ declined to extend the protection of the ETD to homosexuals primarily on the basis that there was no common European consensus to afford equality of treatment to those in homosexual relationships with heterosexual relationships. Differential treatment on the basis of sexual orientation is, therefore, currently sanctioned by the jurisprudence of the European Courts and denied the status of unlawful discrimination however, this will always need to be reviewed in light of the particular facts of any case and emphasis must be placed upon evidence showing that relocation elsewhere is impossible (legal impediment) or unreasonable given the links with the UK or the difficulties arising in other countries particularly if those are related to discriminatory laws or other treatment. Current social attitudes and practice which is also highly relevant. In some jurisdictions the changes in social attitude is beginning to be reflected in decisions according equality of protection to homosexuals and lesbians[18].

In our domestic courts recent indicators of judicial attitudes suggest an increasingly progressive approach reflecting changed societal attitudes in the UK. The high point is the judgment of Ward LJ in *Fitzpatrick v Sterling Housing Association* [1998] Ch 304[19]. Judgment in the House of Lords is expected, but see also the observations of the majority in *Fitzpatrick* as well as Simon Brown in *R v Ministry of Defence, ex p Smith* [1996] QB[19]. The rights of gay and lesbian couples to adopt was recognised *Re W (a minor) (adoption: homosexual adopter)* [1997] Fam 58.

16 See *Dugeon* and *Norris* (supra).
17 See, however, X,Y Z v UK in which the European Court did hold that there was family life between a child, her natural mother and a transsexual father.
18 See *Baehr v Lewin* 852 P 2d 44 (Supreme Court of Haiwai 1993) discussed in Griffin 'Another Case Another Clause' [1997] Public Law 315; *Vriend v Alberta* (1998) 4 BHRC 140; *Romer v Evans* (1996) 1 BHRC 178; *National Coalition for Gay and Lesbian Equality v Minister of Home Affairs* (12 February 1999, unreported) South African High Court.
19 See also the observations of the majority in *Fitzpatrick* in the Court of Appeal (judgment in the House of Lords is awaited) and Simon Brown in *R v Ministry of Defence, ex p Smith* [1996] QB 517. The rights of gay and lesbian couples to adopt was recognised in *Re W (a minor) (adoption: homosexual adopter)* [1997] Fam 58.

5.5 Illegitimacy and nationality

The British Nationality Act 1981, section 50(9), expressly denies British nationality to children born outside marriage in certain cases since such children cannot rely upon their father to establish acquisition by birth or descent. The judgment of the European Court in *Marckx v Belgium* offers hope of establishing this provision to be incompatible with the ECHR obligations (if a claim could be brought within the ambit of a substantive obligation; obviously article 8, but also possibly article 3 (degrading treatment))[20].

5.6 Asylum

Since an asylum claim will invariably include a claim to article 3 protection the processing of an asylum claim may give scope to argue for change or if not challenge practice where women asylum seekers are subjected to less favourable circumstances in which to effectively pursue their claims such as absence of female interviewers, interpreters, or presenting officers particularly in cases involving rape and other sexual violence.

Greater force may now be brought to bear in respect of anecdotal evidence of discriminatory practice in respect of detention of particular nationalities/racial groups of asylum seekers. The recent experience of the discriminate detention of the male heads of Roma families as a deliberate Home Office policy purporting to act as a deterrent to absconding provides a good illustration of how article 14 could be effectively used in the context of an infringement of the substantive right to family life engaged in these cases.

6. Conclusion

The purpose of this paper as set out above whilst setting out the ambit of article 14 is about possibilities with a limited assessment of the prospect of success. Article 14 is subsidiary and will remain so to the substantive obligations, however, to properly inform practice it should be seen as integral to the exercise of the fundamental rights of the Convention and, therefore, to the effective representation of those effected by and subjected to immigration control in all its many aspects. It at least gives a legal language and currency to articulating the injustice that underpins much of immigration law and practice. It should not, however be accepted as a substitute and needs to be complemented by the inclusion of the decisions and actions of public servants within the ambit of the domestic Sex and Race Discrimination Acts.

---

20 For a detailed consideration of the impact on nationality law, see chapter 8. Also see chapter 8 for a reference to illegitimacy under the European Convention on Nationality 1997.

CHAPTER 7

Free movement of persons under rights conferred by European Union law

Nuala Mole, Director, The AIRE Centre, Advice on Individual Rights in Europe[†]

As has already been noted in previous chapters, the Human Rights Act 1998, intended to '*give further effect* to the rights and freedoms guaranteed under the European Convention on Human Rights 1998 is of wide constitutional and juridical significance and applicability. It should be remembered, however, that in deference to Parliamentary sovereignty, the Act does not incorporate in the strictest sense the Convention or the rights it contains. Rather, in an 'ingenious' attempt to avoid this conflict and yet make human rights claims justiciable before the courts, it allows domestic courts to examine the compatibility of domestic law with Convention standards and affords a right to individuals to pursue and rely upon Convention rights in those same courts. Just how far the higher courts will be willing to make declarations of incompatibility and how the courts will interpret and receive Convention principles remains to be seen.

In relation to the Community law rights, the subject of this paper, the Act will bring together in domestic courts two legal orders: one pro-active, facilitating the removal of all obstacles to achieving European Union, the other a safety net preventing states from falling below a lowest common denominator of standards.

1. Rights of entry and residence under EU law

As originally conceived, the provisions relating to the free movement of persons in the Community were designed to promote the achievement of purely economic goals and were framed in the context of the promotion of a common market. The rights thus associated with this aim were necessarily defined by reference to their primarily economic function. Since then, as the Community aims have been re-appraised, the Commission and Court of the European Communities has adopted a broader approach in defining the beneficiaries of these rights, reflecting these changing political realities and the human and socio-economic context.

The rights to freedom of movement under European Union (EU) law fall into a series of broad categories. As regards nationals of European Economic Area (EEA) countries, the economically active enjoy a right of free movement:

[†]   The author would like to thank Navtej S Ahluwalia, AIRE Assistant Director, in the preparation of this chapter.

workers[1], the self-employed and the providers and receivers of services[2]. In addition, the economically inactive but with sufficient funds so as to avoid becoming a burden on the social assistance of the state are also entitled to move freely within the Member States of the Community: students[3], retired pensioners[4] and those who exercise a general right of residence[5].

Recognising this 'human' element, those *connected* with EEA nationals also enjoy a right, flowing directly from the exercise of the EEA national's community activity, to install themselves, *irrespective of their nationality*, with the EEA national. They can be said to enjoy derivative rights. The qualifying family members of such persons who have a right to enter and reside with the EEA national are the spouse and descendants who are under the age of 21 or who are dependants and dependant relatives in the ascending line[6].

Member States shall *facilitate* (*favour* in some provisions) other members of the household[7]. Under these provisions, only the spouse of an EEA national has the right to accompany the EEA national and at present the term spouse does not extend to fiancées, common law spouses or same sex partners. However, under the rule in *Reed*[8], *where* national law permits 'family' reunion for the common law spouses or same sex partners of its own nationals, that facility must also be accorded to the equivalent partners of EEA nationals. It may therefore only be a matter of time before the ECJ extends the concept of spouse to include such relationships. The European Convention organs have chosen to regard same sex relationships under the rubric of *private rather* than *family life* and have not so far protected them in immigration cases[9].

---

1 Regulation 1612/68 of 15 October 1968 on the Free movement of workers in the Community (OJ 1612 L257/14).
2 Directive 73/148 of 21 May 1973 on the abolition of Restrictions on Movement and Residence within the Community for Nationals of Member States with regard to Establishment and Services (OJ 1973 L172/14).
3 Directive 93/96 of 29 October 1993 on the right of Residence for Students(OJ 1993 L317/59).
4 Directive 90/365 of 28 June 1990 on the Rights of Residence for Employees and Self-employed Persons who have Ceased their Occupational Activity ((OJ 1990 L180/30).
5 Directive 90/364 of 28 June 1990 on the Right of Residence (OJ 1990 L180/26).
6 See article 10(1) of Regulation 1612/68 which reads:

> The following shall have the right, irrespective of their nationality to install themselves with a worker who is a national of one Member State and who is employed in the territory of another member State:
> (a) his souse and their descendants who are under the age of 21 years or are dependants;
> (b) dependant relatives in the ascending line of the worker and his spouse.

Equally, article 1(1) of Directive 73/148 reads:

> Member States shall, acting as provided in this Directive, abolish restrictions on the movement and residence of:...
> (c) the spouse and children under twenty-one years of age of such nationals, irrespective of their nationality
> (d) the relatives in the ascending and descending lines of such nationals and of the spouse of such nationals, which relatives are dependant on them, irrespective of their nationality.

See further common articles 1(2) of Directives 90/364 and 90/365. Note however, that only the spouse and dependant children are entitled to the right of residence along with the EEA student under Directive 93/96.
7 See article 10(2) of Directive 1612/68 and article 1(2) of Directive 73/148.
8 [1986] ECR 1283.
9 See *B v United Kingdom* 64 DR 278; Application 12513/97 *X and Y v United Kingdom* unreported.

In addition, following the typically creative decisions of the Court of Justice in *Rush Portuguesa*[10], and *Vander Elst*[11], workers posted by a Community company established in one Member State to the territory of another whether or not EEA nationals are entitled to enter and reside in Community states. Their position is likely to be clarified by the adoption of the Posted Workers Directive 1998, due to enter into force in September 1999.

As early as the 1960s, the Community was seriously contemplating agreements with its neighbouring states with a view to enlargement of the Community. The Turkish Association Agreement of 1963[12], its additional protocol[13] and the decisions of the Association Council[14] were originally conceived to create a framework by which Turkey's accession to the Community could be considered. Changes on the political scene have prevented accession. Turkish citizens who are entitled to work in the Community under the national law of individual Member States, are granted the right to remain in the State to continue employment. The Agreement does not, however, grant them the right to enter any Member State.[15]

In the 1970s the Community concluded a less ambitious set of agreements with the Maghreb states: Algeria[16], Morocco[17] and Tunisia[18]. These were aimed at promoting economic and trade co-operation between the states and the Community in order that those states conform with their international obligations. Nationals of such states were only guaranteed therefore the rights of equal treatment and freedom from discrimination as to working conditions and remuneration as compared with host national workers[19].

Following the fall of the Berlin wall in 1989, the Community moved quickly to strengthen relations with Central and Eastern Europe announcing a programme to support the process of political and economic reform with the states of this region. Part of this programme included Association agreements with, Hungary[20] and Poland[1]

---

10 *Rush Portuguesa v Office National d'Immigration* [1990] ECR-I 1417.
11 *Vander Elst v Office des Migrations Internationales* [1994] ECR I-3803.
12 Agreement Establishing an Association between the EEC and Turkey (OJ 1977 L361/29).
13 Additional Protocol of 1970 (OJ 1977 L361/69).
14 Council of Association Decisions 2/76 of 20 December 1976 and Decisions 1/80 and 3/80 of 19 September 1980.
15 See articles 6 and 7 of Council Decision 1/80:

> 'As the law stands now, however, Turkish nationals are not entitled to move freely within the community but enjoy certain rights in the host Member States whose territory thy have lawfully entered and where they have been in legal employment for a specified period.'

> (*Tetik v Land Berlin* [1997] ECR I-329 and *Günaydin v Friestaat Bayern* C-36/96 [1998] 1 CMLR 871.

16 Co-operation Agreement between the European Economic Community and the Republic of Algeria, of 26 April 1976 (OJ 1978 L265/2).
17 Co-operation Agreement between the European Economic Community and the Kingdom of Morocco, of 27 April 1976 (OJ L264/2).
18 Co-operation Agreement between the European Economic Community and the Republic of Tunisia of 25 April 1976 (OJ L263/2).
19 For example, article 40 Of Moroccon Co-operation Agreement reads:

> 'The treatment accorded by each Member State to workers of Moroccan nationality employed in its territory shall be free from any discrimination based on nationality, as regards working conditions or remuneration, in relation to its own nationals.'

20 Europe Agreement establishing an Association between the European Community and their Member States on the one part and Hungary on the other part, 1991 (OJ 1993 L347/1).
1 Europe Agreement establishing an Association between the European Community and their Member States on the one part and Poland on the other part, 1991 (OJ 1993 L348/1).

in 1991, the Czech[2] and Slovak[3] Republics following their split, Bulgaria[4] and Romania[5] in 1993 and the Baltic States of Estonia, Latvia and Lithuania[6] following independence in 1995. A further agreement was concluded with Slovenia in 1996[7]. Under these agreements, the Member States of the Community provide a right of establishment for companies by means of setting up or managing subsidiaries, branches or agencies, and the right to send 'key personnel' (a term defined in the agreements) to carry out these activities. In addition, the agreements afford a right of individuals to pursue economic activities as self-employed persons to set up and manage undertakings which they effectively control.

It is unlikely that the incorporation of the Convention into domestic law will have any effect on claims to family reunion for the categories of person who enter the United Kingdom as posted workers or under any of the Europe Agreements. Community law does not provide for family reunion for such persons[8] and the question which the Strasbourg organs consider is whether it is reasonable to conduct family life elsewhere. As has been noted elsewhere, the Commission and Court do not consider that article 8 of the Convention permits couples to choose their country of residence. In *Choudhry v United Kingdom*[9], the European Commission found that there was no violation of the Convention when a couple, one of whom was seriously disabled and the other suffered from acute psychiatric disturbance, was obliged to uproot themselves from the UK and move to another Member State to escape deportation to Pakistan. The Commission found the case inadmissible, in that there was no obstacle to them conducting their family in the other Member State and thus no interference:

> 'The Commission does not consider that the availability of the "community law route" embarked upon by the applicants to obtain residence rights in the United Kingdom is sufficient to render the decision of the United Kingdom to issue a deportation order against the second applicant a disproportionate measure for the purposes of Article 8 of the Convention.'

Since they found the case inadmissible because there was no interference they did not have to consider the question of proportionality.

The case of *Demirel*[10] concerned the rights to family reunion of Turkish nationals established in a Member State under the Turkish Agreement. It concerned in particular Article 7 of the Agreement which stated that Contracting Parties must refrain from any measures liable to jeopardise the attainment of the objectives of the agreement.

2 Europe Agreement establishing an Association between the European Community and their Member States on the one part and the Czech Republic on the other part, 1993 (OJ 1994 L360/1).
3 Europe Agreement establishing an Association between the European Community and their Member States on the one part and the Slovak Republic on the other part, 1993 (OJ 1994 L359/1).
4 Europe Agreement establishing an Association between the European Community and their Member States on the one part and Bulgaria on the other part, 1993 (OJ 1994 L358/1).
5 Europe Agreement establishing an Association between the European Community and their Member States on the one part and Romania on the other part, 1993 (OJ 1994 L357/1).
6 See *A Guide to the Right of Establishment,* Elspeth Guild, Bailey Shaw & Gillet, 1996.
7 Europe Agreement establishing an Association between the European Community and their Member States on the one part and Slovenia on the other part, 1996 (COM (95) 41).
8 See for example, *Demirel v Stadt Schwäbisch Gmünd* [1989] 1 CMLR 421 and *Selma Kadiman v Friestaat Bayern* [1997] ECR I-2133.
9 Application 27949/95 (13 May 1996, unreported).
10 Above.

The Court held that the question of family reunion was outside the scope of community law as far as Turkish nationals were concerned and they did not therefore need to examine the compatibility of German national law with article 8 of the Convention.

Since *Gul v Switzerland*[11] established that even those with long temporary residence (ten years) in a state could not demand family reunion unless they could prove the impossibility of conducting family life in their own country, it is unlikely that the Convention will assist those who are in the U.K. temporarily exercising EU based rights.

2. Types of EU law

Regulations are binding on all Member States and are directly applicable by them. They are the primary legislation of the EU whilst the treaties are the constitution norms. They form part of the domestic law of each state without the need for any further action on the part of the state. Article 10(2) which provides for facilitating the admission of other household members is enshrined in Regulation 1612/68, and is thus directly enforceable in the courts of the UK and the courts must protect that right. Convention jurisprudence on which family members are considered as forming a part of the family entity which is entitled to respect, may be pertinent to the application of this paragraph.

Member States are under a duty not to '*obstruct the direct applicability of regulations*'[12]. Any instrument, including for example, the EEA Order 1994, which appears to distort any provision of a Regulation is therefore arguably illegal.

Thus under paragraph 2(2) of the EEA Order 1994 'a spouse does not include a party to a marriage of convenience'. Such a definition arguably breaches Community law in so far as Community law provides for no such exclusion. In the context of an arguable Convention law right relating to family reunion for an EEA national, there may be situations where the decision taken is not *in accordance with the law* for the purpose of article 8 of the Convention.

Directives are binding as to the end to be achieved but leave the state some choice as to the form and method which it upon.

The ECJ has recognised a limited '*margin of discretion*' in EU law[13], but it is narrowly construed. It is a fundamental tenet of EU law that it should be applied uniformly across the Union. The *margin of appreciation* permitted to Member States of the Council of Europe under the Convention is wide and only exclusions which clearly breach the minimum Convention standards will be treated a violations.

3. The inter-relationship between the two legal orders

The two European courts – the European Court of Human Rights and the European Court of Justice – are the authorities on the interrelationship between the two legal

---

11 RJD 1996-I No 3; (1996) 22 EHRR 93.
12 *Variola v Amministrazione delle Finanze* [1973] ECR 981.
13 Cf *Van Duyn v Home Office* [1974] ECR 1337. The margin is reflected in article 3 of Directive 64/221 which permits exclusions on public policy or public security grounds. For the margin of error in Strasbourg jurisprudence, see p 16.

orders. Each approaches the matter from its own jurisdictional viewpoint. That is each tribunal looks at the significance of the other legal order for the interpretation of its own treaty.

4. The case law of the ECHR on EU law

The case of *M v Germany*[14] remains the leading authority in Convention jurisprudence on state responsibility under the Convention for acts of the Community institutions. However it never progressed beyond admissibility and so its jurisprudential value remains low.

In *M* the Commission held that an application could not be brought against a state relating to its execution of a judgment of the European Court of Justice. Moreover the state was not required under article 6 of the Convention, guaranteeing the right to a fair trial, to satisfy itself that the provisions of that article had been observed by the Community institutions in any proceedings which then had to be executed by the domestic courts. It was not therefore open to the applicants to bring a complaint to Strasbourg alleging that it was a breach of the Convention for a state to carry out the action required of it under EU law to enforce a fine imposed by the EC Commission. The adopted approach is consistent with Convention jurisprudence. In *Drozd and Janousek v France and Spain*[15] the Court considered that State parties to the Convention are not obliged, in executing judgements of other states, to determine whether Convention standards have been met by courts in states not party to the Convention. The Commission in *M* found that:

> '... a transfer of powers does not necessarily exclude a State's responsibility under the Convention with regard to the exercise of the transferred powers. Otherwise the guarantees of the Convention could wantonly be limited or excluded and thus be deprived of their peremptory character.'

They went on to explain that:

> '... the transfer of powers to an international organisation is not incompatible with the Convention provided that within the organisation fundamental rights will receive [sic] equivalent protection.'

A number of cases have come before the Commission concerning the Community legal order which were concerned with obligations under article 3, Protocol No 1, (the obligation upon states to hold free elections) concerning elections to the European Parliament. The Commission had either side stepped the issue or considered the European Parliament was not a legislature for the purposes of article 3 of Protocol 1[16].

The recent judgment of the Court in *Matthews v United Kingdom*, concerned the exclusion of Gibraltarians from participation in the European Parliament elections.

---

1   64 DR 138.
15 (1992) 14 EHRR 745.
16 See, for example, *Heinz v Contracting States also Parties to the European Patent Convention* 76-A DR 125.

In its argument before the Commission and Court the British Government submitted that the EU Act on Direct Elections fell within the Community legal order and were therefore not subject to review by the Convention organs. The majority of the Commission did not find it necessary to address this argument, but one member of the Commission in a separate dissenting opinion underlined that:

'Contracting States remain responsible for infringement of human rights if they do not provide for adequate protection of those rights by the institutions to which powers are transferred.'

It would seem politically inconceivable that the Court of Human Rights would ever hold that the European Union institutions did not provide the adequate protection to which the Commission Member referred.

However, the Court in *Matthews* found that the EU Act on Direct Elections and its Annexes of 1976 was an international treaty, freely entered into by the United Kingdom and was not an act of the Community institutions. In 1976 the European Parliament did not constitute a legislature within the meaning of article 3 of Protocol No 1. The Maastricht Treaty, which extended the powers of the European Parliament, was a similar Treaty, also freely entered into, but after the extension of Protocol No 1 to Gibraltar on 25 February 1988. Maastricht invested the European Parliament with powers which now made it a legislature within the meaning of Protocol No 1. The failure of the United Kingdom to secure access to that institution for the citizens of Gibraltar constituted a violation of the Convention.

Analogous arguments may present themselves in relation to the compatibility of the United Kingdom's obligations under the Convention where it claims to be acting in compliance with the obligations it freely entered into with its other EU partners in, for example, the Dublin Convention, or under the Treaty of Amsterdam. The European Court is currently considering a complaint relating to the compatibility with the Convention of action being taken under the Dublin Convention[17].

Once the Human Rights Act is in force, domestic courts will be required under sections 2 and 3 and 6 and 7 to determine many of these issues.

The Convention organs otherwise seem to have decided that they will not pierce the 'community veil' in order to determine whether matters which fall squarely (and even exclusively) within the ambit of EU law also comply with Convention standards.

In immigration matters this is of little significance. EU law does not normally oblige states to exclude those whom Convention law would oblige them to admit. The reverse is the more frequently found scenario. This situation may change when the Third Pillar instruments move, after the entry into force of the Amsterdam Treaty, into the First Pillar. The provisions of article 30 of the Vienna Convention on the Law of Treaties will then apply. In international law, under that Article, the provisions of the earlier treaty (ie the European Convention) will normally apply only to the extent that its provisions are compatible with those of a later treaty. However the important role accorded to the Convention under the EU treaties and the special nature of fundamental human rights treaties would make it inconceivable that a provision of Community law could be interpreted in a way which was in clear conflict with Strasbourg case law. As a matter of domestic law the courts will be obliged to strive to find an interpretation of EU law which is consistent with the ECHR as it will be reflected in English law by the Human Rights Act 1998.

17 Application No 43844/98 *TI v United Kingdom* – pre-admissibility.

5. Discrimination in favour of EEA nationals as against other aliens – article 14 ECHR

In *Moustaquim v Belgium*[18] the question arose as to whether the expulsion of a long term resident, second generation immigrant was a violation of article 8 of the Convention, when, it was argued, he would not have been expelled for the same conduct had he been an EU citizen. The Court held that the European Community constituted a *separate* and *special legal order* and that there was an *objective and reasonable justification* for the preferential treatment given to EEA national. As a result there was no breach of Article 14 in connection with Article 8.

6. Right to a remedy

The European Commission and Court have always held that judicial review constitutes an effective remedy for a decision to exclude for the purposes of article 13[19]. These decisions have always related to cases concerning potential violations of article 3 and the Court has been persuaded that the *'most anxious scrutiny'* test applied in domestic law do provide the effective degree of control demanded by the Convention. In the joined cases of *Shingara and Radiom*[20] the ECJ also found that judicial review was an effective remedy, but posed some questions as to the absence of a review on the merits. It is not, however, established in Strasbourg jurisprudence that judicial review is an effective remedy in family life cases and where the application of EU law is denied, thereby excluding individuals from the appeal process, issues may arise under the Convention.

As has already been noted, the Human Rights Act will not actually *incorporate* the ECHR into domestic law. Rather, it is seen as a piece of interpretative legislation.

It is designed instead to enable the domestic courts to apply directly those provisions of the Convention set out in the Act, that is those parts of the Convention to which the United Kingdom is a party. But, unlike most of the old member states of the Council of Europe and all of the new ones, the United Kingdom is not a party to all the Protocols to the Convention, which provide additional substantive rights to those protected under articles 1–18. In particular, it is not a party to Protocol No 4. Article 3 of Protocol 4 states:

> No-one shall be expelled, by means either of an individual or of a collective measure, from the territory of the state of which he is a national.
> No-one shall be deprived of the right to enter the territory of the state of which he is a national.

Since the judgement of the ECJ in *Surinder Singh*[1] many British citizens have taken advantage of their free movement rights to benefit their family members who would

---

18 (1991) 13 EHRR 802. See also chapter 6 on discrimination generally.
19 See, for example, *Soering v United Kingdom* (1989) 11 EHRR 439; *Vivarajah v United Kingdom* (1991) 14 EHRR 248.
20 *R v Secretary of State for the Home Department, ex p Shingara and Radiom* [1997] ECR I-3341.
1   *R v Immigration Appeal Tribunal and Surinder Singh, ex p Secretary of State for the Home Department* [1992] ECR I-4265.

not be entitled to live with them under domestic law. They move to another EU country in the exercise of their treaty rights and their return to the Member State then comes under the more generous provisions for family reunion of EU law. The case of *Surinder Singh* concerned reverse discrimination. It determined that a British citizen returning to the UK after exercising treaty rights in another Member State must be accorded treatment at least equal to that which other EU nationals enjoy. This included the full package of EU rights relating to family reunion. Thus, under the rule in *Diatta v Land Berlin*[2] a separated spouse can still benefit from EU family reunion rules until the marriage has dissolved or the partner has left the UK. The ECJ in *Singh* expressed the erroneous belief that the spouses of British citizens would have no difficulty establishing themselves in the United Kingdom if they were parties to a subsisting genuine marriage.[3] The ECJ also appeared to be under the erroneous impression that the Protocol No 4 to the Convention had been accepted by the United Kingdom. Although a signatory to the Protocol it has not ratified the same. It cannot therefore be invoked as a matter of Convention law nor as a matter of Community law against the United Kingdom[4].

The decision of the ECJ in *Singh* made it clear that EU law prohibits reverse discrimination against its own nationals returning who exercise treaty rights. The failure to ratify Protocol No 4 means that incorporation will not confer any additional rights on those who can use their British Citizenship in the context of exercising EU rights.

Union citizenship is recognised in article 8A of the Maastricht Treaty. EU citizens are those who have the citizenship of a Member State. The UK stated that, as far as British citizenship is concerned, this only refers to British citizens and British Dependant Territories citizens with a Gibraltar connection. The other classes are excluded from the benefits of citizenship of the Union. The validity of the exclusion of British Overseas citizens from inclusion as European citizens has been referred to the ECJ and the ruling is awaited.[5]

Where the right to enter or remain is regulated by EU rather than domestic law the impact of the Human Rights Act will be less significant than in other areas of immigration law. This is because it has always been possible to apply appropriate ECHR standards to matters which are regulated by EU law.

Article F of the Treaty of Maastricht stated that the Union shall respect fundamental rights as guaranteed by the ECHR as general principles of law. The Treaty of Amsterdam has gone a little further and provided for a higher emphasis on the observance of human rights within EU law. This emphasis has been introduced largely with a view to vetting the accession or continued membership of the Union of states with unsatisfactory human rights records.

The Court of Human Rights made a cursory glance at the extent of EU free movement provisions in *Piermont v France*[6]. An MEP, who was an outspoken critic of French policy and practice in relation to nuclear testing in the Pacific, was

2   [1986] ECR 567.
3   The 'primary purpose' rule was in full force at the time.
4   The case of *Nold, Kohlen-unf Baustoffgrofshundlung v EC Commission* ([1974] ECR 491) did, however suggest that the *common legal heritage of the Member States* included those treaties in which they had collaborated, as well as those which they had ratified. This would reflect the normal interpretation of Article 18 of the Vienna Convention on the law of treaties which obliges a state to act in good faith so as to refrain from acts calculated to frustrate the object of a treaty (including a protocol) which it has signed subject to ratification.
5   *Ex p Manjit Kaur* (11 December 1998, unreported). See p 127.
6   (1995) 20 EHRR 301.

prevented from speaking on these subjects in French Polynesia and New Caledonia. The free movement provisions of the EU did not apply to French Overseas Territories and she could not therefore claim to have been lawfully on the territory of either French Polynesia or New Caledonia once measures excluding her from those territories had been served on her. The applicant based her argument in part on her status as a European citizen, and claimed that she could not therefore be treated as an alien under article 16 of the Convention[7]. The Court found that as *'the Community treaties did not at the time recognise any such citizenship'*, it could not accept the argument based on Union Citizenship. It did however find that her possession of a nationality of a Member State of the European Union and her status as a member of the European Parliament meant that article 16 could not be invoked against her.

7.   Procedural delays

In *Hornsby v Greece*[8] the Court held that the delay by the Greek authorities in executing a judgment delivered in accordance with a ruling of the ECJ constituted a breach of article 6. However as the Court has frequently held that article 6 does not apply to immigration measures, which are administrative matters and not determinative of 'civil rights', this will be of little advantage[9]. Whilst not disturbing this principle the Strasbourg authorities are increasingly emphasising the procedural elements which are inherent in other substantive rights including those under articles 2, 3 and 8[10]. The inordinate delays in processing EEA family permits may not only engage the responsibilities of the Home Office under article 5 of Directive 64/221 but also under article 8 of the Convention

The case of *Konstantinidis v Stadt Altensteigstandesamt*[11] concerned a Greek Citizen resident in the Federal Republic of Germany who found himself in difficulties because of the system of transliteration of Greek names used under the ISO Convention. This effectively rendered Mr Konstantinidis' name unrecognisable to his potential and actual clientele. The view of Advocate General Jacobs was detailed and instructive. He noted that the decision in *ERT* did not establish clearly whether the applicant could invoke the protection of his fundamental rights as a matter of Community law. Advocate-General Jacobs was however of the view that a:

> 'Community national who goes to another Member State as a worker or self employed
> person under Article 48, 52, or 59 EEC is entitled not just to pursue his trade or profession
> and to enjoy the same living and working conditions as nationals of the host states: he
> is in addition entitled to assume that wherever he goes to earn his living in the European
> Community, he will be treated in accordance with a common code of fundamental values,
> in particular those laid down in the ECHR. In other words, he is entitled to say civic
> europeus sum and to invoke that status in order to oppose any violation of his fundamental
> rights.'

---

7   Article 16 reads 'Nothing in Articles 10, 11 and 14 shall be regarded as preventing the High
     Contracting Parties from imposing restrictions on the political activity of aliens.'
8   (1997) 24 EHRR 250.
9   See, for example, *Agee v United Kingdom* (1976) 7 DR 164; *Bozano v France* (1984) 39 DR
     119; and Application 26373/95 *Aksar v United Kingdom* (16 October 1995, unreported).
10   See, for example, *Akdivar v Turkey* (1996) 1 BHRC 137; *Assenov v Bulgaria*, Judgment 28
     October 1998; and *Bronda v Italy*, Judgment, 8 June 1998.
11   [1993] ECR I-1191.

The Advocate General saw his proposition through to its logical consequence and noted that:

'... it follows *ex hypothesi* that a Member State may in certain circumstances be obliged to treat producers or workers from other Member States more favourably than it treats its own producers and workers'.

Unfortunately the Court did not find itself called upon to endorse the Advocate General's opinion, and has not been called upon since to do so. However it did not refute it and as a thesis it has some support.

His opinion in *Konstandtinidis* was of some importance in the UK prior to incorporation since it was a means of importing the Convention by the back door. After the Act comes into force the Convention will have entered EU law in the English Courts through the front door and speculative concepts such as were found in the case will hopefully no longer be needed.

In conclusion, it would appear, given that the provisions of free movement of workers are already generous, it is unlikely to be significantly changed after the entry into force of the Human Rights Act 1998. Rather, relevant provisions of the Convention will best serve to assist immigration practitioners in reinforcing Community law rights arguments before national authorities. It seems likely that the demarcation between the two legal orders will remain.

CHAPTER 8

The Human Rights Act[1] and British Nationality

Laurie Fransman

1. Introduction

The ECHR itself[2], signed in 1950, contains no nationality-based rights or freedoms but 13 years later the Fourth Protocol[3] protected the immigration rights that nationals enjoy under international law in respect of their own countries. The UK did not ratify the Protocol as immigration controls had just been introduced in respect of certain of its own nationals[4] and this control was extended and entrenched in the years that followed[5]. Although Protocol 4 is not ratified and therefore not incorporated into domestic law by the HRA, the British nationals who would have benefited are not necessarily without a human rights remedy after commencement. Protocol 4 might be imported via Community law and, further, as there can be so much overlap between Convention rights, those that are available through incorporation could in at least some cases protect individuals with nationality-related problems, including those normally associated with Protocol 4. The prevailing attitudes of the international community and, particularly, the Council of Europe on nationality issues may give guidance as to when a nationality-related problem may engage with the incorporated rights.

2. A right to British nationality?

2.1 The position in international law and under the Convention

In international law everyone has the right to a nationality[6] but this naturally does not mean any person can demand British nationality. Rather, it is a statement of

---

1 Referred to throughout as the HRA, and references to the Convention are to the Convention and Protocols unless the contrary is indicated.
2 ETS 5.
3 ETS 46. Opened for signature (and signed by the UK) on 16 September 1963 at Strasbourg. In force on 2 May 1968 (but not as yet ratified by or, therefore, in force in respect of, the UK). For an Explanatory Report drafted in February 1963 by the Committee of Experts that drafted Protocol 4, see Chapter III of Council of Europe document H(71)11, pp 25-46.
4 The Commonwealth Immigrants Act 1962, abrogating the common law immigration rights of British subjects for the first time.
5 Commonwealth Immigrants Act 1968; Immigration Act 1971, ss 1-3.
6 Eg the Universal Declaration of Human Rights 1948, art 15; the ICCPR (International Covenant on Civil and Political Rights) 1966, art 24(3); the American Convention on Human Rights

principle that might be prayed in aid of specific arguments. The right to a nationality is clarified by subsidiary instruments such as the Convention on the Reduction of Statelessness 1961[7] and the Convention on the Nationality of Married Women 1957[8] and may be relied upon, for example, to argue that there is a responsibility within the international community for each state to confer nationality on its peoples (such as in cases of state succession[9] or the independence of colonies[10]). Also, where an individual is establishing ever stronger connections with a state there might come a point at which the right to a nationality is offended if that status continues to be withheld (particularly if the individual does not have the nationality of any other country).

The right to a nationality is not a right incorporated by the HRA or protected at all by the ECHR or any of its Protocols. Nevertheless, when giving effect to the rights and freedoms that are protected, it cannot be overlooked that 'everyone has the right to a nationality' under article 4a[11] of the Council of Europe's 1997 European Convention on Nationality[12] and 'Every child has the right to acquire a nationality' under article 24(3) of the ICCPR[13], and that nothing in the ECHR limits the rights and freedoms of any other treaty to which the state is a party[14].

Consequently, apart from the circumstances in which there actually is a right to British nationality under domestic law, there may be situations in which the right, as a principle of international law generally and Council of Europe treaty law particularly, may be relevant to determining whether a provision of legislation or an act of a public authority is compatible with the incorporated rights.

2.2 Meaning of British nationality

Arguably the demands of international human rights law are such that there must in at least some circumstances be an opportunity for people to have access to British nationality, but the meaning of the term is not clear. In current British nationality law there are British citizens, British Dependent Territories citizens (BDTCs), British Overseas citizens (BOCs), British subjects, British Nationals (Overseas) (BN(O)s) and British Protected Persons (BPPs), but some may be 'British nationals' for one purpose and not for another.

For the purposes of general international law the term should include all the aforesaid save for BPPs, as strictly speaking they were and remain protected aliens,

---

1969, art 20; the Convention on the Rights of the Child 1989, art 7; the European Convention on Nationality 1997 (ETS 166), art 4a. See also *Proposed Amendments to the Naturalization Provisions of the Constitution of Costa Rica*, Advisory Opinion OC-4/84, 19 January 1984, Series A No 4, para 32.

7 Which clarifies that, generally, nationality must be granted to persons born in a state, and to the children of one of their nationals, if they would otherwise be stateless.

8 Which provides that women shall not automatically acquire or lose nationality as the result of marriage or divorce or the husband's change of nationality during marriage.

9 The right to the nationality of a succeeding state (see, eg, the European Convention on Nationality 1997, Ch VI).

10 The right to the nationality of the newly independent state.

11 In respect of which no reservation is possible – see art 29(1).

12 Adopted 6 November 1997 in Strasbourg. The UK has not yet signed but is believed to intend to sign and ratify in due course.

13 And the UK has ratified the ICCPR (on 20 May 1976). See also note 6.

14 ECHR, art 53. This opens the door to, eg, ICCPR, art 24(3).

not British. For the purposes of Community law the UK has unilaterally declared its nationals to be British citizens, BDTCs (but only those deriving the status from Gibraltar) and British subjects (but only those with the right of abode in the UK), and no-one else[15]. In domestic law there may now be an argument that all, even BPPs, are included because although traditionally BPPs were not[16], British nationality law excludes them from the definition of aliens[17] and, increasingly, modern legislation is positively including BPPs as nationals[18].

These disparities cast serious doubt on what definition the term might have for the purposes of the Convention and Protocols. The UK has not had to address the issue this far as it does not arise in respect of the Convention itself or the ratified Protocols, but will need to do so if it is ever to accede to Protocol 4. The Commission accepted in *East African Asians v United Kingdom*[19] that BPPs were not UK nationals, but by the same token accepted that citizens of the UK and Colonies[20] certainly were, and those persons became British citizens, BDTCs and BOCs when the category was redefined[1]. It would seem unlikely, therefore, that the term would exclude any BDTCs or BOCs. On the other hand, the Strasbourg Court has not yet had to consider the meaning of 'national' in the context of Protocol 4 at all and when required to do so might possibly decline to follow any existing definition and give the term an autonomous meaning[2].

Further consideration is given below to the minimum adjustments the UK would have to make in order to ratify and incorporate Protocol 4. For the moment, though, the point is whether there is a sufficient opportunity for people to have access to the categories of nationality provided for in domestic law.

2.3 Access to British citizenship

There does not seem to be a persistent practical problem regarding access to British citizenship, the main British nationality. It is or has been widely available under the 1981 and 1983 Acts[3] and the Hong Kong Acts of 1990, 1996 and 1997[4]. The permanent rules governing acquisition of British citizenship cover birth and descent (on a modified *jus sanguinis* basis), registration (including a broad discretion to register any minor) and the naturalisation of persons of full age (based on up to five years' lawful residence).

However, at the time of writing there are proposals for the amendment of British nationality laws. The White Paper *Partnership for Progress and Prosperity – Britain*

---

15 OJ C 23, 28 January 1983; Cmnd 9062. The legality of this declaration has at the date of writing been referred to the ECJ under art 177: *Manjit Kaur* (1998) 11 December (CO/0985/98) – see section 3.3, p 139, below.
16 *R v Secretary of State for the Home Department, ex p Thakrar* [1974] 2 All ER 261, CA.
17 BNA 1981, s 50(1).
18 See, eg, the definition of UK nationals in the Antarctic Act 1994, Chemical Weapons Act 1996, s 3(4) and Outer Space Act 1986.
19 (1973) 3 EHRR 76.
20 Under the BNA 1948. From 1 January 1949 to 31 December 1982, inclusive, the primary British nationals were 'citizens of the UK and Colonies' (CUKCs) but from 1962 onwards only some, corresponding to today's British citizens, remained outside the scope of UK immigration controls.
1 Upon the commencement of the BNA 1981 on 1 January 1983; see ss 11, 23, 26.
2 See chapter 1, section 4.3, p 10.
3 The BNA 1981; the British Nationality (Falkland Islands) Act 1983.
4 The British Nationality (Hong Kong) Act 1990; the Hong Kong (War Wives and Widows) Act 1996; the British Nationality (Hong Kong) Act 1997.

and the Overseas Territories[5] may raise new problems regarding access to British citizenship and is discussed below. The White Paper *Fairer, Faster and Firmer – a Modern Approach to Immigration and Asylum*[6] proposes changes to the residence requirements of British citizenship applications but they are unlikely to engage human rights issues.

2.4 Access to other British nationalities

British Dependent Territories citizenship is also widely available (under the 1981 Act only) and on equivalent terms to British citizenship. However, there is some evidence that in at least one dependent territory long-term residents have been kept on time restrictions with the result that they never qualify for naturalisation under the Act[7]. This concerned Moroccan migrants in Gibraltar. In such a situation, and depending upon the consequences of nationality being withheld, one might argue this violates article 3 (degrading treatment), article 5 (the right to security[8]) and article 8 (private life) – in conjunction with article 14 if a class such as the Moroccan migrants is involved. The First Protocol might also be relevant, depending on the circumstances: article 2 (the right to education) and possibly even article 3 (right to free elections). There are individual rights within article 3 (of Protocol 1) though they are not easily ascertainable[9]. Perhaps it might therefore be possible to make the necessary link between article 3 and the fact that it presupposes a democratic society, yet denying access to nationality may also be a denial of political rights and so lead to a democratic deficit within the society. Supportive soft law would include article 3(3) of the 1955 European Convention on Establishment[10], which provides that nationals of a state party[11] lawfully residing for more than ten years in the territory of another party may only be expelled for reasons of national security or for certain other reasons of a particularly serious nature. Even more significantly, article 6(3) of the 1997 European Convention on Nationality provides:

> 'Each State Party shall provide in its internal law for the possibility of naturalisation of persons lawfully and habitually resident on its territory. In establishing the conditions for naturalisation, it shall not provide for a period of residence exceeding ten years before the lodging of an application'.

Regarding British Overseas citizenship, apart from certain special cases[12] it is now only available to minors on an application to be registered at the Secretary of State's discretion[13]. However, the policy has always been to exercise this discretion very sparingly

---

5 March 1999; Cm 4264.
6 July 1998; Cm 4018, at para 10.7.
7 BNA 1981, s 18(1), Sch 2, para 5(2)(c).
8 Though it would be novel to detach this right from the right to liberty.
9 *Law of the European Convention on Human Rights*, Harris, O'Boyle & Warbrick (1995, Butterworths) p 551.
10 ETS 19.
11 Although only nationals of a state party are protected, UK policy has long been to extend it to all nationals (hence the so-called 'long residence concession').
12 Persons from Hong Kong who became BOCs *ex lege* on 1 July 1997 to prevent statelessness (see the Hong Kong (British Nationality) Order 1986, SI 1986/948, art 6(1)) and certain others who would be stateless (see BNA 1981, Sch 2, para 1(1)).
13 BNA, s 27(1).

indeed not even a stateless child with BOC parents can expect to be registered[14]. Depending on the circumstances it may be arguable that the refusal to register is unlawful under section 6(1) of the HRA. Various articles, such as article 3, might be engaged.

The same points may be made in respect of section 32 of the BNA 1981 (providing for the discretionary registration of minors as British subjects).

No point is likely to arise in respect of BPP status, while BN(O) status is no longer even obtainable.

2.5 Equality of access to British nationality

Where there is provision for British nationality to be acquired, is it on equal terms within categories[15] and, if not, could the primary legislation be incompatible with the Convention?

Section 44(1) of the BNA 1981 prohibits discrimination on grounds of 'race, colour or religion'. Section 50(9), the only expressly discriminatory provision of the Act, applies to prevent illegitimate children from relying on their father in order to establish acquisition by birth or descent.

However, article 14 of the Convention prohibits discrimination 'on any ground' and gives the examples of 'sex, race, colour, language, religion, political or other opinion, national or social origin, association with a national minority, property, birth or other status'. The Council of Europe's Nationality Convention appears to disapprove discrimination on grounds of illegitimacy in the nationality context. Its provisions[16] suggest that where access to British nationality is provided for, whether *ex lege* or on application, there is to be sexual equality both in its acquisition and transmission and, by logical extension therefore, irrespective of legitimacy. The continuing discrimination against illegitimate children could be sufficient basis on which to launch an article 3 (degrading treatment) taken together with article 14 argument, given the right case.

So in respect of British citizenship (as well as British Dependent Territories citizenship) there continues to be discrimination against illegitimate children and it is becoming increasingly arguable that this could violate one or more of the incorporated provisions[17]. This could warrant a section 4 declaration of incompatibility under the HRA. Further, the refusal of a section 3(1) registration application, made to avoid the discrimination (and disclosing evidence of paternity) may be an unlawful act under section 6(1) of the HRA.

2.6 Fairness of the application process

The two principal unfairness issues arising in the practice of British nationality law have been the absence of any requirement to give reasons for refusing discretionary applications and the absence of any appeal remedy.

14 See *Fransman's British Nationality Law*, 2nd edn, at 18.2.1.
15 Eg open to men and women equally in the naturalisation category.
16 Arts 2c, 5(1) and 6(1)(a) taken together. See also the reference in chapter 6 to discrimination on grounds of illegitimacy.
17 Though it is reiterated that an art 14 point can only be run in conjunction with at least one of the other articles.

The reasons for refusals issue came to a head in *R v Secretary of State for the Home Department, ex p Fayed*[18] in which the Court of Appeal held that in certain cases the Secretary of State is under a duty to give an applicant notice of his areas of concern (but not that there is a general duty to give reasons). The Secretary of State took the case to the House of Lords but *en route* and, hardly coincidentally, shortly after the European Convention on Nationality was opened for signature, announced that henceforth reasons will be given in all cases[19]. Hardly coincidentally because the Nationality Convention requires all decisions to be reasoned[20].

Were it not for these recent developments, incorporation might have provided a new opportunity to challenge the withholding of reasons.

Incorporation might nevertheless provide an opportunity to challenge the absence of an appeal remedy. At present, judicial review is available but on limited grounds only where discretionary refusals are concerned[1], and there is only an appeal right on merits where an individual claims already to be a British citizen[2]. Now that reasons are to accompany all refusals, the absence of a merits appeal procedure will be felt more acutely. Further, the new Nationality Convention requires all decisions to 'be open to an administrative or judicial review in conformity with its internal law'[3]. However, it is not immediately clear how the lack of an appeal may be linked to the incorporated rights; article 6 (everyone is entitled to a fair and public hearing) seems relevant, but the right only arises in respect of 'civil' rights and obligations and criminal charges, and 'civil' is taken to apply only to private law[4]. An appeal right against nationality refusals, on the face of it, is clearly a public law dispute.

3.   The right of nationals to enter and leave and not be expelled from their country of nationality

3.1   The position in international law and under the ECHR

It is well established in international law that 'Everyone has the right to leave any country, including his own'[5]. As for a state admitting its own nationals, there is in international law, in the relationship between states, a duty on a home state to admit its national expelled from a host state[6]. In international (human rights) law there has also developed, between states and individuals, a duty on the state to admit its own nationals[7]. This duty is

---

18   [1997] 1 All ER 228.
19   Hansard, 22 December 1997, col 564 (written answer to a PQ).
20   Art 11.
1   BNA 1981, s 44(2).
2   The right of appeal (under the Immigration Act 1971, s 13) against the refusal of a certificate of entitlement to the right of abode.
3   Art 12.
4   *König v Germany* (1978) 2 EHRR 170, para 95. See the discussions on art 6 at p 21 and pp 51-52.
5   Eg Universal Declaration of Human Rights 1948, art 13(2); ICCPR 1966, art 12(2).
6   *R v Secretary of State for the Home Department, ex p Thakrar* [1974] 2 All ER 261 at 266, CA.
7   Universal Declaration 1948, art 13(2); ICCPR 1966, art 12(4); International Convention of the Elimination of All Forms of Racial Discrimination 1966, art 5(d)(ii); American Convention on Human Rights 1969, art 22(5); African Charter on Human Rights, art 12(2). See Plender *International Migration Law*, rev 2nd edn, at pp 133-138 generally and at 135 where he lists the many national constitutions which characterise the right to enter one's own country as a fundamental or human right.

considered so important a consequence of nationality 'that it is almost equated with it'[8] and even the ECJ has expressly acknowledged this[9]. Implicit in the right to enter is a right not to be expelled.

As for the ECHR, Protocol 4 provides in article 2(2) 'Everyone shall be free to leave any country, including his own', and in article 3(1) 'No one shall be expelled ... from the territory of the State of which he is a national'. Article 3(2) states:

'No one shall be deprived of the right to enter the territory of the State of which he is a national'.

Article 3(2) does not give a right of entry but protects it. As a member of the Commission has observed[10]:

'(T)he original draft of Article 3(2) read: "Everyone shall be free to enter" the territory of the State of which he is a national. But it was very substantially altered to read in the final text: "No one shall be deprived of the right to enter ...". The difference is obvious and fundamental, the final text being posited on the existence of a right of entry of nationals'.

The UK has declined to ratify Protocol 4 to date but, ironically, there is some suggestion that when convenient to do so the UK relies on the general right of entry of nationals as typified by article 3(2), Protocol 4. In *Surinder Singh*[11] the European Court of Justice said:

'Admittedly, as the United Kingdom submits, a national of a Member State enters and resides in the territory of that State by virtue of the rights attendant upon his nationality and not by virtue of those conferred on him by Community law. In particular, as is provided, moreover, by Article 3 of the Fourth Protocol to the European Convention on Human Rights, a State may not expel one of its own nationals or deny him entry to its territory'.

The right of nationals to enter, leave and not be expelled from their country of nationality or the territory of the state of which they are nationals can raise issues as to the territorial extent of the state (whether the right applies only to the metropolitan state or to its overseas territories as well) and as to the meaning of 'nationals' in relation to the state's different territorial parts.

3.2 The prospect of the UK ratifying Protocol 4

As already indicated, the UK has not ratified Protocol 4 because many British nationals do not have the right of abode in the UK and so are subject to immigration controls. In the White Paper *Rights Brought Home: the Human Rights Bill*[12] the government said Protocol 4 had not been ratified

---

8 Van Panhuys *The Role of Nationality in International Law*, p 56.
9 *Van Duyn v Home Office* [1974] ECR 1337 at 1351.
10 Mr J E S Fawcett in *East African Asians v United Kingdom* (1973) 3 EHRR 76, at para 242.
11 [1992] Imm AR 565, ECJ at para 22; this is a decision of the European Community's Court of Justice in Luxembourg, not the Council of Europe's Court of Human Rights in Strasbourg.
12 October 1997; Cm 3782.

'... because of concerns about what is the exact extent of the obligation regarding a right of entry'[13]

but that Protocol 4 contains 'important rights' and should be ratified

'... if the potential conflicts with our domestic laws can be resolved'[14].

The language employed here ('the exact extent of the obligation') suggests uncertainty about how far the government would have to go in permitting entry to UK nationals in order to meet the article 3(2) obligation. The language also suggests there might nevertheless be a realistic prospect of ratifying the Protocol, so what are the issues?

The different types of British nationality have already been set out[15]. The position regarding entry to the UK by BDTCs, BOCs, BN(O)s, British subjects and BPPs must be considered[16] to gauge whether there is a shortfall of Protocol 4 standards.

BDTCs are in effect the citizens of the remaining colonies and in the main have no other nationality. Those who derive their status from Gibraltar or the Falkland Islands thereby have, or have access to, British citizenship[17] and as British citizenship confers the right of abode[18], they may already enter the UK if they wish. As for (almost all) the rest, the government is now proposing an extension to them of British citizenship (and *ipso facto* the right of abode). In the White Paper *Partnership for Progress and Prosperity – Britain and the Overseas Territories*[19] the government says:

'We have decided that British citizenship – and so the right of abode – should be offered to those British Dependent Territories citizens who do not already enjoy it and who want to take it up'[20].

However, it is not proposed to offer British citizenship to quite all. Excluded are the BDTCs:

'... who owe their status to their association with the Sovereign Base Areas in Cyprus or with the British Indian Ocean Territory. Both are special cases. British usage of these territories is defence-related'[1].

These exclusions are not as easily justifiable as the White Paper tries to suggest. It may or may not be a coincidence that at the time the White Paper was published

---

13 Cm 3782, para. 4.10.
14 Cm 3782, para. 4.11.
15 Above, at 2.2.
16 Without prejudice to any argument that some – BPPs at least – pose no Protocol 4 problem as they are not nationals of this country for ECHR purposes.
17 For the right of a BDTC (Gibraltar) to register as a British citizen, see BNA 1981, s 5; for the automatic acquisition of British citizenship by a BDTC (Falkland Islands), see the British Nationality (Falkland Islands) Act 1983.
18 Immigration Act 1971, s 2(1)(a) as amended by the BNA 1981, s 39(2).
19 March 1999; Cm 4264.
20 Cm 4264, para. 3.7.
1 Cm 4264, para. 3.13. But when the Foreign Secretary introduced the White Paper he said 'We are not extending the offer of citizenship to [BDTCs] who are associated with [BIOT] and the Sovereign Base Areas in Cyprus, *all of whom have alternative nationality*' House of Commons statement, 16 March 1999 (emphasis supplied).

members of a community known as the Ilois were in the process of obtaining leave to apply for judicial review of their exclusion from the British Indian Ocean Territory (BIOT). The Chagos Islands, the largest of which is Diego Garcia, were detached from Mauritius, at the time a British colony, and together with certain other islands were constituted the BIOT Colony in 1965 and promptly made available to the USA for defence purposes. To this end the Chagos Islanders, or Ilois, were rounded up and resettled on Mauritius, an independent country from 1968. The Ilois remained citizens of the UK and Colonies (CUKCs), however, and today the community (still on Mauritius and with dreams of returning home) are a mix of BDTCs by birth and descent. Their plight raises two issues: the one concerns whether the Convention is available to assist them in re-entering BIOT (as to which see 3.4 below), while the other concerns their position in respect of the UK. They did not accidentally or incidentally become CUKCs by, for example, being brought to the American naval base to work as domestics, but pre-date the use of the islands for defence purposes and, with Chagos ancestry going back up to five generations, arguably constitute an indigenous population. Unlike the majority of BDTCs, they are required to live outside their homeland. Assuming the White Paper's proposal on the extension of British citizenship to BDTCs to be a step towards ratification and incorporation of Protocol 4, it seems at least arguably to be a flawed step as the exclusion of the Ilois – and perhaps of BDTCs in a similar position as regards the Cyprus Sovereign Base Areas – may be discriminatory, violate the Protocol or constitute and unfair and inconsistent application of it.

Regarding the admission of BOCs to the UK, the White Paper says:

'We do not intend to offer British citizenship to British Overseas Citizens. Many have access to or have acquired dual nationality. Many have access to the UK through our voucher scheme'[2].

BOCs do not, as a pure consequence of their citizenship, have the right of abode in the UK, a dependent territory or any other place. They have a British nationality status but not an effective nationality and the UK has as good as conceded this[3].

As already indicated, though, the Commission in *East African Asians v United Kingdom*[4] treated all CUKCs as British nationals without distinction and such citizens became British citizens, BDTCs and BOCs when the category was redefined. As the Commission engaged with BOCs in their pre-1983[5] status and as BOCs are patently British nationals under the British Nationality Act 1981, it seems unlikely the UK would be able to exclude them from being nationals of this country for the purposes of Protocol 4. Since 1 January 1983 BOCs have been a shrinking class as there is no provision for the automatic perpetuation of that citizenship[6], but their numbers are still substantial. There were an estimated 1.5 million BOCs on 1 January 1983[7], so probably in excess of 1 million remain. However, the great majority are dual nationals,

---

2   Cm 4264, para. 3.12.
3   See the British Nationality (Hong Kong) Act 1997, s 1(1)-(3) making British citizenship available to certain BOCs, BN(O)s, British subjects and BPPs who but for such citizenship or status would be stateless (and who with it and nothing else are therefore effectively stateless).
4   (1973) 3 EHRR 76.
5   The British Nationality Act 1981 commenced on 1 January 1983.
6   Transitional provisions aside, there is just a discretion to register minors as BOCs: BNA 1981, s 27(1).
7   See statistics in *Fransman's British Nationality Law* 2nd edn, at 1232.

being BOCs and Malaysian[8], and this may give the UK a basis on which to exclude most BOCs from the prospective scope of Protocol 4. Regarding the BOCs with no other nationality, of whom there are probably about 150,000 to 200,000, the government has long provided a special voucher scheme whereby many may be admitted to the UK on a quota basis[9] which might possibly be sufficient for Protocol 4 purposes.

Much the same can be said of BN(O)s – they are a numerically large but shrinking class and those without any other nationality are to some extent already being offered a basis for entering the UK. BN(O)s are those Hong Kong BDTCs who during the period 1 July 1987 to 30 June 1997 registered as BN(O)s[10] to have a British status that would survive the return to China of sovereignty over the Colony. Approximately 3.4 million people became BN(O)s[11], but save for 8,000 to 10,000, they are ethnically Chinese and therefore are dual BN(O)/Chinese nationals[12]. Those who are effectively stateless, being BN(O)s only, and who remained ordinarily resident in Hong Kong are entitled to register as British citizens under the British Nationality (Hong Kong) Act 1997, originally a Private Member's Bill but adopted by the government on 4 February 1997 so as to afford an effective nationality to Hong Kong's ethnic minorities[13].

Regarding British subjects and BPPs, they too are members of shrinking classes[14] though by definition they have no other nationality or citizenship[15] (save as far as Irish British subjects[16] are concerned, but being Irish nationals that group has access to the UK in any event so do not pose a Protocol 4 problem). The government in 1980 guessed there would be 50,000 British subjects under the 1981 Act at commencement[17] which, if right, means there are significantly fewer now, and there are likely to be less than 10,000 remaining BPPs scattered across the globe[18]. To some extent both groups appear to benefit exceptionally from the special voucher scheme for BOCs[19]. At common law BPPs are not British nationals at all, so for that reason alone may not pose a Protocol 4 problem, though to rely on this to exclude such a small group who but for being BPPs would be stateless would not mark the UK's proudest hour.

Overall, the UK might argue that it will satisfy the minimum requirements of Protocol 4 by extending British citizenship to the remaining BDTCs under the White Paper proposals, by continuing to register BN(O)s with no other nationality as British citizens under the 1997 Act and by continuing the special voucher scheme in respect of BOCs with no other nationality as well as British subjects and (if they are treated

---

8   *Ibid.*
9   Immigration Rules HC 395, paras 249-254, and see *Macdonald's Immigration Law and Practice*, 4th edn, 13.10 to 13.21. See also section 3.3 below at note 8.
10 See the Hong Kong (British Nationality) Order 1986, SI 1986/948, art 4.
11 *Fransman's British Nationality Law*, 2nd edn, at p 585.
12 For the applicable Chinese nationality provisions see *ibid* at p 606.
13 *Ibid* at pp 589-591, 604-606.
14 See, respectively, ss 30-32 of the BNA 1981 and the British Protectorates, Protected States and Protected Persons Order 1982, SI 1982/1070 (providing only for acquisition to prevent statelessness).
15 See, respectively, s 35 of the BNA 1981 and art 10 of the British Protectorates, Protected States and Protected Persons Order 1982, SI 1982/1070.
16 BNA 1981, s 31.
17 See the 1980 White Paper, Cmnd 7987, Annex B, para 10.
18 *Fransman's British Nationality Law*, 2nd en, at p 1233.
19 *Macdonald's Immigration Law and Practice*, 4th edn, at para 13.14.

as nationals of this country) BPPs. However, there must be grave doubts as to whether this would suffice. The exclusion of BDTCs from BIOT and, possibly, the Sovereign Base Areas of Cyprus may be indefensible and the limitations of the 1997 Act (applying only to those satisfying ordinary residence requirements) and special voucher scheme (applying, for example, only to heads of households) may leave unacceptable gaps in the coverage Protocol 4 would require. While it is surely the case that the UK would not need to go so far as to grant British citizenship to all those British nationals likely to fall within the scope of Protocol 4 (as a permission rather than entitlement to enter may suffice in practice), it is suggested it would be preferable to do so nonetheless as an effective nationality is preferable to an ineffective one compensated by an uncertain and easily removed permission to enter.

3.3   Non-Protocol 4 challenges to UK exclusions[20] and expulsions[1] of own nationals

The Protocol 4 right to leave one's own country is not in practice a contentious issue in UK domestic law, therefore the non-incorporation of article 2(2) into domestic law does not leave a noticeable gap in human rights protection. However, the lack of article 3(1) and (2) matters greatly; if these provisions were ratified and therefore incorporated, British nationals[2] would have hard law on which to rely in seeking admission to and resisting removal from the UK. The present deficiencies are illustrated by the anomaly of BOCs and others seeking asylum at UK ports of entry; that is, seeking to be refugees in the country of their own nationality. Hopefully the proposals of the White Paper on the remaining colonies (or overseas territories as they are now styled) signal ratification and incorporation of Protocol 4 in the not too distant future. Meanwhile, though, all is not necessarily lost as at least some of those who would benefit under the Protocol may be able to solve the same problem by relying on other Convention articles instead, supported by the soft (international) law referred to above[3], or by applying Community law to the case and taking a Protocol 4 point in that context.

The case of *Manjit Kaur*[4], still pending at the date of writing, illustrates the latter course. Mrs Kaur, a BOC, argues that she is a European Union (EU) citizen with the right to move and reside freely within the territory of the EU member states under articles 8 and 8a of the EC Treaty as amended by the Treaty on European Union (TEU). She argues that either the UK's unilateral declaration excluding her from being a UK national for Community law purposes[5] is invalid, or as an aid to construing whether she is such a national for article 8 purposes that declaration is outbalanced by the consideration that article 8 should not be construed

'... in a manner which interferes and is incompatible with the fundamental rights of the Applicant and other BOCs. In short the argument runs that the jurisprudence of the ECJ (eg Case C-260/89 *Elliniki Radiophonia Tiléorassi AE* [1991] ECR I-2925 at 2963-4)

---

20   Ie entry refusals.
1   Ie enforcement decisions.
2   See pp 130-131.
3   See pp 134-135.
4   (1998) 11 December (CO/0985/98).
5   See section 2.2 and note 15, p 131.

and Article F(2) of the Treaty (introduced by the TEU) requires respect for fundamental rights; and that one such right protected by Article 3(2) of Protocol No.4 to the European Convention on Human Rights requires respect for the right of a national to enter his own country; that, whilst the UK is not a party to this protocol, it is part of the *corpus* of law to be taken into account by the ECJ in construing the Treaty; and that this requires a construction to be adopted which entitles BOCs to enter and remain in Britain. I shall say no more about this argument than that both parties agree that it should be referred to the ECJ … and in the circumstances I think that it is proper to do so' (paragraph 22).

As for the former course (relying on other Convention articles, pending any incorporation of the Protocol), these other articles would be most likely to include article 3 (degrading treatment) such as in *East African Asians v United Kingdom*[6]. In this case the Commission concluded that:

'… although the right to enter one's country is not [in the case of the UK] protected by the Convention, the refusal of this right may in special circumstances, nevertheless, violate quite independently another right already covered by this treaty. It follows that, in the present cases, the Commission is not being called upon to consider the rights of entry or residence as such, but that it is being invited to examine the different question whether the decisions complained of amount to 'degrading treatment' in the sense of Article 3'.

The Commission in a Report adopted on 14 December 1973 did find article 3 to have been violated (in respect of the 25 applicants who were CUKCs[7], but not the six who were BPPs). On 21 October 1977 the Committee of Ministers, noting that by 1975 the annual quota for special vouchers[8] had been increased to 5,000 (and that the applicants had all been granted settlement), resolved that no further action was called for[9].

It is inarguable that just because article 3 of Protocol 4 cannot be relied upon (outside the Community law context) by a British national seeking admission or resisting removal it is impossible ever to succeed in a situation for which its rights were intended. The Preamble to Protocol 4 does say it concerns rights 'other than those already included' in the Convention, but this does not mean the Convention itself cannot give backdoor protection. The *East African Asians* case stands testimony to this proposition.

Where a case would be ideally suited to article 3 of Protocol 4 it will not always be arguable under another provision, such as the incorporated article 3. However, where the individual does not have the nationality of another country and has a good reason for not using or benefiting under the special voucher scheme, an argument may lie.

Such litigation under the HRA seems particularly likely given the UK's present policy on British nationals. Where, for example, a BOC with no other nationality

---

6 (1973) 3 EHRR 76. This is a Commission decision unofficially reported (ie the Commission Report was never officially published).

7 See note 20, p 131.

8 The scheme to allow British nationals to enter the UK for settlement on a quota basis (see 3.2, n.69). For its history, see the speech of Lord Fraser in *Amin* [1983] 2 AC 818, HL in which the scheme's sex discrimination was held not to be unlawful under the Sex Discrimination Act 1975 and refusals under it were held not to be appealable under the Immigration Act 1971. Incorporation may provide an opportunity to revisit, particularly with arts 3, 6 and 14 in mind, these and other aspects of the scheme.

9 Resolution DH (77) 2.

was in the jurisdiction it did not used to be unduly difficult to obtain indefinite leave to remain. However, policy hardened and the Home Office began to remove such persons wherever it was possible to do so under the removal powers[10]. Where the individual has appeared to the Secretary of State not to be removable under those powers at the present time, he is known to have issued letters explaining that, for the moment, the individual will not be removed but will not be granted leave to enter either. Remaining in this twilight zone indefinitely could well engage article 3 as well as other articles (such as article 8 and the second article of Protocol 1) depending on the circumstances and the Secretary of State is known to have backed down in just such a case once judicial review proceedings were underway[11].

3.4 Non-Protocol 4 challenges to an Overseas Territory's exclusions and expulsions of own nationals

The ECHR has been declared from time to time to apply to various of the UK's territories. The first declaration, of 23 October 1953, provided:

> 'Her Majesty's Government have considered the extension of the European Convention on Human rights to those territories for whose international relations they are responsible and in which that Convention would be applicable'

and went on to specify many, but not all, colonies of the day.

Subsequent declarations amended the list, particularly as a result of territories attaining independence and ceasing to be the UK's responsibility. The most recent declaration, made on 3 April 1984 (following Brunei's independence), applies the Convention to Anguilla, Bermuda, the British Virgin Islands, Cayman Islands, Channel Islands, Falkland Islands, Gibraltar, Isle of Man, Montserrat, St Helena and Turks & Caicos Islands. Therefore just as provisions of the Convention itself might be used to challenge the legality of British nationals being excluded or expelled from the UK, so the same may be said at least of BDTCs in respect of the aforementioned overseas territories.

Additionally, there is an argument that the ECHR may still extend to British overseas territories which are omitted from the latest declaration but were once included. The remaining overseas territories excluded from the 1984 declaration are the British Antarctic Territory, British Indian Ocean Territory (BIOT), the Pitcairn Islands (Pitcairn, Henderson, Ducie and Oeno) and the Sovereign Base Areas of Cyprus. The Pitcairn Islands (the population of which is stated in the White Paper to be 54[12]) were never specified in the declarations so the ECHR never extended to them.

However, the British Antarctic Territory was formerly part of the Falkland Islands dependency and as such included in earlier declarations and the BIOT was formerly part of the Colony of Mauritius and as such also included[13]. The Sovereign Base

---

10 Removal under the Immigration Act 1971, Sch 2, para 8(1)(c) or Sch 3, para 1(1) to a country 'to which there is reason to believe that he will be admitted'. See *Patel* [1993] Imm AR 392, CA.
11 *Lakhani v Immigration Appeal Tribunal* [1988] Imm AR 474.
12 Cm 4264 at p 62.
13 Mauritius was included in the declaration of 12 August 1964, made just before the Chagos Islands were detached from it to constitute a separate colony.

Areas of Cyprus were formerly part of Cyprus Colony and so were included in a reference to Cyprus that appeared in the original declaration. It is undoubtedly true that the British Antarctic Territory, BIOT and Sovereign Base Areas are now populated, if at all, by scientific expeditions or defence personnel, but there may be instances where a practical issue arises. Such is the case in respect of the Ilois – BDTCs by association with BIOT who are excluded from that overseas territory but wish to return there (see above). Article 3 and other arguments under the Convention itself could avail such persons if it is right that once the Convention has extended to them, its rights and freedoms cannot be withdrawn.

The proposition is untested in ECHR jurisprudence, but in 1992 the Human Rights Committee (established under the ICCPR[14]) made a potentially landmark decision (reported at 15 EHRR 233). The editor's note reads as follows:

> 'The Human Rights Committee held an extremely significant discussion of the obligations of the successor States to the former Yugoslavia under the ICCPR. ... Records of the discussion are published in full below. The position taken by the Human Rights Committee is important and authoritative; it may well prove influential in the consideration of any State succession issues by other International Human Rights bodies such as the European Commission and Court of Human Rights'.

The decision in essence concerned the requirement of states that have ratified the ICCPR to report to the Committee (about every five years). The Human Rights Committee decided that because Yugoslavia had been a party to the ICCPR the successor states were bound by it and therefore were required to submit reports. This decision has been respected in practice as the states concerned have submitted reports as if bound by the ICCPR. The other parties to the ICCPR (such as the UK) have to date not protested the 1992 decision. This has set a trend which the former Soviet Union states have followed; they have been lodging declarations of succession with the Human Rights Committee rather than acts of ratification.

The principle is an important one in international human rights law and might be expected to be applied to Council of Europe treaty law, particularly the ECHR. In the context of the BDTCs from the British Indian Ocean Territory, they could argue the ECHR extended to them when their islands formed part of Mauritius and therefore continued to do so when BIOT was established in 1965 and even after the independence of Mauritius in 1968 (by which time the UK had even accepted the right of individual petition and recognised the Court's jurisdiction[15]).

14 See chapter 1, section 1.3, note 3, p 3.
15 See chapter 1, section 7.3, p 25. These steps were taken on 14 January 1966.

Appendix

Human Rights Act 1998

1998 Chapter 42

An Act to give further effect to rights and freedoms guaranteed under the European Convention on Human Rights; to make provision with respect to holders of certain judicial offices who become judges of the European Court of Human Rights; and for connected purposes.

[9th November 1998]

BE IT ENACTED by the Queen's most Excellent Majesty, by and with the advice and consent of the Lords Spiritual and Temporal, and Commons, in this present Parliament assembled, and by the authority of the same, as follows—

Introduction

1 The Convention Rights

(1)   In this Act "the Convention rights" means the rights and fundamental freedoms set out in—
(a) Articles 2 to 12 and 14 of the Convention,
(b) Articles 1 to 3 of the First Protocol, and
(c) Articles 1 and 2 of the Sixth Protocol,
as read with Articles 16 to 18 of the Convention.

(2)   Those Articles are to have effect for the purposes of this Act subject to any designated derogation or reservation (as to which see sections 14 and 15).

(3)   The Articles are set out in Schedule 1.

(4)   The Secretary of State may by order make such amendments to this Act as he considers appropriate to reflect the effect, in relation to the United Kingdom, of a protocol.

(5)   In subsection (4) "protocol" means a protocol to the Convention—
(a) which the United Kingdom has ratified; or
(b) which the United Kingdom has signed with a view to ratification.

(6) No amendment may be made by an order under subsection (4) so as to come into force before the protocol concerned is in force in relation to the United Kingdom.

Notes
Initial Commencement
To be appointed
To be appointed: see s 22(3).

2 Interpretation of Convention rights

(1)   A court or tribunal determining a question which has arisen in connection with a Convention right must take into account any—

(a) judgment, decision, declaration or advisory opinion of the European Court of Human Rights,

(b) opinion of the Commission given in a report adopted under Article 31 of the Convention,

(c) decision of the Commission in connection with Article 26 or 27(2) of the Convention, or

(d) decision of the Committee of Ministers taken under Article 46 of the Convention, whenever made or given, so far as, in the opinion of the court or tribunal, it is relevant to the proceedings in which that question has arisen.

(2)   Evidence of any judgment, decision, declaration or opinion of which account may have to be taken under this section is to be given in proceedings before any court or tribunal in such manner as may be provided by rules.

(3)   In this section "rules" means rules of court or, in the case of proceedings before a tribunal, rules made for the purposes of this section—

(a) by the Lord Chancellor or the Secretary of State, in relation to any proceedings outside Scotland;

(b) by the Secretary of State, in relation to proceedings in Scotland; or

(c) by a Northern Ireland department, in relation to proceedings before a tribunal in Northern Ireland—

(i) which deals with transferred matters; and

(ii) for which no rules made under paragraph (a) are in force.

Notes
Initial Commencement
To be appointed
To be appointed: see s 22(3).

Legislation

3 Interpretation of legislation

(1)   So far as it is possible to do so, primary legislation and subordinate legislation must be read and given effect in a way which is compatible with the Convention rights.

(2)   This section—

(a) applies to primary legislation and subordinate legislation whenever enacted;

(b) does not affect the validity, continuing operation or enforcement of any incompatible primary legislation; and

(c) does not affect the validity, continuing operation or enforcement of any incompatible subordinate legislation if (disregarding any possibility of revocation) primary legislation prevents removal of the incompatibility.

Notes
Initial Commencement
To be appointed
To be appointed: see s 22(3).

4 Declaration of incompatibility

(1)   Subsection (2) applies in any proceedings in which a court determines whether a provision of primary legislation is compatible with a Convention right.

(2)   If the court is satisfied that the provision is incompatible with a Convention right, it may make a declaration of that incompatibility.

(3)   Subsection (4) applies in any proceedings in which a court determines whether a provision of subordinate legislation, made in the exercise of a power conferred by primary legislation, is compatible with a Convention right.

(4)   If the court is satisfied—
(a) that the provision is incompatible with a Convention right, and
(b) that (disregarding any possibility of revocation) the primary legislation concerned prevents removal of the incompatibility,
it may make a declaration of that incompatibility.

(5)   In this section "court" means—
(a) the House of Lords;
(b) the Judicial Committee of the Privy Council;
(c) the Courts-Martial Appeal Court;
(d) in Scotland, the High Court of Justiciary sitting otherwise than as a trial court or the Court of Session;
(e) in England and Wales or Northern Ireland, the High Court or the Court of Appeal

(6)   A declaration under this section ("a declaration of incompatibility")—
(a) does not affect the validity, continuing operation or enforcement of the provision in respect of which it is given; and
(b) is not binding on the parties to the proceedings in which it is made.

Notes
Initial Commencement
To be appointed
To be appointed: see s 22(3).

5 Right of Crown to intervene

(1)   Where a court is considering whether to make a declaration of incompatibility, the Crown is entitled to notice in accordance with rules of court.

(2)   In any case to which subsection (1) applies—
(a) a Minister of the Crown (or a person nominated by him),

(b) a member of the Scottish Executive,

(c) a Northern Ireland Minister,

(d) a Northern Ireland department,

is entitled, on giving notice in accordance with rules of court, to be joined as a party to the proceedings.

(3)   Notice under subsection (2) may be given at any time during the proceedings.

(4)   A person who has been made a party to criminal proceedings (other than in Scotland) as the result of a notice under subsection (2) may, with leave, appeal to the House of Lords against any declaration of incompatibility made in the proceedings.

(5)   In subsection (4)—

"criminal proceedings" includes all proceedings before the Courts-Martial Appeal Court; and

"leave" means leave granted by the court making the declaration of incompatibility or by the House of Lords.

Notes

Initial Commencement
To be appointed
To be appointed: see s 22(3).

Public authorities

6   Acts of public authorities

(1)   It is unlawful for a public authority to act in a way which is incompatible with a Convention right.

(2)   Subsection (1) does not apply to an act if—

(a) as the result of one or more provisions of primary legislation, the authority could not have acted differently; or

(b) in the case of one or more provisions of, or made under, primary legislation which cannot be read or given effect in a way which is compatible with the Convention rights, the authority was acting so as to give effect to or enforce those provisions.

(3)   In this section "public authority" includes—

(a) a court or tribunal, and

(b) any person certain of whose functions are functions of a public nature,

but does not include either House of Parliament or a person exercising functions in connection with proceedings in Parliament.

(4)   In subsection (3) "Parliament" does not include the House of Lords in its judicial capacity.

(5)   In relation to a particular act, a person is not a public authority by virtue only of subsection (3)(b) if the nature of the act is private.

(6)   "An act" includes a failure to act but does not include a failure to—

(a) introduce in, or lay before, Parliament a proposal for legislation; or

(b) make any primary legislation or remedial order.

Notes

Initial Commencement

To be appointed

To be appointed: see s 22(3).

7   Proceedings

(1)   A person who claims that a public authority has acted (or proposes to act) in a way which is made unlawful by section 6(1) may—

(a) bring proceedings against the authority under this Act in the appropriate court or tribunal, or

(b) rely on the Convention right or rights concerned in any legal proceedings,

but only if he is (or would be) a victim of the unlawful act.

(2)   In subsection (1)(a) "appropriate court or tribunal" means such court or tribunal as may be determined in accordance with rules; and proceedings against an authority include a counterclaim or similar proceeding.

(3)   If the proceedings are brought on an application for judicial review, the applicant is to be taken to have a sufficient interest in relation to the unlawful act only if he is, or would be, a victim of that act.

(4)   If the proceedings are made by way of a petition for judicial review in Scotland, the applicant shall be taken to have title and interest to sue in relation to the unlawful act only if he is, or would be, a victim of that act.

(5)   Proceedings under subsection (1)(a) must be brought before the end of—

(a) the period of one year beginning with the date on which the act complained of took place; or

(b) such longer period as the court or tribunal considers equitable having regard to all the circumstances,

but that is subject to any rule imposing a stricter time limit in relation to the procedure in question.

(6)   In subsection (1)(b) "legal proceedings" includes—

(a) proceedings brought by or at the instigation of a public authority; and

(b) an appeal against the decision of a court or tribunal.

(7)   For the purposes of this section, a person is a victim of an unlawful act only if he would be a victim for the purposes of Article 34 of the Convention if proceedings were brought in the European Court of Human Rights in respect of that act.

(8)   Nothing in this Act creates a criminal offence.

(9)   In this section "rules" means—

(a) in relation to proceedings before a court or tribunal outside Scotland, rules made by the Lord Chancellor or the Secretary of State for the purposes of this section or rules of court,

(b) in relation to proceedings before a court or tribunal in Scotland, rules made by the Secretary of State for those purposes,

(c) in relation to proceedings before a tribunal in Northern Ireland—

(i) which deals with transferred matters; and

(ii) for which no rules made under paragraph (a) are in force,

rules made by a Northern Ireland department for those purposes,

and includes provision made by order under section 1 of the Courts and Legal Services Act 1990.

(10) In making rules, regard must be had to section 9.

(11) The Minister who has power to make rules in relation to a particular tribunal may, to the extent he considers it necessary to ensure that the tribunal can provide an appropriate remedy in relation to an act (or proposed act) of a public authority which is (or would be) unlawful as a result of section 6(1), by order add to—

(a) the relief or remedies which the tribunal may grant; or

(b) the grounds on which it may grant any of them.

(12) An order made under subsection (11) may contain such incidental, supplemental, consequential or transitional provision as the Minister making it considers appropriate.

(13) "The Minister" includes the Northern Ireland department concerned.

Notes
Initial Commencement
To be appointed
To be appointed: see s 22(3).

8 Judicial remedies

(1) In relation to any act (or proposed act) of a public authority which the court finds is (or would be) unlawful, it may grant such relief or remedy, or make such order, within its powers as it considers just and appropriate.

(2) But damages may be awarded only by a court which has power to award damages, or to order the payment of compensation, in civil proceedings.

(3) No award of damages is to be made unless, taking account of all the circumstances of the case, including—

(a) any other relief or remedy granted, or order made, in relation to the act in question (by that or any other court), and

(b) the consequences of any decision (of that or any other court) in respect of that act,

the court is satisfied that the award is necessary to afford just satisfaction to the person in whose favour it is made.

(4)   In determining—
(a) whether to award damages, or
(b) the amount of an award,
the court must take into account the principles applied by the European Court of Human Rights in relation to the award of compensation under Article 41 of the Convention.

(5)   A public authority against which damages are awarded is to be treated—
(a) in Scotland, for the purposes of section 3 of the Law Reform (Miscellaneous Provisions) (Scotland) Act 1940 as if the award were made in an action of damages in which the authority has been found liable in respect of loss or damage to the person to whom the award is made;
(b) for the purposes of the Civil Liability (Contribution) Act 1978 as liable in respect of damage suffered by the person to whom the award is made.

(6)   In this section—
"court" includes a tribunal;
"damages" means damages for an unlawful act of a public authority; and
"unlawful" means unlawful under section 6(1).

Notes
Initial Commencement
To be appointed
To be appointed: see s 22(3).

9   Judicial acts

(1)   Proceedings under section 7(1)(a) in respect of a judicial act may be brought only—
(a) by exercising a right of appeal;
(b) on an application (in Scotland a petition) for judicial review; or
(c) in such other forum as may be prescribed by rules.

(2)   That does not affect any rule of law which prevents a court from being the subject of judicial review.

(3)   In proceedings under this Act in respect of a judicial act done in good faith, damages may not be awarded otherwise than to compensate a person to the extent required by Article 5(5) of the Convention.

(4)   An award of damages permitted by subsection (3) is to be made against the Crown; but no award may be made unless the appropriate person, if not a party to the proceedings, is joined.

(5)   In this section—
"appropriate person" means the Minister responsible for the court concerned, or a person or government department nominated by him;
"court" includes a tribunal;
"judge" includes a member of a tribunal, a justice of the peace and a clerk or other officer entitled to exercise the jurisdiction of a court;

"judicial act" means a judicial act of a court and includes an act done on the instructions, or on behalf, of a judge; and

"rules" has the same meaning as in section 7(9).

Notes
Initial Commencement
To be appointed
To be appointed: see s 22(3).

Remedial action

10   Power to take remedial action

(1)   This section applies if—

(a) a provision of legislation has been declared under section 4 to be incompatible with a Convention right and, if an appeal lies—

  (i) all persons who may appeal have stated in writing that they do not intend to do so;

  (ii) the time for bringing an appeal has expired and no appeal has been brought within that time; or

  (iii) an appeal brought within that time has been determined or abandoned; or

(b) it appears to a Minister of the Crown or Her Majesty in Council that, having regard to a finding of the European Court of Human Rights made after the coming into force of this section in proceedings against the United Kingdom, a provision of legislation is incompatible with an obligation of the United Kingdom arising from the Convention.

(2)   If a Minister of the Crown considers that there are compelling reasons for proceeding under this section, he may by order make such amendments to the legislation as he considers necessary to remove the incompatibility.

(3)   If, in the case of subordinate legislation, a Minister of the Crown considers—

(a) that it is necessary to amend the primary legislation under which the subordinate legislation in question was made, in order to enable the incompatibility to be removed, and

(b) that there are compelling reasons for proceeding under this section,

he may by order make such amendments to the primary legislation as he considers necessary.

(4)   This section also applies where the provision in question is in subordinate legislation and has been quashed, or declared invalid, by reason of incompatibility with a Convention right and the Minister proposes to proceed under paragraph 2(b) of Schedule 2.

(5)   If the legislation is an Order in Council, the power conferred by subsection (2) or (3) is exercisable by Her Majesty in Council.

(6)   In this section "legislation" does not include a Measure of the Church Assembly or of the General Synod of the Church of England.

(7)   Schedule 2 makes further provision about remedial orders.

Notes
Initial Commencement
To be appointed
To be appointed: see s 22(3).

Other rights and proceedings

11 Safeguard for existing human rights

A person's reliance on a Convention right does not restrict—
(a) any other right or freedom conferred on him by or under any law having effect in any part of the United Kingdom; or
(b) his right to make any claim or bring any proceedings which he could make or bring apart from sections 7 to 9.

Notes
Initial Commencement
To be appointed
To be appointed: see s 22(3).

12 Freedom of expression

(1)   This section applies if a court is considering whether to grant any relief which, if granted, might affect the exercise of the Convention right to freedom of expression.

(2)   If the person against whom the application for relief is made ("the respondent") is neither present nor represented, no such relief is to be granted unless the court is satisfied—
(a) that the applicant has taken all practicable steps to notify the respondent; or
(b) that there are compelling reasons why the respondent should not be notified.

(3)   No such relief is to be granted so as to restrain publication before trial unless the court is satisfied that the applicant is likely to establish that publication should not be allowed.

(4)   The court must have particular regard to the importance of the Convention right to freedom of expression and, where the proceedings relate to material which the respondent claims, or which appears to the court, to be journalistic, literary or artistic material (or to conduct connected with such material), to—
(a) the extent to which—
    (i) the material has, or is about to, become available to the public; or
    (ii) it is, or would be, in the public interest for the material to be published;
(b) any relevant privacy code.

(5)   In this section—
"court" includes a tribunal; and
"relief" includes any remedy or order (other than in criminal proceedings).

Notes
Initial Commencement
To be appointed
To be appointed: see s 22(3).

13 Freedom of thought, conscience and religion

(1)   If a court's determination of any question arising under this Act might affect the exercise by a religious organisation (itself or its members collectively) of the Convention right to freedom of thought, conscience and religion, it must have particular regard to the importance of that right.

(2)   In this section "court" includes a tribunal.

Notes
Initial Commencement
To be appointed
To be appointed: see s 22(3).

Derogations and reservations

14 Derogations

(1)   In this Act "designated derogation" means—

(a) the United Kingdom's derogation from Article 5(3) of the Convention; and

(b) any derogation by the United Kingdom from an Article of the Convention, or of any protocol to the Convention, which is designated for the purposes of this Act in an order made by the Secretary of State.

(2)   The derogation referred to in subsection (1)(a) is set out in Part I of Schedule 3.

(3)   If a designated derogation is amended or replaced it ceases to be a designated derogation.

(4)   But subsection (3) does not prevent the Secretary of State from exercising his power under subsection (1)(b) to make a fresh designation order in respect of the Article concerned.

(5)   The Secretary of State must by order make such amendments to Schedule 3 as he considers appropriate to reflect—

(a) any designation order; or

(b) the effect of subsection (3).

(6)   A designation order may be made in anticipation of the making by the United Kingdom of a proposed derogation.

Notes
Initial Commencement
To be appointed
To be appointed: see s 22(3).

15 Reservations

(1)   In this Act "designated reservation" means—

(a) the United Kingdom's reservation to Article 2 of the First Protocol to the Convention; and

(b) any other reservation by the United Kingdom to an Article of the Convention, or of any protocol to the Convention, which is designated for the purposes of this Act in an order made by the Secretary of State.

(2)   The text of the reservation referred to in subsection (1)(a) is set out in Part II of Schedule 3.

(3)   If a designated reservation is withdrawn wholly or in part it ceases to be a designated reservation.

(4)   But subsection (3) does not prevent the Secretary of State from exercising his power under subsection (1)(b) to make a fresh designation order in respect of the Article concerned.

(5)   The Secretary of State must by order make such amendments to this Act as he considers appropriate to reflect—
(a) any designation order; or
(b) the effect of subsection (3).

Notes
Initial Commencement
To be appointed
To be appointed: see s 22(3).

16   Period for which designated derogations have effect

(1)   If it has not already been withdrawn by the United Kingdom, a designated derogation ceases to have effect for the purposes of this Act—
(a) in the case of the derogation referred to in section 14(1)(a), at the end of the period of five years beginning with the date on which section 1(2) came into force;
(b) in the case of any other derogation, at the end of the period of five years beginning with the date on which the order designating it was made.

(2)   At any time before the period—
(a) fixed by subsection (1)(a) or (b), or
(b) extended by an order under this subsection,
comes to an end, the Secretary of State may by order extend it by a further period of five years.

(3)   An order under section 14(1)(b) ceases to have effect at the end of the period for consideration, unless a resolution has been passed by each House approving the order.

(4)   Subsection (3) does not affect—
(a) anything done in reliance on the order; or
(b) the power to make a fresh order under section 14(1)(b).

(5)   In subsection (3) "period for consideration" means the period of forty days beginning with the day on which the order was made.

(6)   In calculating the period for consideration, no account is to be taken of any time during which—

(a) Parliament is dissolved or prorogued; or

(b) both Houses are adjourned for more than four days.

(7)   If a designated derogation is withdrawn by the United Kingdom, the Secretary of State must by order make such amendments to this Act as he considers are required to reflect that withdrawal.

Notes
Initial Commencement
To be appointed
To be appointed: see s 22(3).

17   Periodic review of designated reservations

(1)   The appropriate Minister must review the designated reservation referred to in section 15(1)(a)—

(a) before the end of the period of five years beginning with the date on which section 1(2) came into force; and

(b) if that designation is still in force, before the end of the period of five years beginning with the date on which the last report relating to it was laid under subsection (3).

(2)   The appropriate Minister must review each of the other designated reservations (if any)—

(a) before the end of the period of five years beginning with the date on which the order designating the reservation first came into force; and

(b) if the designation is still in force, before the end of the period of five years beginning with the date on which the last report relating to it was laid under subsection (3).

(3)   The Minister conducting a review under this section must prepare a report on the result of the review and lay a copy of it before each House of Parliament.

Notes
Initial Commencement
To be appointed
To be appointed: see s 22(3).

Judges of the European Court of Human Rights

18   Appointment to European Court of Human Rights

(1)   In this section "judicial officc" means the office of—

(a) Lord Justice of Appeal, Justice of the High Court or Circuit judge, in England and Wales;

(b) judge of the Court of Session or sheriff, in Scotland;

(c) Lord Justice of Appeal, judge of the High Court or county court judge, in Northern Ireland.

(2)   The holder of a judicial office may become a judge of the European Court of Human Rights ("the Court") without being required to relinquish his office.

(3)   But he is not required to perform the duties of his judicial office while he is a judge of the Court.

(4)   In respect of any period during which he is a judge of the Court—
(a) a Lord Justice of Appeal or Justice of the High Court is not to count as a judge of the relevant court for the purposes of section 2(1) or 4(1) of the Supreme Court Act 1981 (maximum number of judges) nor as a judge of the Supreme Court for the purposes of section 12(1) to (6) of that Act (salaries etc);
(b) a judge of the Court of Session is not to count as a judge of that court for the purposes of section 1(1) of the Court of Session Act 1988 (maximum number of judges) or of section 9(1)(c) of the Administration of Justice Act 1973 ("the 1973 Act") (salaries etc);
(c) a Lord Justice of Appeal or judge of the High Court in Northern Ireland is not to count as a judge of the relevant court for the purposes of section 2(1) or 3(1) of the Judicature (Northern Ireland) Act 1978 (maximum number of judges) nor as a judge of the Supreme Court of Northern Ireland for the purposes of section 9(1)(d) of the 1973 Act (salaries etc);
(d) a Circuit judge is not to count as such for the purposes of section 18 of the Courts Act 1971 (salaries etc);
(e) a sheriff is not to count as such for the purposes of section 14 of the Sheriff Courts (Scotland) Act 1907 (salaries etc);
(f) a county court judge of Northern Ireland is not to count as such for the purposes of section 106 of the County Courts Act (Northern Ireland) 1959 (salaries etc).

(5)   If a sheriff principal is appointed a judge of the Court, section 11(1) of the Sheriff Courts (Scotland) Act 1971 (temporary appointment of sheriff principal) applies, while he holds that appointment, as if his office is vacant.

(6)   Schedule 4 makes provision about judicial pensions in relation to the holder of a judicial office who serves as a judge of the Court.

(7)   The Lord Chancellor or the Secretary of State may by order make such transitional provision (including, in particular, provision for a temporary increase in the maximum number of judges) as he considers appropriate in relation to any holder of a judicial office who has completed his service as a judge of the Court.

Notes
Initial Commencement
Royal Assent
Royal Assent: 9 November 1998: see s 22(2).

Parliamentary procedure

19   Statements of compatibility

(1)   A Minister of the Crown in charge of a Bill in either House of Parliament must, before Second Reading of the Bill—

(a) make a statement to the effect that in his view the provisions of the Bill are compatible with the Convention rights ("a statement of compatibility"); or

(b) make a statement to the effect that although he is unable to make a statement of compatibility the government nevertheless wishes the House to proceed with the Bill.

(2)   The statement must be in writing and be published in such manner as the Minister making it considers appropriate.

Notes
Initial Commencement
To be appointed
To be appointed: see s 22(3).
Appointment
Appointment: 24 November 1998: see SI 1998/2882, art 2.

Supplemental
20   Orders etc under this Act

(1)   Any power of a Minister of the Crown to make an order under this Act is exercisable by statutory instrument.

(2)   The power of the Lord Chancellor or the Secretary of State to make rules (other than rules of court) under section 2(3) or 7(9) is exercisable by statutory instrument.

(3)   Any statutory instrument made under section 14, 15 or 16(7) must be laid before Parliament.

(4)   No order may be made by the Lord Chancellor or the Secretary of State under section 1(4), 7(11) or 16(2) unless a draft of the order has been laid before, and approved by, each House of Parliament.

(5)   Any statutory instrument made under section 18(7) or Schedule 4, or to which subsection (2) applies, shall be subject to annulment in pursuance of a resolution of either House of Parliament.

(6)   The power of a Northern Ireland department to make—
(a) rules under section 2(3)(c) or 7(9)(c), or
(b) an order under section 7(11),
is exercisable by statutory rule for the purposes of the Statutory Rules (Northern Ireland) Order 1979.

(7)   Any rules made under section 2(3)(c) or 7(9)(c) shall be subject to negative resolution; and section 41(6) of the Interpretation Act (Northern Ireland) 1954 (meaning of "subject to negative resolution") shall apply as if the power to make the rules were conferred by an Act of the Northern Ireland Assembly.

(8)   No order may be made by a Northern Ireland department under section 7(11) unless a draft of the order has been laid before, and approved by, the Northern Ireland Assembly.

Notes
Initial Commencement
Royal Assent
Royal Assent: 9 November 1998: see s 22(2).

21 Interpretation, etc

(1)   In this Act—

"amend" includes repeal and apply (with or without modifications);

"the appropriate Minister" means the Minister of the Crown having charge of the appropriate authorised government department (within the meaning of the Crown Proceedings Act 1947);

"the Commission" means the European Commission of Human Rights;

"the Convention" means the Convention for the Protection of Human Rights and Fundamental Freedoms, agreed by the Council of Europe at Rome on 4th November 1950 as it has effect for the time being in relation to the United Kingdom;

"declaration of incompatibility" means a declaration under section 4;

"Minister of the Crown" has the same meaning as in the Ministers of the Crown Act 1975;

"Northern Ireland Minister" includes the First Minister and the deputy First Minister in Northern Ireland;

"primary legislation" means any—

    (a) public general Act;

    (b) local and personal Act;

    (c) private Act;

    (d) Measure of the Church Assembly;

    (e) Measure of the General Synod of the Church of England;

    (f) Order in Council—

        (i) made in exercise of Her Majesty's Royal Prerogative;

        (ii) made under section 38(1)(a) of the Northern Ireland Constitution Act 1973 or the corresponding provision of the Northern Ireland Act 1998; or

        (iii) amending an Act of a kind mentioned in paragraph (a), (b) or (c);

and includes an order or other instrument of made under primary legislation (otherwise than by the National Assembly for Wales, a member of the Scottish Executive, a Northern Ireland Minister or a Northern Ireland department) to the extent to which it operates to bring one or more provisions of that legislation into force or amends any primary legislation;

"the First Protocol" means the protocol to the Convention agreed at Paris on 20th March 1952;

"the Sixth Protocol" means the protocol to the Convention agreed at Strasbourg on 28th April 1983;

"the Eleventh Protocol" means the protocol to the Convention (restructuring the control machinery established by the Convention) agreed at Strasbourg on 11th May 1994;

"remedial order" means an order under section 10;

"subordinate legislation" means any—

    (a) Order in Council other than one—

        (i) made in exercise of Her Majesty's Royal Prerogative;

        (ii) made under section 38(1)(a) of the Northern Ireland Constitution Act 1973 or the corresponding provision of the Northern Ireland Act 1998; or

      (iii) amending an Act of a kind mentioned in the definition of primary legislation;

  (b) Act of the Scottish Parliament;

  (c) Act of the Parliament of Northern Ireland;

  (d) Measure of the Assembly established under section 1 of the Northern Ireland Assembly Act 1973;

  (e) Act of the Northern Ireland Assembly;

  (f) order, rules, regulations, scheme, warrant, byelaw or other instrument made under primary legislation (except to the extent to which it operates to bring one or more provisions of that legislation into force or amends any primary legislation);

  (g) order, rules, regulations, scheme, warrant, byelaw or other instrument made under legislation mentioned in paragraph (b), (c), (d) or (e) or made under an Order in Council applying only to Northern Ireland;

  (h) order, rules, regulations, scheme, warrant, byelaw or other instrument made by a member of the Scottish Executive, a Northern Ireland Minister or a Northern Ireland department in exercise of prerogative or other executive functions of Her Majesty which are exercisable by such a person on behalf of Her Majesty;

"transferred matters" has the same meaning as in the Northern Ireland Act 1998; and

"tribunal" means any tribunal in which legal proceedings may be brought.

(2)   The references in paragraphs (b) and (c) of section 2(1) to Articles are to Articles of the Convention as they had effect immediately before the coming into force of the Eleventh Protocol.

(3)   The reference in paragraph (d) of section 2(1) to Article 46 includes a reference to Articles 32 and 54 of the Convention as they had effect immediately before the coming into force of the Eleventh Protocol.

(4)   The references in section 2(1) to a report or decision of the Commission or a decision of the Committee of Ministers include references to a report or decision made as provided by paragraphs 3, 4 and 6 of Article 5 of the Eleventh Protocol (transitional provisions).

(5)   Any liability under the Army Act 1955, the Air Force Act 1955 or the Naval Discipline Act 1957 to suffer death for an offence is replaced by a liability to imprisonment for life or any less punishment authorised by those Acts; and those Acts shall accordingly have effect with the necessary modifications.

Notes
Initial Commencement
Royal Assent
Sub-s (5): Royal Assent: 9 November 1998: see s 22(2).
To be appointed
Sub-ss (1)–(4): To be appointed: see s 22(3).

22   Short title, commencement, application and extent

(1)   This Act may be cited as the Human Rights Act 1998.

(2)   Sections 18, 20 and 21(5) and this section come into force on the passing of this Act.

(3)   The other provisions of this Act come into force on such day as the Secretary of State may by order appoint; and different days may be appointed for different purposes

(4)   Paragraph (b) of subsection (1) of section 7 applies to proceedings brought by or at the instigation of a public authority whenever the act in question took place; but otherwise that subsection does not apply to an act taking place before the coming into force of that section.

(5)   This Act binds the Crown.

(6)   This Act extends to Northern Ireland.

(7)   Section 21(5), so far as it relates to any provision contained in the Army Act 1955, the Air Force Act 1955 or the Naval Discipline Act 1957, extends to any place to which that provision extends.

Notes
Initial Commencement
Royal Assent
Royal Assent: 9 November 1998: see s 22(2).

SCHEDULE 1
The Articles

Section 1(3)

Part I
The Convention

Rights and Freedoms

Article 2
Right to life

1

Everyone's right to life shall be protected by law. No one shall be deprived of his life intentionally save in the execution of a sentence of a court following his conviction of a crime for which this penalty is provided by law.

2

Deprivation of life shall not be regarded as inflicted in contravention of this Article when it results from the use of force which is no more than absolutely necessary:
(a) in defence of any person from unlawful violence;
(b) in order to effect a lawful arrest or to prevent the escape of a person lawfully detained;
(c) in action lawfully taken for the purpose of quelling a riot or insurrection.

Article 3
Prohibition of torture

No one shall be subjected to torture or to inhuman or degrading treatment or punishment.

Article 4
Prohibition of slavery and forced labour

1

No one shall be held in slavery or servitude.

2

No one shall be required to perform forced or compulsory labour.

3

For the purpose of this Article the term "forced or compulsory labour" shall not include:
(a) any work required to be done in the ordinary course of detention imposed according to the provisions of Article 5 of this Convention or during conditional release from such detention;
(b) any service of a military character or, in case of conscientious objectors in countries where they are recognised, service exacted instead of compulsory military service;
(c) any service exacted in case of an emergency or calamity threatening the life or well-being of the community;
(d)   any work or service which forms part of normal civic obligations.

Article 5
Right to liberty and security

1

Everyone has the right to liberty and security of person. No one shall be deprived of his liberty save in the following cases and in accordance with a procedure prescribed by law:
(a) the lawful detention of a person after conviction by a competent court;
(b) the lawful arrest or detention of a person for non-compliance with the lawful order of a court or in order to secure the fulfilment of any obligation prescribed by law;
(c) the lawful arrest or detention of a person effected for the purpose of bringing him before the competent legal authority on reasonable suspicion of having committed an offence or when it is reasonably considered necessary to prevent his committing an offence or fleeing after having done so;
(d) the detention of a minor by lawful order for the purpose of educational supervision or his lawful detention for the purpose of bringing him before the competent legal authority;
(e) the lawful detention of persons for the prevention of the spreading of infectious diseases, of persons of unsound mind, alcoholics or drug addicts or vagrants;

(f) the lawful arrest or detention of a person to prevent his effecting an unauthorised entry into the country or of a person against whom action is being taken with a view to deportation or extradition.

2

Everyone who is arrested shall be informed promptly, in a language which he understands, of the reasons for his arrest and of any charge against him.

3

Everyone arrested or detained in accordance with the provisions of paragraph 1(c) of this Article shall be brought promptly before a judge or other officer authorised by law to exercise judicial power and shall be entitled to trial within a reasonable time or to release pending trial. Release may be conditioned by guarantees to appear for trial.

4

Everyone who is deprived of his liberty by arrest or detention shall be entitled to take proceedings by which the lawfulness of his detention shall be decided speedily by a court and his release ordered if the detention is not lawful.

5

Everyone who has been the victim of arrest or detention in contravention of the provisions of this Article shall have an enforceable right to compensation.

Article 6
Right to a fair trial

1

In the determination of his civil rights and obligations or of any criminal charge against him, everyone is entitled to a fair and public hearing within a reasonable time by an independent and impartial tribunal established by law. Judgment shall be pronounced publicly but the press and public may be excluded from all or part of the trial in the interest of morals, public order or national security in a democratic society, where the interests of juveniles or the protection of the private life of the parties so require, or to the extent strictly necessary in the opinion of the court in special circumstances where publicity would prejudice the interests of justice.

2

Everyone charged with a criminal offence shall be presumed innocent until proved guilty according to law.

3

Everyone charged with a criminal offence has the following minimum rights:
(a) to be informed promptly, in a language which he understands and in detail, of the nature and cause of the accusation against him;

(b) to have adequate time and facilities for the preparation of his defence;
(c) to defend himself in person or through legal assistance of his own choosing or, if he has not sufficient means to pay for legal assistance, to be given it free when the interests of justice so require;
(d) to examine or have examined witnesses against him and to obtain the attendance and examination of witnesses on his behalf under the same conditions as witnesses against him;
(e) to have the free assistance of an interpreter if he cannot understand or speak the language used in court.

Article 7
No punishment without law

1

No one shall be held guilty of any criminal offence on account of any act or omission which did not constitute a criminal offence under national or international law at the time when it was committed. Nor shall a heavier penalty be imposed than the one that was applicable at the time the criminal offence was committed.

2

This Article shall not prejudice the trial and punishment of any person for any act or omission which, at the time when it was committed, was criminal according to the general principles of law recognised by civilised nations.

Article 8
Right to respect for private and family life

1

Everyone has the right to respect for his private and family life, his home and his correspondence.

2

There shall be no interference by a public authority with the exercise of this right except such as is in accordance with the law and is necessary in a democratic society in the interests of national security, public safety or the economic well-being of the country, for the prevention of disorder or crime, for the protection of health or morals, or for the protection of the rights and freedoms of others.

Article 9
Freedom of thought, conscience and religion

1

Everyone has the right to freedom of thought, conscience and religion; this right includes freedom to change his religion or belief and freedom, either alone or in community with others and in public or private, to manifest his religion or belief, in worship, teaching, practice and observance.

2

Freedom to manifest one's religion or beliefs shall be subject only to such limitations as are prescribed by law and are necessary in a democratic society in the interests of public safety, for the protection of public order, health or morals, or for the protection of the rights and freedoms of others.

Article 10
Freedom of expression

1

Everyone has the right to freedom of expression. This right shall include freedom to hold opinions and to receive and impart information and ideas without interference by public authority and regardless of frontiers. This Article shall not prevent States from requiring the licensing of broadcasting, television or cinema enterprises.

2

The exercise of these freedoms, since it carries with it duties and responsibilities, may be subject to such formalities, conditions, restrictions or penalties as are prescribed by law and are necessary in a democratic society, in the interests of national security, territorial integrity or public safety, for the prevention of disorder or crime, for the protection of health or morals, for the protection of the reputation or rights of others, for preventing the disclosure of information received in confidence, or for maintaining the authority and impartiality of the judiciary.

Article 11
Freedom of assembly and association

1

Everyone has the right to freedom of peaceful assembly and to freedom of association with others, including the right to form and to join trade unions for the protection of his interests

2

No restrictions shall be placed on the exercise of these rights other than such as are prescribed by law and are necessary in a democratic society in the interests of national security or public safety, for the prevention of disorder or crime, for the protection of health or morals or for the protection of the rights and freedoms of others. This Article shall not prevent the imposition of lawful restrictions on the exercise of these rights by members of the armed forces, of the police or of the administration of the State.

Article 12
Right to marry

Men and women of marriageable age have the right to marry and to found a family, according to the national laws governing the exercise of this right.

Article 14
Prohibition of discrimination

The enjoyment of the rights and freedoms set forth in this Convention shall be secured without discrimination on any ground such as sex, race, colour, language, religion, political or other opinion, national or social origin, association with a national minority, property, birth or other status.

Article 16
Restrictions on political activity of aliens

Nothing in Articles 10, 11 and 14 shall be regarded as preventing the High Contracting Parties from imposing restrictions on the political activity of aliens.

Article 17
Prohibition of abuse of rights

Nothing in this Convention may be interpreted as implying for any State, group or person any right to engage in any activity or perform any act aimed at the destruction of any of the rights and freedoms set forth herein or at their limitation to a greater extent than is provided for in the Convention.

Article 18
Limitation on use of restrictions on rights

The restrictions permitted under this Convention to the said rights and freedoms shall not be applied for any purpose other than those for which they have been prescribed.

Notes
Initial Commencement
To be appointed
To be appointed: see s 22(3).

Part II
The First Protocol

Article 1
Protection of property

Every natural or legal person is entitled to the peaceful enjoyment of his possessions. No one shall be deprived of his possessions except in the public interest and subject to the conditions provided for by law and by the general principles of international law.

The preceding provisions shall not, however, in any way impair the right of a State to enforce such laws as it deems necessary to control the use of property in accordance with the general interest or to secure the payment of taxes or other contributions or penalties.

Article 2
Right to education

No person shall be denied the right to education. In the exercise of any functions which it assumes in relation to education and to teaching, the State shall respect the right of parents to ensure such education and teaching in conformity with their own religious and philosophical convictions.

Article 3
Right to free elections

The High Contracting Parties undertake to hold free elections at reasonable intervals by secret ballot, under conditions which will ensure the free expression of the opinion of the people in the choice of the legislature.

Notes
Initial Commencement
To be appointed
To be appointed: see s 22(3).

Part III
The Sixth Protocol

Article 1
Abolition of the death penalty

The death penalty shall be abolished. No one shall be condemned to such penalty or executed.

Article 2
Death penalty in time of war

A State may make provision in its law for the death penalty in respect of acts committed in time of war or of imminent threat of war; such penalty shall be applied only in the instances laid down in the law and in accordance with its provisions. The State shall communicate to the Secretary General of the Council of Europe the relevant provisions of that law.

Notes
Initial Commencement
To be appointed
To be appointed: see s 22(3).

SCHEDULE 2
Remedial Orders

Section 10

Orders

1

(1)   A remedial order may—

(a) contain such incidental, supplemental, consequential or transitional provision as the person making it considers appropriate;
(b) be made so as to have effect from a date earlier than that on which it is made;
(c) make provision for the delegation of specific functions;
(d) make different provision for different cases.

(2)   The power conferred by sub-paragraph (1)(a) includes—
(a) power to amend primary legislation (including primary legislation other than that which contains the incompatible provision); and
(b) power to amend or revoke subordinate legislation (including subordinate legislation other than that which contains the incompatible provision).

(3)   A remedial order may be made so as to have the same extent as the legislation which it affects.

(4)   No person is to be guilty of an offence solely as a result of the retrospective effect of a remedial order.

Procedure

2

No remedial order may be made unless—
(a) a draft of the order has been approved by a resolution of each House of Parliament made after the end of the period of 60 days beginning with the day on which the draft was laid; or
(b) it is declared in the order that it appears to the person making it that, because of the urgency of the matter, it is necessary to make the order without a draft being so approved.

Orders laid in draft

3

(1)   No draft may be laid under paragraph 2(a) unless—
(a) the person proposing to make the order has laid before Parliament a document which contains a draft of the proposed order and the required information; and
(b) the period of 60 days, beginning with the day on which the document required by this sub-paragraph was laid, has ended.

(2)   If representations have been made during that period, the draft laid under paragraph 2(a) must be accompanied by a statement containing—
(a) a summary of the representations; and
(b) if, as a result of the representations, the proposed order has been changed, details of the changes.

Urgent cases

4

(1)   If a remedial order ("the original order") is made without being approved in draft, the person making it must lay it before Parliament, accompanied by the required information, after it is made.

(2)   If representations have been made during the period of 60 days beginning with the day on which the original order was made, the person making it must (after the end of that period) lay before Parliament a statement containing—
(a) a summary of the representations; and
(b) if, as a result of the representations, he considers it appropriate to make changes to the original order, details of the changes.

(3)   If sub-paragraph (2)(b) applies, the person making the statement must—
(a) make a further remedial order replacing the original order; and
(b) lay the replacement order before Parliament.

(4)   If, at the end of the period of 120 days beginning with the day on which the original order was made, a resolution has not been passed by each House approving the original or replacement order, the order ceases to have effect (but without that affecting anything previously done under either order or the power to make a fresh remedial order).

Definitions

5

In this Schedule—
"representations" means representations about a remedial order (or proposed remedial order) made to the person making (or proposing to make) it and includes any relevant Parliamentary report or resolution; and
"required information" means—
(a) an explanation of the incompatibility which the order (or proposed order) seeks to remove, including particulars of the relevant declaration, finding or order; and
(b) a statement of the reasons for proceeding under section 10 and for making an order in those terms.

Calculating periods

6

In calculating any period for the purposes of this Schedule, no account is to be taken of any time during which—
(a) Parliament is dissolved or prorogued; or
(b) both Houses are adjourned for more than four days.

Notes
Initial Commencement

To be appointed
To be appointed: see s 22(3).

SCHEDULE 3
Derogation and Reservation

Sections 14 and 15

Part I
Derogation

The 1988 notification

The United Kingdom Permanent Representative to the Council of Europe presents his compliments to the Secretary General of the Council, and has the honour to convey the following information in order to ensure compliance with the obligations of Her Majesty's Government in the United Kingdom under Article 15(3) of the Convention for the Protection of Human Rights and Fundamental Freedoms signed at Rome on 4 November 1950.

There have been in the United Kingdom in recent years campaigns of organised terrorism connected with the affairs of Northern Ireland which have manifested themselves in activities which have included repeated murder, attempted murder, maiming, intimidation and violent civil disturbance and in bombing and fire raising which have resulted in death, injury and widespread destruction of property. As a result, a public emergency within the meaning of Article 15(1) of the Convention exists in the United Kingdom.

The Government found it necessary in 1974 to introduce and since then, in cases concerning persons reasonably suspected of involvement in terrorism connected with the affairs of Northern Ireland, or of certain offences under the legislation, who have been detained for 48 hours, to exercise powers enabling further detention without charge, for periods of up to five days, on the authority of the Secretary of State. These powers are at present to be found in Section 12 of the Prevention of Terrorism (Temporary Provisions) Act 1984, Article 9 of the Prevention of Terrorism (Supplemental Temporary Provisions) Order 1984 and Article 10 of the Prevention of Terrorism (Supplemental Temporary Provisions) (Northern Ireland) Order 1984.

Section 12 of the Prevention of Terrorism (Temporary Provisions) Act 1984 provides for a person whom a constable has arrested on reasonable grounds of suspecting him to be guilty of an offence under Section 1, 9 or 10 of the Act, or to be or to have been involved in terrorism connected with the affairs of Northern Ireland, to be detained in right of the arrest for up to 48 hours and thereafter, where the Secretary of State extends the detention period, for up to a further five days. Section 12 substantially re-enacted Section 12 of the Prevention of Terrorism (Temporary Provisions) Act 1976 which, in turn, substantially re-enacted Section 7 of the Prevention of Terrorism (Temporary Provisions) Act 1974.

Article 10 of the Prevention of Terrorism (Supplemental Temporary Provisions) (Northern Ireland) Order 1984 (SI 1984/417) and Article 9 of the Prevention of

Terrorism (Supplemental Temporary Provisions) Order 1984 (SI 1984/418) were both made under Sections 13 and 14 of and Schedule 3 to the 1984 Act and substantially re-enacted powers of detention in Orders made under the 1974 and 1976 Acts. A person who is being examined under Article 4 of either Order on his arrival in, or on seeking to leave, Northern Ireland or Great Britain for the purpose of determining whether he is or has been involved in terrorism connected with the affairs of Northern Ireland, or whether there are grounds for suspecting that he has committed an offence under Section 9 of the 1984 Act, may be detained under Article 9 or 10, as appropriate, pending the conclusion of his examination. The period of this examination may exceed 12 hours if an examining officer has reasonable grounds for suspecting him to be or to have been involved in acts of terrorism connected with the affairs of Northern Ireland.

Where such a person is detained under the said Article 9 or 10 he may be detained for up to 48 hours on the authority of an examining officer and thereafter, where the Secretary of State extends the detention period, for up to a further five days.

In its judgment of 29 November 1988 in the Case of *Brogan and Others*, the European Court of Human Rights held that there had been a violation of Article 5(3) in respect of each of the applicants, all of whom had been detained under Section 12 of the 1984 Act. The Court held that even the shortest of the four periods of detention concerned, namely four days and six hours, fell outside the constraints as to time permitted by the first part of Article 5(3). In addition, the Court held that there had been a violation of Article 5(5) in the case of each applicant.

Following this judgment, the Secretary of State for the Home Department informed Parliament on 6 December 1988 that, against the background of the terrorist campaign, and the over-riding need to bring terrorists to justice, the Government did not believe that the maximum period of detention should be reduced. He informed Parliament that the Government were examining the matter with a view to responding to the judgment. On 22 December 1988, the Secretary of State further informed Parliament that it remained the Government's wish, if it could be achieved, to find a judicial process under which extended detention might be reviewed and where appropriate authorised by a judge or other judicial officer. But a further period of reflection and consultation was necessary before the Government could bring forward a firm and final view.

Since the judgment of 29 November 1988 as well as previously, the Government have found it necessary to continue to exercise, in relation to terrorism connected with the affairs of Northern Ireland, the powers described above enabling further detention without charge for periods of up to 5 days, on the authority of the Secretary of State, to the extent strictly required by the exigencies of the situation to enable necessary enquiries and investigations properly to be completed in order to decide whether criminal proceedings should be instituted. To the extent that the exercise of these powers may be inconsistent with the obligations imposed by the Convention the Government has availed itself of the right of derogation conferred by Article 15(1) of the Convention and will continue to do so until further notice.

Dated 23 December 1988.

The 1989 notification

The United Kingdom Permanent Representative to the Council of Europe presents his compliments to the Secretary General of the Council, and has the honour to convey the following information.

In his communication to the Secretary General of 23 December 1988, reference was made to the introduction and exercise of certain powers under section 12 of the Prevention of Terrorism (Temporary Provisions) Act 1984, Article 9 of the Prevention of Terrorism (Supplemental Temporary Provisions) Order 1984 and Article 10 of the Prevention of Terrorism (Supplemental Temporary Provisions) (Northern Ireland) Order 1984.

These provisions have been replaced by section 14 of and paragraph 6 of Schedule 5 to the Prevention of Terrorism (Temporary Provisions) Act 1989, which make comparable provision. They came into force on 22 March 1989. A copy of these provisions is enclosed.

The United Kingdom Permanent Representative avails himself of this opportunity to renew to the Secretary General the assurance of his highest consideration.

23 March 1989.

Notes
Initial Commencement
To be appointed
To be appointed: see s 22(3).

Part II
Reservation

At the time of signing the present (First) Protocol, I declare that, in view of certain provisions of the Education Acts in the United Kingdom, the principle affirmed in the second sentence of Article 2 is accepted by the United Kingdom only so far as it is compatible with the provision of efficient instruction and training, and the avoidance of unreasonable public expenditure.

Dated 20 March 1952. Made by the United Kingdom Permanent Representative to the Council of Europe.

Notes
Initial Commencement
To be appointed
To be appointed: see s 22(3).

SCHEDULE 4
Judicial Pensions

Section 18(6)

Duty to make orders about pensions

1

(1)   The appropriate Minister must by order make provision with respect to pensions payable to or in respect of any holder of a judicial office who serves as an ECHR judge.

(2)   A pensions order must include such provision as the Minister making it considers is necessary to secure that—

(a) an ECHR judge who was, immediately before his appointment as an ECHR judge, a member of a judicial pension scheme is entitled to remain as a member of that scheme;

(b) the terms on which he remains a member of the scheme are those which would have been applicable had he not been appointed as an ECHR judge; and

(c) entitlement to benefits payable in accordance with the scheme continues to be determined as if, while serving as an ECHR judge, his salary was that which would (but for section 18(4)) have been payable to him in respect of his continuing service as the holder of his judicial office.

Contributions

2

A pensions order may, in particular, make provision—

(a) for any contributions which are payable by a person who remains a member of a scheme as a result of the order, and which would otherwise be payable by deduction from his salary, to be made otherwise than by deduction from his salary as an ECHR judge; and

(b) for such contributions to be collected in such manner as may be determined by the administrators of the scheme.

Amendments of other enactments

3

A pensions order may amend any provision of, or made under, a pensions Act in such manner and to such extent as the Minister making the order considers necessary or expedient to ensure the proper administration of any scheme to which it relates.

Definitions

4

In this Schedule—

"appropriate Minister" means—

    (a) in relation to any judicial office whose jurisdiction is exercisable exclusively in relation to Scotland, the Secretary of State; and

    (b) otherwise, the Lord Chancellor;

"ECHR judge" means the holder of a judicial office who is serving as a judge of the Court;

"judicial pension scheme" means a scheme established by and in accordance with a pensions Act;

"pensions Act" means—

    (a) the County Courts Act (Northern Ireland) 1959;

    (b) the Sheriffs' Pensions (Scotland) Act 1961;

    (c) the Judicial Pensions Act 1981; or

    (d) the Judicial Pensions and Retirement Act 1993; and

"pensions order" means an order made under paragraph 1.

Notes

Initial Commencement
To be appointed
To be appointed: see s 22(3).

Convention for the Protection of Human Rights and Fundamental Freedoms

Rome, 4.XI.1950

"The text of the Convention had been amended according to the provisions of Protocol No 3 (ETS No 45), which entered into force on 21 September 1970, of Protocol No 5 (ETS No 55), which entered into force on 20 December 1971 and of Protocol No 8 (ETS No 118), which entered into force on 1 January 1990, and comprised also the text of Protocol No 2 (ETS No 44) which, in accordance with Article 5, paragraph 3 thereof, had been an integral part of the Convention since its entry into force on 21 September 1970. All provisions which had been amended or added by these Protocols are replaced by Protocol No 11 (ETS No 155), as from the date of its entry into force on 1 November 1998. As from that date, Protocol n° 9 (ETS No 140), which entered into force on 1 October 1994, is repealed and Protocol n° 10 (ETS No 146), which has not entered into force, has lost its purpose."

The governments signatory hereto, being members of the Council of Europe,

Considering the Universal Declaration of Human Rights proclaimed by the General Assembly of the United Nations on 10th December 1948;

Considering that this Declaration aims at securing the universal and effective recognition and observance of the Rights therein declared;

Considering that the aim of the Council of Europe is the achievement of greater unity between its members and that one of the methods by which that aim is to be pursued is the maintenance and further realisation of human rights and fundamental freedoms;

Reaffirming their profound belief in those fundamental freedoms which are the foundation of justice and peace in the world and are best maintained on the one hand by an effective political democracy and on the other by a common understanding and observance of the human rights upon which they depend;

Being resolved, as the governments of European countries which are like-minded and have a common heritage of political traditions, ideals, freedom and the rule of law, to take the first steps for the collective enforcement of certain of the rights stated in the Universal Declaration,

Have agreed as follows:

Article 1[1] – Obligation to respect human rights

The High Contracting Parties shall secure to everyone within their jurisdiction the rights and freedoms defined in Section I of this Convention.

Section I
Rights and freedoms

Article 2[1] – Right to life

1   Everyone's right to life shall be protected by law. No one shall be deprived of his life intentionally save in the execution of a sentence of a court following his conviction of a crime for which this penalty is provided by law.

2   Deprivation of life shall not be regarded as inflicted in contravention of this article when it results from the use of force which is no more than absolutely necessary:
(a) in defence of any person from unlawful violence;
(b) in order to effect a lawful arrest or to prevent the escape of a person lawfully detained;
(c) in action lawfully taken for the purpose of quelling a riot or insurrection.

Article 3[1] – Prohibition of torture

No one shall be subjected to torture or to inhuman or degrading treatment or punishment.

Article 4[1] – Prohibition of slavery and forced labour

1   No one shall be held in slavery or servitude.

2   No one shall be required to perform forced or compulsory labour.

3   For the purpose of this article the term "forced or compulsory labour" shall not include:
(a) any work required to be done in the ordinary course of detention imposed according to the provisions of Article 5 of this Convention or during conditional release from such detention;
(b) any service of a military character or, in case of conscientious objectors in countries where they are recognised, service exacted instead of compulsory military service;
(c) any service exacted in case of an emergency or calamity threatening the life or well-being of the community;
(d) any work or service which forms part of normal civic obligations.

Article 5[1] – Right to liberty and security

1   Everyone has the right to liberty and security of person. No one shall be deprived of his liberty save in the following cases and in accordance with a procedure prescribed by law:
(a) the lawful detention of a person after conviction by a competent court;
(b) the lawful arrest or detention of a person for non- compliance with the lawful order of a court or in order to secure the fulfilment of any obligation prescribed by law;
(c) the lawful arrest or detention of a person effected for the purpose of bringing him before the competent legal authority on reasonable suspicion of having committed an offence or when it is reasonably considered necessary to prevent his committing an offence or fleeing after having done so;

(d) the detention of a minor by lawful order for the purpose of educational supervision or his lawful detention for the purpose of bringing him before the competent legal authority;
(e) the lawful detention of persons for the prevention of the spreading of infectious diseases, of persons of unsound mind, alcoholics or drug addicts or vagrants;
(f) the lawful arrest or detention of a person to prevent his effecting an unauthorised entry into the country or of a person against whom action is being taken with a view to deportation or extradition.

2   Everyone who is arrested shall be informed promptly, in a language which he understands, of the reasons for his arrest and of any charge against him.

3   Everyone arrested or detained in accordance with the provisions of paragraph 1.c of this article shall be brought promptly before a judge or other officer authorised by law to exercise judicial power and shall be entitled to trial within a reasonable time or to release pending trial. Release may be conditioned by guarantees to appear for trial.

4   Everyone who is deprived of his liberty by arrest or detention shall be entitled to take proceedings by which the lawfulness of his detention shall be decided speedily by a court and his release ordered if the detention is not lawful.

5   Everyone who has been the victim of arrest or detention in contravention of the provisions of this article shall have an enforceable right to compensation.

Article 6[1] – Right to a fair trial

1   In the determination of his civil rights and obligations or of any criminal charge against him, everyone is entitled to a fair and public hearing within a reasonable time by an independent and impartial tribunal established by law. Judgment shall be pronounced publicly but the press and public may be excluded from all or part of the trial in the interests of morals, public order or national security in a democratic society, where the interests of juveniles or the protection of the private life of the parties so require, or to the extent strictly necessary in the opinion of the court in special circumstances where publicity would prejudice the interests of justice.

2   Everyone charged with a criminal offence shall be presumed innocent until proved guilty according to law.

3   Everyone charged with a criminal offence has the following minimum rights:
(a) to be informed promptly, in a language which he understands and in detail, of the nature and cause of the accusation against him;
(b) to have adequate time and facilities for the preparation of his defence;
(c) to defend himself in person or through legal assistance of his own choosing or, if he has not sufficient means to pay for legal assistance, to be given it free when the interests of justice so require;
(d) to examine or have examined witnesses against him and to obtain the attendance and examination of witnesses on his behalf under the same conditions as witnesses against him;
(e) to have the free assistance of an interpreter if he cannot understand or speak the language used in court.

Article 7[1] – No punishment without law

1   No one shall be held guilty of any criminal offence on account of any act or omission which did not constitute a criminal offence under national or international law at the time when it was committed. Nor shall a heavier penalty be imposed than the one that was applicable at the time the criminal offence was committed.

2   This article shall not prejudice the trial and punishment of any person for any act or omission which, at the time when it was committed, was criminal according to the general principles of law recognised by civilised nations.

Article 8[1] – Right to respect for private and family life

1   Everyone has the right to respect for his private and family life, his home and his correspondence.

2   There shall be no interference by a public authority with the exercise of this right except such as is in accordance with the law and is necessary in a democratic society in the interests of national security, public safety or the economic well-being of the country, for the prevention of disorder or crime, for the protection of health or morals, or for the protection of the rights and freedoms of others.

Article 9[1] – Freedom of thought, conscience and religion

1   Everyone has the right to freedom of thought, conscience and religion; this right includes freedom to change his religion or belief and freedom, either alone or in community with others and in public or private, to manifest his religion or belief, in worship, teaching, practice and observance.

2   Freedom to manifest one's religion or beliefs shall be subject only to such limitations as are prescribed by law and are necessary in a democratic society in the interests of public safety, for the protection of public order, health or morals, or for the protection of the rights and freedoms of others.

Article 10[1] – Freedom of expression

1   Everyone has the right to freedom of expression. This right shall include freedom to hold opinions and to receive and impart information and ideas without interference by public authority and regardless of frontiers. This article shall not prevent States from requiring the licensing of broadcasting, television or cinema enterprises.

2   The exercise of these freedoms, since it carries with it duties and responsibilities, may be subject to such formalities, conditions, restrictions or penalties as are prescribed by law and are necessary in a democratic society, in the interests of national security, territorial integrity or public safety, for the prevention of disorder or crime, for the protection of health or morals, for the protection of the reputation or rights of others, for preventing the disclosure of information received in confidence, or for maintaining the authority and impartiality of the judiciary.

Article 11[1] – Freedom of assembly and association

1   Everyone has the right to freedom of peaceful assembly and to freedom of association with others, including the right to form and to join trade unions for the protection of his interests.

2   No restrictions shall be placed on the exercise of these rights other than such as are prescribed by law and are necessary in a democratic society in the interests of national security or public safety, for the prevention of disorder or crime, for the protection of health or morals or for the protection of the rights and freedoms of others. This article shall not prevent the imposition of lawful restrictions on the exercise of these rights by members of the armed forces, of the police or of the administration of the State.

Article 12[1] – Right to marry

Men and women of marriageable age have the right to marry and to found a family, according to the national laws governing the exercise of this right.

Article 13[1] – Right to an effective remedy

Everyone whose rights and freedoms as set forth in this Convention are violated shall have an effective remedy before a national authority notwithstanding that the violation has been committed by persons acting in an official capacity.

Article 14[1] – Prohibition of discrimination

The enjoyment of the rights and freedoms set forth in this Convention shall be secured without discrimination on any ground such as sex, race, colour, language, religion, political or other opinion, national or social origin, association with a national minority, property, birth or other status.

Article 15[1] – Derogation in time of emergency

1   In time of war or other public emergency threatening the life of the nation any High Contracting Party may take measures derogating from its obligations under this Convention to the extent strictly required by the exigencies of the situation, provided that such measures are not inconsistent with its other obligations under international law.

2   No derogation from Article 2, except in respect of deaths resulting from lawful acts of war, or from Articles 3, 4 (paragraph 1) and 7 shall be made under this provision.

3   Any High Contracting Party availing itself of this right of derogation shall keep the Secretary General of the Council of Europe fully informed of the measures which it has taken and the reasons therefor. It shall also inform the Secretary General of the Council of Europe when such measures have ceased to operate and the provisions of the Convention are again being fully executed.

Article 16[1] – Restrictions on political activity of aliens

Nothing in Articles 10, 11 and 14 shall be regarded as preventing the High Contracting Parties from imposing restrictions on the political activity of aliens.

Article 17[1] – Prohibition of abuse of rights

Nothing in this Convention may be interpreted as implying for any State, group or person any right to engage in any activity or perform any act aimed at the destruction of any of the rights and freedoms set forth herein or at their limitation to a greater extent than is provided for in the Convention.

Article 18[1] – Limitation on use of restrictions on rights

The restrictions permitted under this Convention to the said rights and freedoms shall not be applied for any purpose other than those for which they have been prescribed.

Section II
European Court of Human Rights[2]

Article 19 – Establishment of the Court

To ensure the observance of the engagements undertaken by the High Contracting Parties in the Convention and the Protocols thereto, there shall be set up a European Court of Human Rights, hereinafter referred to as "the Court". It shall function on a permanent basis.

Article 20 – Number of judges

The Court shall consist of a number of judges equal to that of the High Contracting Parties.

Article 21 – Criteria for office

1   The judges shall be of high moral character and must either possess the qualifications required for appointment to high judicial office or be jurisconsults of recognised competence.

2   The judges shall sit on the Court in their individual capacity.

3   During their term of office the judges shall not engage in any activity which is incompatible with their independence, impartiality or with the demands of a full-time office; all questions arising from the application of this paragraph shall be decided by the Court.

Article 22 – Election of judges

1   The judges shall be elected by the Parliamentary Assembly with respect to each High Contracting Party by a majority of votes cast from a list of three candidates nominated by the High Contracting Party.

2   The same procedure shall be followed to complete the Court in the event of the accession of new High Contracting Parties and in filling casual vacancies.

Article 23 – Terms of office

1   The judges shall be elected for a period of six years. They may be re-elected. However, the terms of office of one-half of the judges elected at the first election shall expire at the end of three years.

2 The judges whose terms of office are to expire at the end of the initial period of three years shall be chosen by lot by the Secretary General of the Council of Europe immediately after their election.

3 In order to ensure that, as far as possible, the terms of office of one-half of the judges are renewed every three years, the Parliamentary Assembly may decide, before proceeding to any subsequent election, that the term or terms of office of one or more judges to be elected shall be for a period other than six years but not more than nine and not less than three years.

4 In cases where more than one term of office is involved and where the Parliamentary Assembly applies the preceding paragraph, the allocation of the terms of office shall be effected by a drawing of lots by the Secretary General of the Council of Europe immediately after the election.

5 A judge elected to replace a judge whose term of office has not expired shall hold office for the remainder of his predecessor's term.

6 The terms of office of judges shall expire when they reach the age of 70.

7 The judges shall hold office until replaced. They shall, however, continue to deal with such cases as they already have under consideration.

Article 24 – Dismissal

No judge may be dismissed from his office unless the other judges decide by a majority of two-thirds that he has ceased to fulfil the required conditions.

Article 25 – Registry and legal secretaries

The Court shall have a registry, the functions and organisation of which shall be laid down in the rules of the Court. The Court shall be assisted by legal secretaries.

Article 26 – Plenary Court

The plenary Court shall
(a) elect its President and one or two Vice-Presidents for a period of three years; they may be re-elected;
(b) set up Chambers, constituted for a fixed period of time;
(c) elect the Presidents of the Chambers of the Court; they may be re-elected;
(d) adopt the rules of the Court, and
(e) elect the Registrar and one or more Deputy Registrars.

Article 27 – Committees, Chambers and Grand Chamber

1 To consider cases brought before it, the Court shall sit in committees of three judges, in Chambers of seven judges and in a Grand Chamber of seventeen judges. The Court's Chambers shall set up committees for a fixed period of time.

2 There shall sit as an ex officio member of the Chamber and the Grand Chamber the judge elected in respect of the State Party concerned or, if there is none or if he is unable to sit, a person of its choice who shall sit in the capacity of judge.

3 The Grand Chamber shall also include the President of the Court, the Vice-Presidents, the Presidents of the Chambers and other judges chosen in accordance with the rules of the Court. When a case is referred to the Grand Chamber under Article 43, no judge from the Chamber which rendered the judgment shall sit in the Grand Chamber, with the exception of the President of the Chamber and the judge who sat in respect of the State Party concerned.

Article 28 – Declarations of inadmissibility by committees

A committee may, by a unanimous vote, declare inadmissible or strike out of its list of cases an application submitted under Article 34 where such a decision can be taken without further examination. The decision shall be final.

Article 29 – Decisions by Chambers on admissibility and merits

1 If no decision is taken under Article 28, a Chamber shall decide on the admissibility and merits of individual applications submitted under Article 34.

2 A Chamber shall decide on the admissibility and merits of inter-State applications submitted under Article 33.

3 The decision on admissibility shall be taken separately unless the Court, in exceptional cases, decides otherwise.

Article 30 – Relinquishment of jurisdiction to the Grand Chamber

Where a case pending before a Chamber raises a serious question affecting the interpretation of the Convention or the protocols thereto, or where the resolution of a question before the Chamber might have a result inconsistent with a judgment previously delivered by the Court, the Chamber may, at any time before it has rendered its judgment, relinquish jurisdiction in favour of the Grand Chamber, unless one of the parties to the case objects.

Article 31 – Powers of the Grand Chamber

The Grand Chamber shall
(a) determine applications submitted either under Article 33 or Article 34 when a Chamber has relinquished jurisdiction under Article 30 or when the case has been referred to it under Article 43; and
(b) consider requests for advisory opinions submitted under Article 47.

Article 32 – Jurisdiction of the Court

1 The jurisdiction of the Court shall extend to all matters concerning the interpretation and application of the Convention and the protocols thereto which are referred to it as provided in Articles 33, 34 and 47.

2 In the event of dispute as to whether the Court has jurisdiction, the Court shall decide.

Article 33 – Inter-State cases

Any High Contracting Party may refer to the Court any alleged breach of the provisions of the Convention and the protocols thereto by another High Contracting Party.

Article 34 – Individual applications

The Court may receive applications from any person, non-governmental organisation or group of individuals claiming to be the victim of a violation by one of the High Contracting Parties of the rights set forth in the Convention or the protocols thereto. The High Contracting Parties undertake not to hinder in any way the effective exercise of this right.

Article 35 – Admissibility criteria

1   The Court may only deal with the matter after all domestic remedies have been exhausted, according to the generally recognised rules of international law, and within a period of six months from the date on which the final decision was taken.

2   The Court shall not deal with any application submitted under Article 34 that
(a) is anonymous; or
(b) is substantially the same as a matter that has already been examined by the Court or has already been submitted to another procedure of international investigation or settlement and contains no relevant new information.

3   The Court shall declare inadmissible any individual application submitted under Article 34 which it considers incompatible with the provisions of the Convention or the protocols thereto, manifestly ill-founded, or an abuse of the right of application.

4   The Court shall reject any application which it considers inadmissible under this Article. It may do so at any stage of the proceedings.

Article 36 – Third party intervention

1   In all cases before a Chamber of the Grand Chamber, a High Contracting Party one of whose nationals is an applicant shall have the right to submit written comments and to take part in hearings.

2   The President of the Court may, in the interest of the proper administration of justice, invite any High Contracting Party which is not a party to the proceedings or any person concerned who is not the applicant to submit written comments or take part in hearings.

Article 37 – Striking out applications

1   The Court may at any stage of the proceedings decide to strike an application out of its list of cases where the circumstances lead to the conclusion that
(a) the applicant does not intend to pursue his application; or
(b) the matter has been resolved; or
(c) for any other reason established by the Court, it is no longer justified to continue the examination of the application.
However, the Court shall continue the examination of the application if respect for human rights as defined in the Convention and the protocols thereto so requires.

2   The Court may decide to restore an application to its list of cases if it considers that the circumstances justify such a course.

Article 38 – Examination of the case and friendly settlement proceedings

1   If the Court declares the application admissible, it shall

(a) pursue the examination of the case, together with the representatives of the parties, and if need be, undertake an investigation, for the effective conduct of which the States concerned shall furnish all necessary facilities;

(b) place itself at the disposal of the parties concerned with a view to securing a friendly settlement of the matter on the basis of respect for human rights as defined in the Convention and the protocols thereto.

2   Proceedings conducted under paragraph 1.b shall be confidential.

Article 39 – Finding of a friendly settlement

If a friendly settlement is effected, the Court shall strike the case out of its list by means of a decision which shall be confined to a brief statement of the facts and of the solution reached.

Article 40 – Public hearings and access to documents

1   Hearings shall be in public unless the Court in exceptional circumstances decides otherwise.

2   Documents deposited with the Registrar shall be accessible to the public unless the President of the Court decides otherwise.

Article 41 – Just satisfaction

If the Court finds that there has been a violation of the Convention or the protocols thereto, and if the internal law of the High Contracting Party concerned allows only partial reparation to be made, the Court shall, if necessary, afford just satisfaction to the injured party.

Article 42 – Judgments of Chambers

Judgments of Chambers shall become final in accordance with the provisions of Article 44, paragraph 2.

Article 43 – Referral to the Grand Chamber

1   Within a period of three months from the date of the judgment of the Chamber, any party to the case may, in exceptional cases, request that the case be referred to the Grand Chamber.

2   A panel of five judges of the Grand Chamber shall accept the request if the case raises a serious question affecting the interpretation or application of the Convention or the protocols thereto, or a serious issue of general importance.

3   If the panel accepts the request, the Grand Chamber shall decide the case by means of a judgment.

Article 44 – Final judgments

1 The judgment of the Grand Chamber shall be final.

2 The judgment of a Chamber shall become final
(a) when the parties declare that they will not request that the case be referred to the Grand Chamber; or
(b) three months after the date of the judgment, if reference of the case to the Grand Chamber has not been requested; or
(c) when the panel of the Grand Chamber rejects the request to refer under Article 43.

3 The final judgment shall be published.

Article 45 – Reasons for judgments and decisions

1 Reasons shall be given for judgments as well as for decisions declaring applications admissible or inadmissible.

2 If a judgment does not represent, in whole or in part, the unanimous opinion of the judges, any judge shall be entitled to deliver a separate opinion.

Article 46 – Binding force and execution of judgments

1 The High Contracting Parties undertake to abide by the final judgment of the Court in any case to which they are parties.

2 The final judgment of the Court shall be transmitted to the Committee of Ministers, which shall supervise its execution.

Article 47 – Advisory opinions

1 The Court may, at the request of the Committee of Ministers, give advisory opinions on legal questions concerning the interpretation of the Convention and the protocols thereto.

2 Such opinions shall not deal with any question relating to the content or scope of the rights or freedoms defined in Section I of the Convention and the protocols thereto, or with any other question which the Court or the Committee of Ministers might have to consider in consequence of any such proceedings as could be instituted in accordance with the Convention.

3 Decisions of the Committee of Ministers to request an advisory opinion of the Court shall require a majority vote of the representatives entitled to sit on the Committee.

Article 48 – Advisory jurisdiction of the Court

The Court shall decide whether a request for an advisory opinion submitted by the Committee of Ministers is within its competence as defined in Article 47.

Article 49 – Reasons for advisory opinions

1 Reasons shall be given for advisory opinions of the Court.

2 If the advisory opinion does not represent, in whole or in part, the unanimous opinion of the judges, any judge shall be entitled to deliver a separate opinion.

3 Advisory opinions of the Court shall be communicated to the Committee of Ministers.

Article 50 – Expenditure on the Court

The expenditure on the Court shall be borne by the Council of Europe.

Article 51 – Privileges and immunities of judges

The judges shall be entitled, during the exercise of their functions, to the privileges and immunities provided for in Article 40 of the Statute of the Council of Europe and in the agreements made thereunder.

Section III
Miscellaneous provisions[3, 1]

Article 52[1] – Inquiries by the Secretary General

On receipt of a request from the Secretary General of the Council of Europe any High Contracting Party shall furnish an explanation of the manner in which its internal law ensures the effective implementation of any of the provisions of the Convention.

Article 53[1] – Safeguard for existing human rights

Nothing in this Convention shall be construed as limiting or derogating from any of the human rights and fundamental freedoms which may be ensured under the laws of any High Contracting Party or under any other agreement to which it is a Party.

Article 54[1] – Powers of the Committee of Ministers

Nothing in this Convention shall prejudice the powers conferred on the Committee of Ministers by the Statute of the Council of Europe.

Article 55[1] – Exclusion of other means of dispute settlement

The High Contracting Parties agree that, except by special agreement, they will not avail themselves of treaties, conventions or declarations in force between them for the purpose of submitting, by way of petition, a dispute arising out of the interpretation or application of this Convention to a means of settlement other than those provided for in this Convention.

Article 56[1] – Territorial application

1[4] Any State may at the time of its ratification or at any time thereafter declare by notification addressed to the Secretary General of the Council of Europe that the present Convention shall, subject to paragraph 4 of this Article, extend to all or any of the territories for whose international relations it is responsible.

2 The Convention shall extend to the territory or territories named in the notification as from the thirtieth day after the receipt of this notification by the Secretary General of the Council of Europe.

3 The provisions of this Convention shall be applied in such territories with due regard, however, to local requirements.

4[4] Any State which has made a declaration in accordance with paragraph 1 of this article may at any time thereafter declare on behalf of one or more of the territories to which the declaration relates that it accepts the competence of the Court to receive applications from individuals, non-governmental organisations or groups of individuals as provided by Article 34 of the Convention.

Article 57[1] – Reservations

1 Any State may, when signing this Convention or when depositing its instrument of ratification, make a reservation in respect of any particular provision of the Convention to the extent that any law then in force in its territory is not in conformity with the provision. Reservations of a general character shall not be permitted under this article.

2 Any reservation made under this article shall contain a brief statement of the law concerned.

Article 58[1] – Denunciation

1 A High Contracting Party may denounce the present Convention only after the expiry of five years from the date on which it became a party to it and after six months' notice contained in a notification addressed to the Secretary General of the Council of Europe, who shall inform the other High Contracting Parties.

2 Such a denunciation shall not have the effect of releasing the High Contracting Party concerned from its obligations under this Convention in respect of any act which, being capable of constituting a violation of such obligations, may have been performed by it before the date at which the denunciation became effective.

3 Any High Contracting Party which shall cease to be a member of the Council of Europe shall cease to be a Party to this Convention under the same conditions.

4[4] The Convention may be denounced in accordance with the provisions of the preceding paragraphs in respect of any territory to which it has been declared to extend under the terms of Article 56.

Article 59[1] – Signature and ratification

1 This Convention shall be open to the signature of the members of the Council of Europe. It shall be ratified. Ratifications shall be deposited with the Secretary General of the Council of Europe.

2 The present Convention shall come into force after the deposit of ten instruments of ratification.

3 As regards any signatory ratifying subsequently, the Convention shall come into force at the date of the deposit of its instrument of ratification.

4 The Secretary General of the Council of Europe shall notify all the members of the Council of Europe of the entry into force of the Convention, the names of the High Contracting Parties who have ratified it, and the deposit of all instruments of ratification which may be effected subsequently.

Done at Rome this 4th day of November 1950, in English and French, both texts being equally authentic, in a single copy which shall remain deposited in the archives of the Council of Europe. The Secretary General shall transmit certified copies to each of the signatories.

Footnotes
1. Heading added according to the provisions of Protocol No 11 (ETS No 155).
2. New Section II according to the provisions of Protocol No 11 (ETS No 155).
3. The articles of this Section are renumbered according to the provisions of Protocol No 11 (ETS No 155).
4. Text amended according to the provisions of Protocol No 11 (ETS No 155).

PROTOCOL TO THE CONVENTION FOR THE PROTECTION OF HUMAN RIGHTS AND FUNDAMENTAL FREEDOMS, AS AMENDED BY PROTOCOL No 11

Paris, 20.III.1952

Headings of articles added and text amended according to the provisions of Protocol No 11 (ETS No 155) as of its entry into force on 1 November 1998.

The governments signatory hereto, being members of the Council of Europe,

Being resolved to take steps to ensure the collective enforcement of certain rights and freedoms other than those already included in Section I of the Convention for the Protection of Human Rights and Fundamental Freedoms signed at Rome on 4 November 1950 (hereinafter referred to as "the Convention"),

Have agreed as follows:

Article 1 - Protection of property

Every natural or legal person is entitled to the peaceful enjoyment of his possessions. No one shall be deprived of his possessions except in the public interest and subject to the conditions provided for by law and by the general principles of international law.

The preceding provisions shall not, however, in any way impair the right of a State to enforce such laws as it deems necessary to control the use of property in accordance with the general interest or to secure the payment of taxes or other contributions or penalties.

Article 2 - Right to education

No person shall be denied the right to education. In the exercise of any functions which it assumes in relation to education and to teaching, the State shall respect the right of parents to ensure such education and teaching in conformity with their own religious and philosophical convictions.

Article 3 - Right to free elections

The High Contracting Parties undertake to hold free elections at reasonable intervals by secret ballot, under conditions which will ensure the free expression of the opinion of the people in the choice of the legislature.

Article 4[1] - Territorial application

Any High Contracting Party may at the time of signature or ratification or at any time thereafter communicate to the Secretary General of the Council of Europe a declaration stating the extent to which it undertakes that the provisions of the present Protocol shall apply to such of the territories for the international relations of which it is responsible as are named therein.

Any High Contracting Party which has communicated a declaration in virtue of the preceding paragraph may from time to time communicate a further declaration modifying the terms of any former declaration or terminating the application of the provisions of this Protocol in respect of any territory.

A declaration made in accordance with this article shall be deemed to have been made in accordance with paragraph 1 of Article 56 of the Convention.

Article 5 - Relationship to the Convention

As between the High Contracting Parties the provisions of Articles 1, 2, 3 and 4 of this Protocol shall be regarded as additional articles to the Convention and all the provisions of the Convention shall apply accordingly.

Article 6 - Signature and ratification

This Protocol shall be open for signature by the members of the Council of Europe, who are the signatories of the Convention. It shall be ratified at the same time as or after the ratification of the Convention. It shall enter into force after the deposit of ten instruments of ratification. As regards any signatory ratifying subsequently, the Protocol shall enter into force at the date of the deposit of its instrument of ratification.

The instruments of ratification shall be deposited with the Secretary General of the Council of Europe, who will notify all members of the names of those who have ratified.

Done at Paris on the 20th day of March 1952, in English and French, both texts being equally authentic, in a single copy which shall remain deposited in the archives of the Council of Europe. The Secretary General shall transmit certified copies to each of the signatory governments.

Footnotes
1. Text amended according to the provisions of Protocol No 11 (ETS No 155).

PROTOCOL No 2 TO THE CONVENTION FOR THE PROTECTION OF HUMAN RIGHTS AND FUNDAMENTAL FREEDOMS, CONFERRING UPON THE EUROPEAN COURT OF HUMAN RIGHTS COMPETENCE TO GIVE ADVISORY OPINIONS

Strasbourg, 6.V.1963

"Protocol No 2 (ETS No 44) had been an integral part of theConvention since its entry into force on 21 September 1970. However, all provisions which had been amended or added by this Protocol are replaced by Protocol No 11 (ETS No 155), as from the date of its entry into force, on 1 November 1998."

Preamble

The member States of the Council of Europe signatory hereto,

Having regard to the provisions of the Convention for the Protection of Human Rights and Fundamental Freedoms signed at Rome on 4th November 1950 (hereinafter referred to as "the Convention") and, in particular, Article 19 instituting, among other bodies, a European Court of Human Rights (hereinafter referred to as "the Court");

Considering that it is expedient to confer upon the Court competence to give advisory opinions subject to certain conditions,

Have agreed as follows:

Article 1

1   The Court may, at the request of the Committee of Ministers, give advisory opinions on legal questions concerning the interpretation of the Convention and the Protocols thereto.

2   Such opinions shall not deal with any question relating to the content or scope of the rights or freedoms defined in Section 1 of the Convention and in the Protocols thereto, or with any other question which the Commission, the Court or the Committee of Ministers might have to consider in consequence of any such proceedings as could be instituted in accordance with the Convention.

3   Decisions of the Committee of Ministers to request an advisory opinion of the Court shall require a two-thirds majority vote of the representatives entitled to sit on the Committee.

Article 2

The Court shall decide whether a request for an advisory opinion submitted by the Committee of Ministers is within its consultative competence as defined in Article 1 of this Protocol.

Article 3

1   For the consideration of requests for an advisory opinion, the Court shall sit in plenary session.

2   Reasons shall be given for advisory opinions of the Court.

3   If the advisory opinion does not represent in whole or in part the unanimous opinion of the judges, any judge shall be entitled to deliver a separate opinion.

4   Advisory opinions of the Court shall be communicated to the Committee of Ministers.

Article 4

The powers of the Court under Article 55 of the Convention shall extend to the drawing up of such rules and the determination of such procedure as the Court may think necessary for the purposes of this Protocol.

Article 5

1   This Protocol shall be open to signature by member States of the Council of Europe, signatories to the Convention, who may become Parties to it by:
(a) signature without reservation in respect of ratification or acceptance;
(b) signature with reservation in respect of ratification or acceptance, followed by ratification or acceptance.
Instruments of ratification or acceptance shall be deposited with the Secretary General of the Council of Europe.

2   This Protocol shall enter into force as soon as all States Parties to the Convention shall have become Parties to the Protocol, in accordance with the provisions of paragraph 1 of this Article.

3   From the date of the entry into force of this Protocol, Articles 1 to 4 shall be considered an integral part of the Convention.

4   The Secretary General of the Council of Europe shall notify the member States of the Council of:
(a) any signature without reservation in respect of ratification or acceptance;
(b) any signature with reservation in respect of ratification or acceptance;
(c) the deposit of any instrument of ratification or acceptance;
(d) the date of entry into force of this Protocol in accordance with paragraph 2 of this Article.
In witness whereof, the undersigned, being duly authorised thereto, have signed this Protocol.

Done at Strasbourg, this 6th day of May 1963, in English and in French, both texts being equally authoritative, in a single copy which shall remain deposited in the archives of the Council of Europe. The Secretary General shall transmit certified copies to each of the signatory States.

PROTOCOL No 3 TO THE CONVENTION FOR THE PROTECTION OF HUMAN RIGHTS AND FUNDAMENTAL FREEDOMS, AMENDING ARTICLES 29, 30 AND 34 OF THE CONVENTION

Strasbourg, 6.V.1963

"The original text of the Convention had been amended according to the text of Protocol No 3 (ETS No 45) which entered into force on 21 September 1970. All provisions which had been amended or added by this Protocol are replaced by Protocol No 11 (ETS No 155), as from the date of its entry into force, on 1 November 1998."

The member States of the Council of Europe, signatories to this Protocol,

Considering that it is advisable to amend certain provisions of the Convention for the Protection of Human Rights and Fundamental Freedoms signed at Rome on 4th November 1950 (hereinafter referred to as "the Convention") concerning the procedure of the European Commission of Human Rights,

Have agreed as follows:

Article 1

1 Article 29 of the Convention is deleted.

2 The following provision shall be inserted in the Convention:

> "**Article 29**
> After it has accepted a petition submitted under Article 25, the Commission may nevertheless decide unanimously to reject the petition if, in the course of its examination, it finds that the existence of one of the grounds for non-acceptance provided for in Article 27 has been established.
> In such a case, the decision shall be communicated to the parties."

Article 2

In Article 30 of the Convention, the word "Sub-Commission" shall be replaced by the word "Commission".

Article 3

1 At the beginning of Article 34 of the Convention, the following shall be inserted: "Subject to the provisions of Article 29..."
2 At the end of the same Article, the sentence "the Sub-Commission shall take its decisions by a majority of its members" shall be deleted.

Article 4

1 This Protocol shall be open to signature by the member States of the Council of Europe signatories to the Convention, who may become Parties to it either by:
(a) signature without reservation in respect of ratification or acceptance, or
(b) signature with reservation in respect of ratification or acceptance, followed by ratification or acceptance.
Instruments of ratification or acceptance shall be deposited with the Secretary General of the Council of Europe.

2 This Protocol shall enter into force as soon as all States Parties to the Convention shall have become Parties to the Protocol, in accordance with the provisions of paragraph 1 of this Article.

3   The Secretary General of the Council of Europe shall notify the member States of the Council of:
(a) any signature without reservation in respect of ratification or acceptance;
(b) any signature with reservation in respect of ratification or acceptance;
(c) the deposit of any instrument of ratification or acceptance;
(d) the date of entry into force of this Protocol in accordance with paragraph 2 of this Article.
In witness whereof, the undersigned, being duly authorised thereto, have signed this Protocol.

Done at Strasbourg, this 6th day of May 1963, in English and in French, both texts being equally authoritative, in a single copy which shall remain deposited in the archives of the Council of Europe. The Secretary General shall transmit certified copies to each of the signatory States.

PROTOCOL No 4 TO THE CONVENTION FOR THE PROTECTION OF HUMAN RIGHTS AND FUNDAMENTAL FREEDOMS, SECURING CERTAIN RIGHTS AND FREEDOMS OTHER THAN THOSE ALREADY INCLUDED IN THE CONVENTION AND IN THE FIRST PROTOCOL THERETO, AS AMENDED BY PROTOCOL NO11

Strasbourg, 16.IX.1963

Headings of articles added and text amended according to the provisions of Protocol No 11 (ETS No 155) as from its entry into force on 1 November 1998.

The governments signatory hereto, being members of the Council of Europe,

Being resolved to take steps to ensure the collective enforcement of certain rights and freedoms other than those already included in Section 1 of the Convention for the Protection of Human Rights and Fundamental Freedoms signed at Rome on 4th November 1950 (hereinafter referred to as the "Convention") and in Articles 1 to 3 of the First Protocol to the Convention, signed at Paris on 20th March 1952,

Have agreed as follows:

Article 1 - Prohibition of imprisonment for debt

No one shall be deprived of his liberty merely on the ground of inability to fulfil a contractual obligation.

Article 2 - Freedom of movement

1   Everyone lawfully within the territory of a State shall, within that territory, have the right to liberty of movement and freedom to choose his residence.

2   Everyone shall be free to leave any country, including his own.

3   No restrictions shall be placed on the exercise of these rights other than such as are in accordance with law and are necessary in a democratic society in the interests of national security or public safety, for the maintenance of ordre public, for the

prevention of crime, for the protection of health or morals, or for the protection of the rights and freedoms of others.

4   The rights set forth in paragraph 1 may also be subject, in particular areas, to restrictions imposed in accordance with law and justified by the public interest in a democratic society.

Article 3 - Prohibition of expulsion of nationals

1 No one shall be expelled, by means either of an individual or of a collective measure, from the territory of the State of which he is a national.

2 No one shall be deprived of the right to enter the territory of the state of which he is a national.

Article 4 - Prohibition of collective expulsion of aliens

Collective expulsion of aliens is prohibited.

Article 5 - Territorial application

1   Any High Contracting Party may, at the time of signature or ratification of this Protocol, or at any time thereafter, communicate to the Secretary General of the Council of Europe a declaration stating the extent to which it undertakes that the provisions of this Protocol shall apply to such of the territories for the international relations of which it is responsible as are named therein.

2   Any High Contracting Party which has communicated a declaration in virtue of the preceding paragraph may, from time to time, communicate a further declaration modifying the terms of any former declaration or terminating the application of the provisions of this Protocol in respect of any territory.

3[1]   A declaration made in accordance with this article shall be deemed to have been made in accordance with paragraph 1 of Article 56 of the Convention.

4   The territory of any State to which this Protocol applies by virtue of ratification or acceptance by that State, and each territory to which this Protocol is applied by virtue of a declaration by that State under this article, shall be treated as separate territories for the purpose of the references in Articles 2 and 3 to the territory of a State.

5[2]   Any State which has made a declaration in accordance with paragraph 1 or 2 of this Article may at any time thereafter declare on behalf of one or more of the territories to which the declaration relates that it accepts the competence of the Court to receive applications from individuals, non-governmental organisations or groups of individuals as provided in Article 34 of the Convention in respect of all or any of Articles 1 to 4 of this Protocol.

Article 6[1] - Relationship to the Convention

As between the High Contracting Parties the provisions of Articles 1 to 5 of this Protocol shall be regarded as additional Articles to the Convention, and all the provisions of the Convention shall apply accordingly.

Article 7 - Signature and ratification

1   This Protocol shall be open for signature by the members of the Council of Europe who are the signatories of the Convention; it shall be ratified at the same time as or after the ratification of the Convention. It shall enter into force after the deposit of five instruments of ratification. As regards any signatory ratifying subsequently, the Protocol shall enter into force at the date of the deposit of its instrument of ratification.

2   The instruments of ratification shall be deposited with the Secretary General of the Council of Europe, who will notify all members of the names of those who have ratified.

In witness whereof the undersigned, being duly authorised thereto, have signed this Protocol.

Done at Strasbourg, this 16th day of September 1963, in English and in French, both texts being equally authoritative, in a single copy which shall remain deposited in the archives of the Council of Europe. The Secretary General shall transmit certified copies to each of the signatory states.

Footnotes
1. Text amended according to the provisions of Protocol No 11 (ETS No 155).
2. Text added according to the provisions of Protocol No 11 (ETS No 155).

PROTOCOL No 5 TO THE CONVENTION FOR THE PROTECTION OF HUMAN RIGHTS AND FUNDAMENTAL FREEDOMS, AMENDING ARTICLES 22 AND 40 OF THE CONVENTION

Strasbourg, 20.I.1966

"The original text of the Convention had been amended according to the text of Protocol No 5 (ETS No 55) which entered into force on 21 December 1970. All provisions which had been amended by this Protocol are replaced by Protocol No 11 (ETS No 155), as from the date of its entry into force, on 1 November 1998."

The governments signatory hereto, being members of the Council of Europe,

Considering that certain inconveniences have arisen in the application of the provisions of Articles 22 and 40 of the Convention for the Protection of Human Rights and Fundamental Freedoms signed at Rome on 4th November 1950 (hereinafter referred to as "the Convention") relating to the length of the terms of office of the members of the European Commission of Human Rights (hereinafter referred to as "the Commission") and of the European Court of Human Rights (hereinafter referred to as "the Court");

Considering that it is desirable to ensure as far as possible an election every three years of one half of the members of the Commission and of one third of the members of the Court;

Considering therefore that it is desirable to amend certain provisions of the Convention,

Have agreed as follows:

Article 1

In Article 22 of the Convention, the following two paragraphs shall be inserted after paragraph 2:

"3 In order to ensure that, as far as possible, one half of the membership of the Commission shall be renewed every three years, the Committee of Ministers may decide, before proceeding to any subsequent election, that the term or terms of office of one or more members to be elected shall be for a period other than six years but not more than nine and not less than three years.
4 In cases where more than one term of office is involved and the Committee of Ministers applies the preceding paragraph, the allocation of the terms of office shall be effected by the drawing of lots by the Secretary General, immediately after the election."

Article 2

In Article 22 of the Convention, the former paragraphs 3 and 4 shall become respectively paragraphs 5 and 6.

Article 3

In Article 40 of the Convention, the following two paragraphs shall be inserted after paragraph 2:

"3 In order to ensure that, as far as possible, one third of the membership of the Court shall be renewed every three years, the Consultative Assembly may decide, before proceeding to any subsequent election, that the term or terms of office of one or more members to be elected shall be for a period other than nine years but not more than twelve and not less than six years.
4 In cases where more than one term of office is involved and the Consultative Assembly applies the preceding paragraph, the allocation of the terms of office shall be effected by the drawing of lots by the Secretary General immediately after the election."

Article 4

In Article 40 of the Convention, the former paragraphs 3 and 4 shall become respectively paragraphs 5 and 6.

Article 5

1   This Protocol shall be open to signature by members of the Council of Europe, signatories to the Convention, who may become Parties to it by:
(a) signature without reservation in respect of ratification or acceptance;
(b) signature with reservation in respect of ratification or acceptance, followed by ratification or acceptance.
Instruments of ratification or acceptance shall be deposited with the Secretary General of the Council of Europe.

2   This Protocol shall enter into force as soon as all Contracting Parties to the Convention shall have become Parties to the Protocol, in accordance with the provisions of paragraph 1 of this article.

3   The Secretary General of the Council of Europe shall notify the members of the Council of:

(a) any signature without reservation in respect of ratification or acceptance;
(b) any signature with reservation in respect of ratification or acceptance;
(c) the deposit of any instrument of ratification or acceptance;
(d) the date of entry into force of this Protocol in accordance with paragraph 2 of this article.

In witness whereof the undersigned, being duly authorised thereto, have signed this Protocol.

Done at Strasbourg, this 20th day of January 1966, in English and in French, both texts being equally authoritative, in a single copy which shall remain deposited in the archives of the Council of Europe. The Secretary General shall transmit certified copies to each of the signatory governments.

PROTOCOL No 6 TO THE CONVENTION FOR THE PROTECTION OF HUMAN RIGHTS AND FUNDAMENTAL FREEDOMS CONCERNING THE ABOLITION OF THE DEATH PENALTY, AS AMENDED BY PROTOCOL No11

Strasbourg, 28.IV.1983

Headings of articles added and text amended according to the provisions of Protocol No 11 (ETS No 155) as from its entry into force on 1 November 1998.

The member States of the Council of Europe, signatory to this Protocol to the Convention for the Protection of Human Rights and Fundamental Freedoms, signed at Rome on 4 November 1950 (hereinafter referred to as "the Convention"),

Considering that the evolution that has occurred in several member States of the Council of Europe expresses a general tendency in favour of abolition of the death penalty;

Have agreed as follows:

Article 1 - Abolition of the death penalty

The death penalty shall be abolished. No-one shall be condemned to such penalty or executed.

Article 2 - Death penalty in time of war

A State may make provision in its law for the death penalty in respect of acts committed in time of war or of imminent threat of war; such penalty shall be applied only in the instances laid down in the law and in accordance with its provisions. The State shall communicate to the Secretary General of the Council of Europe the relevant provisions of that law.

Article 3 - Prohibition of derogations

No derogation from the provisions of this Protocol shall be made under Article 15 of the Convention.

Article 4[1] - Prohibition of reservations

No reservation may be made under Article 57 of the Convention in respect of the provisions of this Protocol.

Article 5 - Territorial application

1 Any State may at the time of signature or when depositing its instrument of ratification, acceptance or approval, specify the territory or territories to which this Protocol shall apply.

2 Any State may at any later date, by a declaration addressed to the Secretary General of the Council of Europe, extend the application of this Protocol to any other territory specified in the declaration. In respect of such territory the Protocol shall enter into force on the first day of the month following the date of receipt of such declaration by the Secretary General.

3 Any declaration made under the two preceding paragraphs may, in respect of any territory specified in such declaration, be withdrawn by a notification addressed to the Secretary General. The withdrawal shall become effective on the first day of the month following the date of receipt of such notification by the Secretary General.

Article 6 - Relationship to the Convention

As between the States Parties the provisions of Articles 1 to 5 of this Protocol shall be regarded as additional articles to the Convention and all the provisions of the Convention shall apply accordingly.

Article 7 - Signature and ratification

The Protocol shall be open for signature by the member States of the Council of Europe, signatories to the Convention. It shall be subject to ratification, acceptance or approval. A member State of the Council of Europe may not ratify, accept or approve this Protocol unless it has, simultaneously or previously, ratified the Convention. Instruments of ratification, acceptance or approval shall be deposited with the Secretary General of the Council of Europe.

Article 8 - Entry into force

1 This Protocol shall enter into force on the first day of the month following the date on which five member States of the Council of Europe have expressed their consent to be bound by the Protocol in accordance with the provisions of Article 7.

2 In respect of any member State which subsequently expresses its consent to be bound by it, the Protocol shall enter into force on the first day of the month following the date of the deposit of the instrument of ratification, acceptance or approval.

Article 9 - Depositary functions

The Secretary General of the Council of Europe shall notify the member States of the Council of:

(a) any signature;
(b) the deposit of any instrument of ratification, acceptance or approval;
(c) any date of entry into force of this Protocol in accordance with Articles 5 and 8;
(d) any other act, notification or communication relating to this Protocol.
In witness whereof the undersigned, being duly authorised thereto, have signed this Protocol.

Done at Strasbourg, this 28th day of April 1983, in English and in French, both texts being equally authentic, in a single copy which shall be deposited in the archives of the Council of Europe. The Secretary General of the Council of Europe shall transmit certified copies to each member State of the Council of Europe.

Footnote
1. Text amended according to the provisions of Protocol No 11 (ETS No 155).

PROTOCOL No 7 TO THE CONVENTION FOR THE PROTECTION OF HUMAN RIGHTS AND FUNDAMENTAL FREEDOMS, AS AMENDED BY PROTOCOL No 11

Strasbourg, 22.XI.1984

Headings of articles added and text amended according to the provisions of Protocol No 11 (ETS No 155) as from its entry into force on 1 November 1998.

The member States of the Council of Europe signatory hereto,

Being resolved to take further steps to ensure the collective enforcement of certain rights and freedoms by means of the Convention for the Protection of Human Rights and Fundamental Freedoms signed at Rome on 4 November 1950 (hereinafter referred to as "the Convention"),

Have agreed as follows :

Article 1   Procedural safeguards relating to expulsion of aliens

1   An alien lawfully resident in the territory of a State shall not be expelled therefrom except in pursuance of a decision reached in accordance with law and shall be allowed:
(a) to submit reasons against his expulsion,
(b) to have his case reviewed, and
(c) to be represented for these purposes before the competent authority or a person or persons designated by that authority.

2   An alien may be expelled before the exercise of his rights under paragraph 1.a, b and c of this Article, when such expulsion is necessary in the interests of public order or is grounded on reasons of national security.

Article 2 - Right of appeal in criminal matters

1   Everyone convicted of a criminal offence by a tribunal shall have the right to have his conviction or sentence reviewed by a higher tribunal. The exercise of this right, including the grounds on which it may be exercised, shall be governed by law.

2 This right may be subject to exceptions in regard to offences of a minor character, as prescribed by law, or in cases in which the person concerned was tried in the first instance by the highest tribunal or was convicted following an appeal against acquittal.

Article 3 - Compensation for wrongful conviction

When a person has by a final decision been convicted of a criminal offence and when subsequently his conviction has been reversed, or he has been pardoned, on the ground that a new or newly discovered fact shows conclusively that there has been a miscarriage of justice, the person who has suffered punishment as a result of such conviction shall be compensated according to the law or the practice of the State concerned, unless it is proved that the non-disclosure of the unknown fact in time is wholly or partly attributable to him.

Article 4 - Right not to be tried or punished twice

1 No one shall be liable to be tried or punished again in criminal proceedings under the jurisdiction of the same State for an offence for which he has already been finally acquitted or convicted in accordance with the law and penal procedure of that State.

2 The provisions of the preceding paragraph shall not prevent the reopening of the case in accordance with the law and penal procedure of the State concerned, if there is evidence of new or newly discovered facts, or if there has been a fundamental defect in the previous proceedings, which could affect the outcome of the case.

3 No derogation from this Article shall be made under Article 15 of the Convention.

Article 5 - Equality between spouses

Spouses shall enjoy equality of rights and responsibilities of a private law character between them, and in their relations with their children, as to marriage, during marriage and in the event of its dissolution. This Article shall not prevent States from taking such measures as are necessary in the interests of the children.

Article 6 - Territorial application

1 Any State may at the time of signature or when depositing its instrument of ratification, acceptance or approval, specify the territory or territories to which the Protocol shall apply and state the extent to which it undertakes that the provisions of this Protocol shall apply to such territory or territories.

2 Any State may at any later date, by a declaration addressed to the Secretary General of the Council of Europe, extend the application of this Protocol to any other territory specified in the declaration. In respect of such territory the Protocol shall enter into force on the first day of the month following the expiration of a period of two months after the date of receipt by the Secretary General of such declaration.

3 Any declaration made under the two preceding paragraphs may, in respect of any territory specified in such declaration, be withdrawn or modified by a notification addressed to the Secretary General. The withdrawal or modification shall become

effective on the first day of the month following the expiration of a period of two months after the date of receipt of such notification by the Secretary General.

4[1]   A declaration made in accordance with this Article shall be deemed to have been made in accordance with paragraph 1 of Article 56 of the Convention.

5   The territory of any State to which this Protocol applies by virtue of ratification, acceptance or approval by that State, and each territory to which this Protocol is applied by virtue of a declaration by that State under this Article, may be treated as separate territories for the purpose of the reference in Article 1 to the territory of a State.

6[2]   Any State which has made a declaration in accordance with paragraph 1 or 2 of this Article may at any time thereafter declare on behalf of one or more of the territories to which the declaration relates that it accepts the competence of the Court to receive applications from individuals, non-governmental organisations or groups of individuals as provided in Article 34 of the Convention in respect of Articles 1 to 5 of this Protocol.

Article 7[1] - Relationship to the Convention

As between the States Parties, the provisions of Article 1 to 6 of this Protocol shall be regarded as additional Articles to the Convention, and all the provisions of the Convention shall apply accordingly.

Article 8 - Signature and ratification

This Protocol shall be open for signature by member States of the Council of Europe which have signed the Convention. It is subject to ratification, acceptance or approval. A member State of the Council of Europe may not ratify, accept or approve this Protocol without previously or simultaneously ratifying the Convention. Instruments of ratification, acceptance or approval shall be deposited with the Secretary General of the Council of Europe.

Article 9 - Entry into force

1   This Protocol shall enter into force on the first day of the month following the expiration of a period of two months after the date on which seven member States of the Council of Europe have expressed their consent to be bound by the Protocol in accordance with the provisions of Article 8.

2   In respect of any member State which subsequently expresses its consent to be bound by it, the Protocol shall enter into force on the first day of the month following the expiration of a period of two months after the date of the deposit of the instrument of ratification, acceptance or approval.

Article 10 - Depositary functions

The Secretary General of the Council of Europe shall notify all the member States of the Council of Europe of:
(a) any signature;
(b) the deposit of any instrument of ratification, acceptance or approval;

(c) any date of entry into force of this Protocol in accordance with Articles 6 and 9;
(d) any other act, notification or declaration relating to this Protocol.
In witness whereof the undersigned, being duly authorised thereto, have signed this Protocol.

Done at Strasbourg, this 22nd day of November 1984, in English and French, both texts being equally authentic, in a single copy which shall be deposited in the archives of the Council of Europe. The Secretary General of the Council of Europe shall transmit certified copies to each member State of the Council of Europe.

Footnotes
1. Text amended according to the provisions of Protocol No 11 (ETS No 155).
2. Text added according to the provisions of Protocol No 11 (ETS No 155).

PROTOCOL No 8 TO THE CONVENTION FOR THE PROTECTION OF HUMAN RIGHTS AND FUNDAMENTAL FREEDOMS

Vienna, 19.III.1985

"The original text of the Convention had been amended according to the text of Protocol No 8 (ETS No 118) which entered into force on 1 January 1990. All provisions which had been amended or added by this Protocol are replaced by Protocol No 11 (ETS No 155), as from the date of its entry into force, on 1 November 1998."

The member States of the Council of Europe, signatories to this Protocol to the Convention for the Protection of Human Rights and Fundamental Freedoms, signed at Rome on 4 November 1950 (hereinafter referred to as "the Convention"),

Considering that it is desirable to amend certain provisions of the Convention with a view to improving and in particular to expediting the procedure of the European Commission of Human Rights,

Considering that it is also advisable to amend certain provisions of the Convention concerning the procedure of the European Court of Human Rights,

Have agreed as follows:

Article 1

The existing text of Article 20 of the Convention shall become paragraph 1 of that article and shall be supplemented by the following four paragraphs:

"2 The Commission shall sit in plenary session. It may, however, set up Chambers, each composed of at least seven members. The Chambers may examine petitions submitted under Article 25 of this Convention which can be dealt with on the basis of established case law or which raise no serious question affecting the interpretation or application of the Convention. Subject to this restriction and to the provisions of paragraph 5 of this article, the Chambers shall exercise all the powers conferred on the Commission by the Convention.

The member of the Commission elected in respect of a High Contracting Party against which a petition has been lodged shall have the right to sit on a Chamber to which that petition has been referred.

3 The Commission may set up committees, each composed of at least three members, with the power, exercisable by a unanimous vote, to declare inadmissible or strike from its list of cases a petition submitted under Article 25, when such a decision can be taken without further examination.

4 A Chamber or committee may at any time relinquish jurisdiction in favour of the plenary Commission, which may also order the transfer to it of any petition referred to a Chamber or committee.

5 Only the plenary Commission can exercise the following powers:
a the examination of applications submitted under Article 24;
b the bringing of a case before the Court in accordance with Article 48.a;
c the drawing up of rules of procedure in accordance with Article 36."

Article 2

Article 21 of the Convention shall be supplemented by the following third paragraph:

"3 The candidates shall be of high moral character and must either possess the qualifications required for appointment to high judicial office or be persons of recognised competence in national or international law."

Article 3

Article 23 of the Convention shall be supplemented by the following sentence:

"During their term of office they shall not hold any position which is incompatible with their independence and impartiality as members of the Commission or the demands of this office."

Article 4

The text, with modifications, of Article 28 of the Convention shall become paragraph 1 of that article and the text, with modifications, of Article 30 shall become paragraph 2. The new text of Article 28 shall read as follows:

"**Article 28**

1 In the event of the Commission accepting a petition referred to it:
a it shall, with a view to ascertaining the facts, undertake together with the representatives of the parties an examination of the petition and, if need be, an investigation, for the effective conduct of which the States concerned shall furnish all necessary facilities, after an exchange of views with the Commission;
b it shall at the same time place itself at the disposal of the parties concerned with a view to securing a friendly settlement of the matter on the basis of respect for human rights as defined in this Convention;

2 If the Commission succeeds in effecting a friendly settlement, it shall draw up a report which shall be sent to the States concerned, to the Committee of Ministers and to the Secretary General of the Council of Europe for publication. This report shall be confined to a brief statement of the facts and of the solution reached."

Article 5

In the first paragraph of Article 29 of the Convention, the word "unanimously" shall be replaced by the words "by a majority of two-thirds of its members".

Article 6

The following provision shall be inserted in the Convention:

"Article 30

1 The Commission may at any stage of the proceedings decide to strike a petition out of its list of cases where the circumstances lead to the conclusion that:
a the applicant does not intend to pursue his petition, or
b the matter has been resolved, or
c for any other reason established by the Commission, it is no longer justified to continue the examination of the petition.
However, the Commission shall continue the examination of a petition if respect for human rights as defined in this Convention so requires.

2 If the Commission decides to strike a petition out of its list after having accepted it, it shall draw up a report which shall contain a statement of the facts and the decision striking out the petition together with the reasons therefor. The report shall be transmitted to the parties, as well as to the Committee of Ministers for information. The Commission may publish it.

3 The Commission may decide to restore a petition to its list of cases if it considers that the circumstances justify such a course."

Article 7

In Article 31 of the Convention, paragraph 1 shall read as follows:

"1 If the examination of a petition has not been completed in accordance with Article 28 (paragraph 2), 29 or 30, the Commission shall draw up a report on the facts and state its opinion as to whether the facts found disclose a breach by the State concerned of its obligations under the Convention. The individual opinions of members of the Commission on this point may be stated in the report."

Article 8

Article 34 of the Convention shall read as follows:

"Subject to the provisions of articles 20 (paragraph 3) and 29, the Commission shall take its decision by a majority of the members present and voting."

Article 9

Article 40 of the Convention shall be supplemented by the following seventh paragraph:

"7 The members of the Court shall sit on the Court in their individual capacity. During their term of office they shall not hold any position which is incompatible with their independence and impartiality as members of the Court or the demands of this office."

Article 10

Article 41 of the Convention shall read as follows:

"The Court shall elect its President and one or two Vice-Presidents for a period of three years. They may be re-elected."

Article 11

In the first sentence of Article 43 of the Convention, the word "seven" shall be replaced by the word "nine".

Article 12

1   This Protocol shall be open for signature by member States of the Council of Europe signatories to the Convention, which may express their consent to be bound by:
(a) signature without reservation as to ratification, acceptance or approval, or
(b) signature subject to ratification, acceptance or approval, followed by ratification, acceptance or approval.

2   Instruments of ratification, acceptance or approval shall be deposited with the Secretary General of the Council of Europe.

Article 13

This Protocol shall enter into force on the first day of the month following the expiration of a period of three months after the date on which all the Parties to the Convention have expressed their consent to be bound by the Protocol in accordance with the provisions of Article 12.

Article 14

The Secretary General of the Council of Europe shall notify the member States of the Council of:
(a) any signature;
(b) the deposit of any instrument of ratification, acceptance or approval;
(c) the date of entry into force of this Protocol in accordance with Article 13;
(d) any other act, notification or communication relating to this Protocol.
In witness whereof the undersigned, being duly authorised thereto, have signed this Protocol.

Done at Vienna, this 19th day of March 1985, in English and French, both texts being equally authentic, in a single copy which shall be deposited in the archives of the Council of Europe. The Secretary General of the Council of Europe shall transmit certified copies to each member State of the Council of Europe

PROTOCOL No 9 TO THE CONVENTION FOR THE PROTECTION OF HUMAN RIGHTS AND FUNDAMENTAL FREEDOMS

Rome, 6.IX.1990

The member States of the Council of Europe, signatories to this Protocol to the Convention for the Protection of Human Rights and Fundamental Freedoms, signed at Rome on 4 November 1950 (hereinafter referred to as "the Convention"),

Being resolved to make further improvements to the procedure under the Convention,

Have agreed as follows:

Article 1

For Parties to the Convention which are bound by this Protocol, the Convention shall be amended as provided in Articles 2 to 5.

Article 2

Article 31, paragraph 2, of the Convention shall read as follows:

> "2. The Report shall be transmitted to the Committee of Ministers. The Report shall also be transmitted to the States concerned and, if it deals with a petition submitted under Article 25, the applicant. The States concerned and the applicant shall not be at liberty to publish it."

Article 3

Article 44 of the Convention shall read as follows:

> "Only the High Contracting Parties, the Commission, and persons, non-governmental organisations or groups of individuals having submitted a petition under Article 25 shall have the right to bring a case before the Court."

Article 4

Article 45 of the Convention shall read as follows:

> "The jurisdiction of the Court shall extend to all cases concerning the interpretation and application of the present Convention which are referred to it in accordance with Article 48."

Article 5

Article 48 of the Convention shall read as follows:

> "1. The following may refer a case to the Court, provided that the High Contracting Party concerned, if there is only one, or the High Contracting Parties concerned, if there is more than one, are subject to the compulsory jurisdiction of the Court or, failing that, with the consent of the High Contracting Party concerned, if there is only one, or of the High Contracting Parties concerned if there is more than one:
> a the Commission;
> b a High Contracting Party whose national is alleged to be a victim;
> c a High Contracting Party which referred the case to the Commission;
> d a High Contracting Party against which the complaint has been lodged;
> e the person, non-governmental organisation or group of individuals having lodged the complaint with the Commission.
>
> 2. If a case is referred to the Court only in accordance with paragraph 1.e, it shall first be submitted to a panel composed of three members of the Court. There shall sit as an ex officio member of the panel the judge elected in respect of the High Contracting Party against which the complaint has been lodged, or, if there is none, a person of its choice who shall sit in the capacity of judge. If the complaint has been lodged against more than one High Contracting Party, the size of the panel shall be increased accordingly.
>
> If the case does not raise a serious question affecting the interpretation or application of the Convention and does not for any other reason warrant consideration by the Court, the panel may, by a unanimous vote, decide that it shall not be considered by the Court. In that event, the Committee of Ministers shall decide, in accordance with the provisions of Article 32, whether there has been a violation of the Convention."

Article 6

1.   This Protocol shall be open for signature by member States of the Council of Europe signatories to the Convention, which may express their consent to be bound by:
(a)   signature without reservation as to ratification, acceptance or approval, or
(b)   signature subject to ratification, acceptance or approval, followed by ratification, acceptance or approval.

2.   The instruments of ratification, acceptance or approval shall be deposited with the Secretary General of the Council of Europe.

Article 7

1.   This Protocol shall enter into force on the first day of the month following the expiration of a period of three months after the date on which ten member States of the Council of Europe have expressed their consent to be bound by the Protocol in accordance with the provisions of Article 6.

2.   In respect of any member State which subsequently expresses its consent to be bound by it, the Protocol shall enter into force on the first day of the month following the expiration of a period of three months after the date of signature or of the deposit of the instrument of ratification, acceptance or approval.

Article 8

The Secretary General of the Council of Europe shall notify all the member States of the Council of Europe of:
(a)   any signature;
(b)   the deposit of any instrument of ratification, acceptance or approval;
(c)   any date of entry into force of this Protocol in accordance with Article 7;
(d)   any other act, notification or declaration relating to this Protocol.
In witness whereof the undersigned, being duly authorised thereto, have signed this Protocol.

Done at Rome, this 6th day of November 1990, in English and French, both texts being equally authentic, in a single copy which shall be deposited in the archives of the Council of Europe. The Secretary General of the Council of Europe shall transmit certified copies to each member State of the Council of Europe.

PROTOCOL No 10 TO THE CONVENTION FOR THE PROTECTION OF HUMAN RIGHTS AND FUNDAMENTAL FREEDOMS

Strasbourg, 25.III.1992

The member States of the Council of Europe, signatories to this Protocol to the Convention for the Protection of Human Rights and Fundamental Freedoms, signed at Rome on 4 November 1950 (hereinafter referred to as "the Convention"),

Considering that it is advisable to amend Article 32 of the Convention with a view to the reduction of the two-thirds majority provided therein,

Have agreed as follows:

Article 1

The words "of two-thirds" shall be deleted from paragraph 1 of Article 32 of the Convention.

Article 2

1.   This Protocol shall be open for signature by member States of the Council of Europe, signatories to the Convention, which may express their consent to be bound by:
(a) signature without reservation as to ratification, acceptance or approval; or
(b) signature subject to ratification, acceptance or approval, followed by ratification, acceptance or approval.

2.   Instruments of ratification, acceptance or approval shall be deposited with the Secretary General of the Council of Europe.

Article 3

This Protocol shall enter into force on the first day of the month following the expiration of a period of three months after the date on which all Parties to the Convention have expressed their consent to be bound by the Protocol in accordance with the provisions of Article 2.

Article 4

The Secretary General of the Council of Europe shall notify the member States of the Council of:
(a) any signature;
(b) the deposit of any instrument of ratification, acceptance or approval;
(c) the date of entry into force of this Protocol in accordance with Article 3;
(d) any other act, notification or communication relating to this Protocol.
In witness whereof the undersigned, being duly authorised thereto, have signed this Protocol.

Done at Strasbourg, this 25th day of March 1992, in English and French, both texts being equally authentic, in a single copy which shall be deposited in the archives of the Council of Europe. The Secretary General of the Council of Europe shall transmit certified copies to each member State of the Council of Europe.

PROTOCOL No 11 TO THE CONVENTION FOR THE PROTECTION OF

HUMAN RIGHTS AND FUNDAMENTAL FREEDOMS,

RESTRUCTURING THE CONTROL MACHINERY ESTABLISHED THEREBY

Strasbourg, 11.V.1994

The member States of the Council of Europe, signatories to this Protocol to the Convention for the Protection of Human Rights and Fundamental Freedoms, signed at Rome on 4 November 1950 (hereinafter referred to as "the Convention"),

Considering the urgent need to restructure the control machinery established by the Convention in order to maintain and improve the efficiency of its protection of human rights and fundamental freedoms, mainly in view of the increase in the number of applications and the growing membership of the Council of Europe;

Considering that it is therefore desirable to amend certain provisions of the Convention with a view, in particular, to replacing the existing European Commission and Court of Human Rights with a new permanent Court;

Having regard to Resolution No 1 adopted at the European Ministerial Conference on Human Rights, held in Vienna on 19 and 20 March 1985;

Having regard to Recommendation 1194 (1992), adopted by the Parliamentary Assembly of the Council of Europe on 6 October 1992;

Having regard to the decision taken on reform of the Convention control machinery by the Heads of State and Government of the Council of Europe member States in the Vienna Declaration on 9 October 1993,

Have agreed as follows:

Article 1

The existing text of Sections II to IV of the Convention (Articles 19 to 56) and Protocol No 2 conferring upon the European Court of Human Rights competence to give advisory opinions shall be replaced by the following Section II of the Convention (Articles 19 to 51):

"Section II
European Court of Human Rights

Article 19   Establishment of the Court

To ensure the observance of the engagements undertaken by the High Contracting Parties in the Convention and the protocols thereto, there shall be set up a European Court of Human Rights, hereinafter referred to as "the Court". It shall function on a permanent basis.

Article 20 - Number of judges

The Court shall consist of a number of judges equal to that of the High Contracting Parties.

Article 21 - Criteria for office

1. The judges shall be of high moral character and must either possess the qualifications required for appointment to high judicial office or be jurisconsults of recognised competence.

2. The judges shall sit on the Court in their individual capacity.

3. During their term of office the judges shall not engage in any activity which is incompatible with their independence, impartiality or with the demands of a full-time office; all questions arising from the application of this paragraph shall be decided by the Court.

Article 22 - Election of judges

1.   The judges shall be elected by the Parliamentary Assembly with respect to each High Contracting Party by a majority of votes cast from a list of three candidates nominated by the High Contracting Party.

2.   The same procedure shall be followed to complete the Court in the event of the accession of new High Contracting Parties and in filling casual vacancies.

Article 23 - Terms of office

1.   The judges shall be elected for a period of six years. They may be re-elected. However, the terms of office of one-half of the judges elected at the first election shall expire at the end of three years.

2.   The judges whose terms of office are to expire at the end of the initial period of three years shall be chosen by lot by the Secretary General of the Council of Europe immediately after their election.

3.   In order to ensure that, as far as possible, the terms of office of one-half of the judges are renewed every three years, the Parliamentary Assembly may decide, before proceeding to any subsequent election, that the term or terms of office of one or more judges to be elected shall be for a period other than six years but not more than nine and not less than three years.

4.   In cases where more than one term of office is involved and where the Parliamentary Assembly applies the preceding paragraph, the allocation of the terms of office shall be effected by a drawing of lots by the Secretary General of the Council of Europe immediately after the election.

5.   A judge elected to replace a judge whose term of office has not expired shall hold office for the remainder of his predecessor's term.

6.   The terms of office of judges shall expire when they reach the age of 70.

7.   The judges shall hold office until replaced. They shall, however, continue to deal with such cases as they already have under consideration.

Article 24 - Dismissal

No judge may be dismissed from his office unless the other judges decide by a majority of two-thirds that he has ceased to fulfil the required conditions.

Article 25 - Registry and legal secretaries

The Court shall have a registry, the functions and organisation of which shall be laid down in the rules of the Court. The Court shall be assisted by legal secretaries.

Article 26 - Plenary Court

The plenary Court shall
(a) elect its President and one or two Vice-Presidents for a period of three years; they may be re-elected;
(b) set up Chambers, constituted for a fixed period of time;
(c) elect the Presidents of the Chambers of the Court; they may be re-elected;
(d) adopt the rules of the Court; and
(e) elect the Registrar and one or more Deputy Registrars.

Article 27 - Committees, Chambers and Grand Chamber

1.   To consider cases brought before it, the Court shall sit in committees of three judges, in Chambers of seven judges and in a Grand Chamber of seventeen judges. The Court's Chambers shall set up committees for a fixed period of time.

2.   There shall sit as an ex officio member of the Chamber and the Grand Chamber the judge elected in respect of the State Party concerned or, if there is none or if he is unable to sit, a person of its choice who shall sit in the capacity of judge.

3. The Grand Chamber shall also include the President of the Court, the Vice-Presidents, the Presidents of the Chambers and other judges chosen in accordance with the rules of the Court. When a case is referred to the Grand Chamber under Article 43, no judge from the Chamber which rendered the judgment shall sit in the Grand Chamber, with the exception of the President of the Chamber and the judge who sat in respect of the State Party concerned.

Article 28 - Declarations of inadmissibility by committees

A committee may, by a unanimous vote, declare inadmissible or strike out of its list of cases an individual application submitted under Article 34 where such a decision can be taken without further examination. The decision shall be final.

Article 29 - Decisions by Chambers on admissibility and merits

1. If no decision is taken under Article 28, a Chamber shall decide on the admissibility and merits of individual applications submitted under Article 34.

2. A Chamber shall decide on the admissibility and merits of inter-State applications submitted under Article 33.

3. The decision on admissibility shall be taken separately unless the Court, in exceptional cases, decides otherwise.

Article 30 - Relinquishment of jurisdiction to the Grand Chamber

Where a case pending before a Chamber raises a serious question affecting the interpretation of the Convention or the protocols thereto, or where the resolution of a question before the Chamber might have a result inconsistent with a judgment previously delivered by the Court, the Chamber may, at any time before it has rendered its judgment, relinquish jurisdiction in favour of the Grand Chamber, unless one of the parties to the case objects.

Article 31 - Powers of the Grand Chamber

The Grand Chamber shall
(a) determine applications submitted either under Article 33 or Article 34 when a Chamber has relinquished jurisdiction under Article 30 or when the case has been referred to it under Article 43; and
(b) consider requests for advisory opinions submitted under Article 47.

Article 32 - Jurisdiction of the Court

1. The jurisdiction of the Court shall extend to all matters concerning the interpretation and application of the Convention and the protocols thereto which are referred to it as provided in Articles 33, 34 and 47.

2. In the event of dispute as to whether the Court has jurisdiction, the Court shall decide.

Article 33 - Inter-State cases

Any High Contracting Party may refer to the Court any alleged breach of the provisions of the Convention and the protocols thereto by another High Contracting Party.

Article 34 - Individual applications

The Court may receive applications from any person, non-governmental organisation or group of individuals claiming to be the victim of a violation by one of the High Contracting Parties of the rights set forth in the Convention or the protocols thereto. The High Contracting Parties undertake not to hinder in any way the effective exercise of this right.

Article 35 - Admissibility criteria

1. The Court may only deal with the matter after all domestic remedies have been exhausted, according to the generally recognised rules of international law, and within a period of six months from the date on which the final decision was taken.

2. The Court shall not deal with any individual application submitted under Article 34 that
(a) is anonymous; or
(b) is substantially the same as a matter that has already been examined by the Court or has already been submitted to another procedure of international investigation or settlement and contains no relevant new information.

3. The Court shall declare inadmissible any individual application submitted under Article 34 which it considers incompatible with the provisions of the Convention or the protocols thereto, manifestly ill-founded, or an abuse of the right of application.

4. The Court shall reject any application which it considers inadmissible under this Article. It may do so at any stage of the proceedings.

Article 36 - Third-party intervention

1. In all cases before a Chamber or the Grand Chamber, a High Contracting Party one of whose nationals is an applicant shall have the right to submit written comments and to take part in hearings.

2. The President of the Court may, in the interest of the proper administration of justice, invite any High Contracting Party which is not a party to the proceedings or any person concerned who is not the applicant to submit written comments or take part in hearings.

Article 37 - Striking out applications

1. The Court may at any stage of the proceedings decide to strike an application out of its list of cases where the circumstances lead to the conclusion that
(a) the applicant does not intend to pursue his application; or
(b) the matter has been resolved; or
(c) for any other reason established by the Court, it is no longer justified to continue the examination of the application.

However, the Court shall continue the examination of the application if respect for human rights as defined in the Convention and the protocols thereto so requires.

2. The Court may decide to restore an application to its list of cases if it considers that the circumstances justify such a course.

Article 38 - Examination of the case and friendly settlement proceedings

1. If the Court declares the application admissible, it shall
(a) pursue the examination of the case, together with the representatives of the parties, and if need be, undertake an investigation, for the effective conduct of which the States concerned shall furnish all necessary facilities;
(b) place itself at the disposal of the parties concerned with a view to securing a friendly settlement of the matter on the basis of respect for human rights as defined in the Convention and the protocols thereto.

2. Proceedings conducted under paragraph 1.b shall be confidential.

Article 39 - Finding of a friendly settlement

If a friendly settlement is effected, the Court shall strike the case out of its list by means of a decision which shall be confined to a brief statement of the facts and of the solution reached.

Article 40 - Public hearings and access to documents

1. Hearings shall be public unless the Court in exceptional circumstances decides otherwise.

2. Documents deposited with the Registrar shall be accessible to the public unless the President of the Court decides otherwise.

Article 41 - Just satisfaction

If the Court finds that there has been a violation of the Convention or the protocols thereto, and if the internal law of the High Contracting Party concerned allows only partial reparation to be made, the Court shall, if necessary, afford just satisfaction to the injured party.

Article 42 - Judgments of Chambers

Judgments of Chambers shall become final in accordance with the provisions of Article 44, paragraph 2.

Article 43 - Referral to the Grand Chamber

1.   Within a period of three months from the date of the judgment of the Chamber, any party to the case may, in exceptional cases, request that the case be referred to the Grand Chamber.

2.   A panel of five judges of the Grand Chamber shall accept the request if the case raises a serious question affecting the interpretation or application of the Convention or the protocols thereto, or a serious issue of general importance.

3.   If the panel accepts the request, the Grand Chamber shall decide the case by means of a judgment.

Article 44 - Final judgments

1.   The judgment of the Grand Chamber shall be final.

2.   The judgment of a Chamber shall become final
(a)   when the parties declare that they will not request that the case be referred to the Grand Chamber; or
(b)   three months after the date of the judgment, if reference of the case to the Grand Chamber has not been requested; or
(c)   when the panel of the Grand Chamber rejects the request to refer under Article 43.

3.   The final judgment shall be published.

Article 45 - Reasons for judgments and decisions

1.   Reasons shall be given for judgments as well as for decisions declaring applications admissible or inadmissible.

2.   If a judgment does not represent, in whole or in part, the unanimous opinion of the judges, any judge shall be entitled to deliver a separate opinion.

Article 46 - Binding force and execution of judgments

1.   The High Contracting Parties undertake to abide by the final judgment of the Court in any case to which they are parties.

2.   The final judgment of the Court shall be transmitted to the Committee of Ministers, which shall supervise its execution.

Article 47 - Advisory opinions

1.   The Court may, at the request of the Committee of Ministers, give advisory opinions on legal questions concerning the interpretation of the Convention and the protocols thereto.

2.   Such opinions shall not deal with any question relating to the content or scope of the rights or freedoms defined in Section I of the Convention and the protocols thereto, or with any other question which the Court or the Committee of Ministers might have to consider in consequence of any such proceedings as could be instituted in accordance with the Convention.

3.   Decisions of the Committee of Ministers to request an advisory opinion of the Court shall require a majority vote of the representatives entitled to sit on the Committee.

Article 48 - Advisory jurisdiction of the Court

The Court shall decide whether a request for an advisory opinion submitted by the Committee of Ministers is within its competence as defined in Article 47.

Article 49 - Reasons for advisory opinions

1.   Reasons shall be given for advisory opinions of the Court.

2.   If the advisory opinion does not represent, in whole or in part, the unanimous opinion of the judges, any judge shall be entitled to deliver a separate opinion.

3.   Advisory opinions of the Court shall be communicated to the Committee of Ministers.

Article 50 - Expenditure on the Court

The expenditure on the Court shall be borne by the Council of Europe.

Article 51 - Privileges and immunities of judges

The judges shall be entitled, during the exercise of their functions, to the privileges and immunities provided for in Article 40 of the Statute of the Council of Europe and in the agreements made thereunder."

Article 2

1.   Section V of the Convention shall become Section III of the Convention; Article 57 of the Convention shall become Article 52 of the Convention; Articles 58 and 59 of the Convention shall be deleted, and Articles 60 to 66 of the Convention shall become Articles 53 to 59 of the Convention respectively.

2.   Section I of the Convention shall be entitled "Rights and freedoms" and new Section III of the Convention shall be entitled "Miscellaneous provisions". Articles 1 to 18 and new Articles 52 to 59 of the Convention shall be provided with headings, as listed in the appendix to this Protocol.

3.   In new Article 56, in paragraph 1, the words ", subject to paragraph 4 of this Article," shall be inserted after the word "shall"; in paragraph 4, the words "Commission to receive petitions" and "in accordance with Article 25 of the present Convention" shall be replaced by the words "Court to receive applications" and "as provided in Article 34 of the Convention" respectively. In new Article 58, paragraph 4, the words "Article 63" shall be replaced by the words "Article 56".

4.   The Protocol to the Convention shall be amended as follows
(a) the Articles shall be provided with the headings listed in the appendix to the present Protocol; and
(b) in Article 4, last sentence, the words "of Article 63" shall be replaced by the words "of Article 56".

5.   Protocol No 4 shall be amended as follows
(a) the Articles shall be provided with the headings listed in the appendix to the present Protocol;
(b) in Article 5, paragraph 3, the words "of Article 63" shall be replaced by the words "of Article 56"; a new paragraph 5 shall be added, which shall read

"Any State which has made a declaration in accordance with paragraph 1 or 2 of this Article may at any time thereafter declare on behalf of one or more of the territories to which the declaration relates that it accepts the competence of the Court to receive applications from individuals, non-governmental organisations or groups of individuals as provided in Article 34 of the Convention in respect of all or any of Articles 1 to 4 of this Protocol."; and c   paragraph 2 of Article 6 shall be deleted.

6.   Protocol No 6 shall be amended as follows
(a) the Articles shall be provided with the headings listed in the appendix to the present Protocol; and
(b) in Article 4 the words "under Article 64" shall be replaced by the words "under Article 57".

7.   Protocol No 7 shall be amended as follows
(a) the Articles shall be provided with the headings listed in the appendix to the present Protocol;
(b) in Article 6, paragraph 4, the words "of Article 63" shall be replaced by the words "of Article 56"; a new paragraph 6 shall be added, which shall read

"Any State which has made a declaration in accordance with paragraph 1 or 2 of this Article may at any time thereafter declare on behalf of one or more of the territories to which the declaration relates that it accepts the competence of the Court to receive applications from individuals, non-governmental organisations or groups of individuals as provided in Article 34 of the Convention in respect of Articles 1 to 5 of this Protocol."; and

c   paragraph 2 of Article 7 shall be deleted.

8.   Protocol No 9 shall be repealed.

Article 3

1.   This Protocol shall be open for signature by member States of the Council of Europe signatories to the Convention, which may express their consent to be bound by
(a) signature without reservation as to ratification, acceptance or approval; or
(b) signature subject to ratification, acceptance or approval, followed by ratification, acceptance or approval.

2.   The instruments of ratification, acceptance or approval shall be deposited with the Secretary General of the Council of Europe.

Article 4

This Protocol shall enter into force on the first day of the month following the expiration of a period of one year after the date on which all Parties to the Convention have expressed their consent to be bound by the Protocol in accordance with the provisions of Article 3. The election of new judges may take place, and any further necessary steps may be taken to establish the new Court, in accordance with the provisions of this Protocol from the date on which all Parties to the Convention have expressed their consent to be bound by the Protocol.

Article 5

1.   Without prejudice to the provisions in paragraphs 3 and 4 below, the terms of office of the judges, members of the Commission, Registrar and Deputy Registrar shall expire at the date of entry into force of this Protocol.

2.   Applications pending before the Commission which have not been declared admissible at the date of the entry into force of this Protocol shall be examined by the Court in accordance with the provisions of this Protocol.

3.   Applications which have been declared admissible at the date of entry into force of this Protocol shall continue to be dealt with by members of the Commission within a period of one year thereafter. Any applications the examination of which has not been completed within the aforesaid period shall be transmitted to the Court which shall examine them as admissible cases in accordance with the provisions of this Protocol.

4.   With respect to applications in which the Commission, after the entry into force of this Protocol, has adopted a report in accordance with former Article 31 of the Convention, the report shall be transmitted to the parties, who shall not be at liberty to publish it. In accordance with the provisions applicable prior to the entry into force of this Protocol, a case may be referred to the Court. The panel of the Grand Chamber shall determine whether one of the Chambers or the Grand Chamber shall decide the case. If the case is decided by a Chamber, the decision of the Chamber shall be final. Cases not referred to the Court shall be dealt with by the Committee of Ministers acting in accordance with the provisions of former Article 32 of the Convention.

5.   Cases pending before the Court which have not been decided at the date of entry into force of this Protocol shall be transmitted to the Grand Chamber of the Court, which shall examine them in accordance with the provisions of this Protocol.

6.   Cases pending before the Committee of Ministers which have not been decided under former Article 32 of the Convention at the date of entry into force of this Protocol shall be completed by the Committee of Ministers acting in accordance with that Article.

Article 6

Where a High Contracting Party had made a declaration recognising the competence of the Commission or the jurisdiction of the Court under former Article 25 or 46 of the Convention with respect to matters arising after or based on facts occurring subsequent to any such declaration, this limitation shall remain valid for the jurisdiction of the Court under this Protocol.

Article 7

The Secretary General of the Council of Europe shall notify the member States of the Council of
(a) any signature;
(b) the deposit of any instrument of ratification, acceptance or approval;
(c) the date of entry into force of this Protocol or of any of its provisions in accordance with Article 4; and
(d) any other act, notification or communication relating to this Protocol.
In witness whereof, the undersigned, being duly authorised thereto, have signed this Protocol.

Done at Strasbourg, this 11th day of May 1994, in English and French, both texts being equally authentic, in a single copy which shall be deposited in the archives of the Council of Europe. The Secretary General of the Council of Europe shall transmit certified copies to each member State of the Council of Europe.

Appendix

Headings ot articles to be inserted into the text of the Convention for the Protection of Human Rights and Fundamental Freedoms and its protocols. See footnote 1

Article 1 - Obligation to respect human rights
Article 2 - Right to life
Article 3 - Prohibition of torture
Article 4 - Prohibition of slavery and forced labour
Article 5 - Right to liberty and security
Article 6 - Right to a fair trial
Article 7 - No punishment without law
Article 8 - Right to respect for private and family life
Article 9 - Freedom of thought, conscience and religion
Article 10 - Freedom of expression
Article 11 - Freedom of assembly and association
Article 12 - Right to marry
Article 13 - Right to an effective remedy
Article 14 - Prohibition of discrimination
Article 15 - Derogation in time of emergency
Article 16 - Restrictions on political activity of aliens
Article 17 - Prohibition of abuse of rights
Article 18 - Limitation on use of restrictions on rights
[...]
Article 52 - Enquiries by the Secretary General
Article 53 - Safeguard for existing human rights
Article 54 - Powers of the Committee of Ministers
Article 55 - Exclusion of other means of dispute settlement
Article 56 - Territorial application
Article 57 - Reservations
Article 58 - Denunciation
Article 59 - Signature and ratification

Protocol
Article 1 - Protection of property
Article 2 - Right to education
Article 3 - Right to free elections
Article 4 - Territorial application
Article 5 - Relationship to the Convention
Article 6 - Signature and ratification

Protocol No 4
Article 1 - Prohibition of imprisonment for debt
Article 2 - Freedom of movement
Article 3 - Prohibition of expulsion of nationals
Article 4 - Prohibition of collective expulsion of aliens

Article 5 - Territorial application
Article 6 - Relationship to the Convention
Article 7 - Signature and ratification

Protocol No 6
Article 1 - Abolition of the death penalty
Article 2 - Death penalty in time of war
Article 3 - Prohibition of derogations
Article 4 - Prohibition of reservations
Article 5 - Territorial application
Article 6 - Relationship to the Convention
Article 7 - Signature and ratification
Article 8 - Entry into force
Article 9 - Depositary functions

Protocol No 7
Article 1 - Procedural safeguards relating to expulsion of aliens
Article 2 - Right of appeal in criminal matters
Article 3 - Compensation for wrongful conviction
Article 4 - Right not to be tried or punished twice
Article 5 - Equality between spouses
Article 6 - Territorial application
Article 7 - Relationship to the Convention
Article 8 - Signature and ratification
Article 9 - Entry into force
Article 10 - Depositary functions

Footnote
1   Headings have already been added to new Articles 19 to 51 of the Convention by the present
    Protocol.

Immigration and Asylum Bill

Human rights

59. Acts made unlawful by section 6(1) of the Human Rights Act 1998.
(1) A person who alleges that an authority has, in taking any decision under the Immigration Acts relating to that person's entitlement to enter or remain in the United Kingdom, acted in breach of his human rights may appeal to an adjudicator against that decision.

(2) For the purposes of this Part, an authority acts in breach of a person's human rights if he acts, or fails to act, in relation to that other person in a way which is made unlawful by section 6(1) of the Human Rights Act 1998.

(3) Subsections (4) and (5) apply if, in proceedings before an adjudicator or the Immigration Appeal Tribunal on an appeal, a question arises as to whether an authority has, in taking any decision under the Immigration Acts relating to the appellant's entitlement to enter or remain in the United Kingdom, acted in breach of the appellant's human rights.

(4) The adjudicator, or the Tribunal, has jurisdiction to consider the question.

(5) If the adjudicator, or the Tribunal, decides that the authority concerned acted in breach of the appellant's human rights, the appeal may be allowed on that ground.

(6) "Authority" means—
(a) the Secretary of State;
(b) an immigration officer;
(c) a person responsible for the grant or refusal of entry clearance.

Extracts from Hansard

(This is a selection of some of the statements made during the Parliamentary debates on the Human Rights Act 1998 by introducing ministers and Special Appeals Commission Bill 1999 where references are made to rights under the ECHR.)

House of Lords, Report Stage

Hansard HL, 29 January 1998, Column 421

The Lord Chancellor (Lord Irvine of Lairg): ... The word 'further' is included in the Long Title because, in our national arrangements, the Convention can, and is, already applied in a variety of different circumstances and is relied on in a range of ways by our own courts.

The Bill will greatly increase the ability of our courts to enforce Convention rights, but it is not introducing a wholly new concept. As I have said before, the Bill as such does not incorporate Convention rights into domestic law but, in accordance with the language of the Long Title, it gives further effect in the United Kingdom to Convention rights by requiring the courts in clause 3(1), 'So far as it is possible to do so' to construe – in the language of the statute, to read and give effect to – primary legislation and subordinate legislation in a way which is compatible with the Convention rights. That is an interpretative principle... I have to make this point absolutely plain. The European Convention on Human Rights under this Bill is not made part of our law. The Bill gives the European Convention on Human Rights a special relationship which will mean that the courts will give effect to the interpretative provisions to which I have already referred, but it does not make the Convention directly justiciable as it would be if it were expressly made part of our law. I want there to be no ambiguity about that ...

[Column 422]

The short point is that if the Convention rights were incorporated into our law, they would be directly justiciable and would be enforced by our courts. That is not the scheme of this Bill. If the courts find it impossible to construe primary legislation in a way which is compatible with the Convention rights, the primary legislation remains in full force and effect. All that the courts may do is to make a declaration of incompatibility.

5 February 1998: Column 839

The Lord Chancellor: My Lords, it is right that this Bill occupies a central position in our programme of constitutional reform. By bringing rights home it will enable people in this country to enforce their Convention rights against public authorities before our domestic courts. I believe that this will have a profound and beneficial effect on our system of law and government and will develop over the years a strong culture of human rights in our country.

The Bill is based on a number of important principles. Legislation should be construed compatibly with the Convention as far as possible. The sovereignty of

Parliament should be disturbed. Where the courts cannot reconcile legislation with Convention rights. Parliament should be able to do so - and more quickly, if thought appropriate, than by enacting primary legislation. Public authorities should comply with Convention rights or face the prospect of legal challenge. Remedies should be available for a breach of Convention rights by a public authority.

… The Bill provides for all legislation, past and future, to be interpreted as far as possible in a way which is compatible with the Convention rights. The Convention rights are the magnetic north and the needle of judicial interpretation will swing towards them.

… the courts are not to set aside primary legislation under the Bill, but the principle of statutory construction is a strong alternative. It will be unlawful for public authorities to act in a way which is incompatible with the Convention rights and that also is a strong and far-reaching provision. Taken together, those measures provide for the Convention rights to have a great effect in our domestic law. I go; in 99 per cent of the cases that will arise, there will be no need for judicial declarations of incompatibility.

… we have not provided for the Convention rights to be directly justiciable in actions between private individuals. We have sought to protect the human rights of individuals against the abuse of power by the state, broadly defined, rather than to protect them against each other.

SECTION 1: THE CONVENTION AND THE FIRST PROTOCOL

House of Lords, Second Reading

Hansard HL, 3 November 1997, Column 1308

The Parliamentary Under-Secretary of State, Home Office (Lord Williams of Mostyn): … Our view is, quite unambiguously, that article 13 is met by the passage of the Bill.

House of Lords, Committee Stage

Hansard HL, 18 November 1997, Column 475

The Lord Chancellor: … The Bill gives effect to article1 by securing to people in the United Kingdom the rights and freedoms of the Convention. It gives effect to article 13 by establishing a scheme under which Convention rights can be raised before our domestic courts. To that end, remedies are provided in clause 8. If the concern is to ensure that the Bill provides an exhaustive code of remedies for those whose Convention rights have been violated, we believe that clause 8 already achieves that and that nothing further is needed.

We have set out in the Bill a scheme to provide remedies for violation of Convention rights and we do not believe that it is necessary to add to it. We also believe that it is undesirable to provide for articles 1 and 13 in the Bill in this way. The courts would be bound to ask themselves what was intended beyond the existing scheme of remedies set out in the Bill. It might lead them to fashion remedies other than the clause 8 remedies, which we regard as sufficient and clear. We believe that clause 8 provides effective remedies before our courts …

Lord Lester of Herne Hill: Is it the intention of the Government that the courts should not be entitled to have regard to article 13 and the case law of the Strasbourg Court on that article in cases where it would otherwise be relevant? ... I give an example. In recent cases brought against Turkey, where there has been torture without adequate police investigations, the European Court has said that regard must be had to article 13 rather than article 6 because it is the former that requires an effective post mortem. Is it the intention of the Government that in cases where the European Court has said that the right provision is article13 and not article 6 our courts should wear blinkers and are not allowed to look at article 13 or the Court's case law?

The Lord Chancellor: One always has in mind *Pepper v Hart* when one is asked questions of that kind. I shall reply as candidly as I may. Clause 2(1) provides:

> 'A court or tribunal determining a question which has arisen under this Act in connection with a Convention right must take into account any ... judgment, decision, declaration or advisory opinion of the European Court of Human Rights.'

That means what it says. The court must take into account such material ...

My response to the second part of the question posed by the noble Lord, Lord Lester, is that the courts may have regard to article 13. In particular, they may wish to do so when considering the very ample provisions of clause 8(1). I remind your Lordships of the terms of that provision:

> 'In relation to any Act (or proposed Act) of a public authority which the court finds is (or would be) unlawful, it may grant such relief or remedy, or make such order, within its jurisdiction as it considers just and appropriate'.

Knowing the remedial amplitude of the law of the United Kingdom, I cannot see any scope for the argument that English or Scots law is incapable within domestic adjectival law of providing effective remedies.

... to incorporate expressly article 13 may lead to the courts fashioning remedies about which we know nothing other than the clause 8 remedies which we regard as sufficient and clear. Until we are told in some specific respect how clause 8 is or may reasonably be anticipated to be deficient we maintain our present position.

House of Commons, Committee Stage

Hansard HC, 20 May 1998, Column 979

Secretary of State for the Home Department (Mr Jack Straw): We decided it was inappropriate to include article 13 for the following reasons.

First and foremost, it is the Bill that gives effect to article 13, so there was an issue of duplication. The Bill sets out clearly how the Convention rights will be given further effect in our domestic law, and what remedies are to be available when a court or tribunal finds that a person has been the victim of an unlawful act ... I will briefly summarise the relevant provisions.

Clause 3 requires legislation to be read and given effect, as far as possible, in accordance with Convention rights. Clause 6 is unlawful for a public authority to act in a way that is incompatible with a Convention right. Clause 7 enables the victim of an unlawful act to rely on his or her Convention rights in any legal proceedings, or to bring proceedings on Convention grounds. Clause 8 provides that a court or tribunal, when it finds that a public authority has acted unlawfully, may grant the victim such relief or remedy, or make such order, within its jurisdiction as it considers just and appropriate.

Those are powerful provisions, as is acknowledged … In our judgment, they afford ample protection for individuals' rights under the Convention. In particular, clause 8(1) gives the courts considerable scope for doing justice when unlawful acts have been committed. Indeed, no one has been able to suggest any respect in which the Bill is deficient in providing effective remedies to those who have been victims of an unlawful act.

… If we were to include article 13 in the Bill in addition to the remedies provided in clauses 3, 6, 7 and 8, the question would inevitably arise what the courts would make of the amendment, which, on the face of it, contains nothing new. I suggest that the amendment would either cause confusion or prompt the courts to act in ways not intended by the Bill – for example, by creating remedies beyond those available in clause 8. Whatever the outcome, the result would be undesirable …

Our overall judgment is that the amendment, which would incorporate article 13, would not add anything much, but might create uncertainties. We see no particular reason to accept it.

We do not believe that those people will be denied an effective remedy. Indeed, as I said, very few people have suggested that the remedies we are providing will be ineffective – however, they must be balanced and proportionate. Ultimately, courts will have to take account of jurisprudence laid down by the court in Strasbourg.

… there is little point including in a Bill additional wording whose probable effect would be not to make any difference, but whose possible effect would be to add uncertainty… I think that he had in mind no more but no less than the fact that the courts would apply clause 2(1), which says

> "A court or tribunal determining a question which has arisen under this Act in connection with a Convention right must take into account"…

not "have regard to" –

> "any … judgment, decision, declaration or advisory opinion of the European Court of Human Rights….whenever made or given, so far as, in the opinion of the court or tribunal, it is relevant to the proceedings in which that question has arisen."

Of course, there is Convention jurisprudence on article 13, as on other articles. Lord Lester made that point in respect of the *Chahal* case, which turned on article 13, and said that it would be taken into account and that regard would be had to it. That point is as much in our favour – suggesting that the specific inclusion of article 13 is unnecessary …

[Column 981]

The Convention has been international law for 50 years, and any tribunal will consider the bare text of any original Convention by considering the way in which its application has developed there is, indeed, a requirement to do so, in practice, the courts must take account of the large body of Convention jurisprudence when considering remedies. Obviously, in doing so, they are bound to take judicial notice of article 13, without specifically being bound by it.

That is my judgment about the way in which the law will work. I wish future Judicial Committees of the House of Lords luck in working through these debates. One sometimes wonders about the wisdom of the *Pepper v Hart* judgment in terms of the work that it has given the higher judiciary. It is a fine point, but since we saw that there was no purpose, and indeed that there were some dangers, in including article 13, we thought that it was best omitted ...

We believe that we are adequately covering the issue of remedies in clauses 3, 6, 7 and 8. We are specifically providing remedies that are understandable in English and Scots law. In determining whether a particular remedy is to be granted in respect of any action, the courts must interpret Convention rights as laid down in clause 2.

If I may labour the point, we do not believe that incorporating article 13 adds anything positive to the Bill that is not already there, that covers the point about the courts having to take judicial notice of article 13 as a basic text without being bound by it. We believe that it could create unnecessary doubt, and that is why it is not sensible to accept the amendment,

[Column 986]

As far as I am concerned we are indeed legislating by black-letter law on the face of the Bill.

[Column 987]

We could have a separate debate about the wisdom of the decision in *Pepper v Hart*: I know why the Judicial Committee made that decision and, to some extent, there is common sense in seeking to tease out the meaning of words where they are ambiguous, but I have always taken the view that what Parliament passes is not what Ministers say, but what is on the face of a Bill. That is of profound importance to the manner in which we make legislation.

SECTION 2: INTERPRETATION OF CONVENTION RIGHTS

House of Lords, Second Reading

Hansard HL, 3 November 1997, Column 1230

The Lord Chancellor (Lord Irvine of Lairg): ... Clause 2 requires courts in the United Kingdom to take account of the decisions of the Convention institutions in Strasbourg in their consideration of Convention points which come before them. It is entirely appropriate that our courts should draw on the wealth of existing jurisprudence on the Convention.

House of Commons, Second Reading

Hansard HC, 16 February 1998, Column 773

The Secretary of State for the Home Department (Mr Jack Straw): The Bill makes the position clear, in clause 6(3) and elsewhere. Clause 6 excludes the Houses of Parliament from the category of public authorities, for very good reasons. What the Bill makes clear is that Parliament is supreme, and that if Parliament wishes to maintain the position enshrined in an Act that it has passed, but which is incompatible with the Convention in the eyes of a British court, it is that Act which will remain in force.

There is, however, a separate question, which is why, in most instances, Parliament and Government will wish to recognise the force of a declaration of incompatibility by the High Court. Let us suppose that a case goes to Strasbourg, where the European Court decides that an action by the British Government, or the British Parliament, is outwith the Convention. According to 50 years of practice on both sides, we always put the action right, and bring it into line with the Convention. One of the questions that will always be before Government, in practice, will be, 'Is it sensible to wait for a further challenge to Strasbourg, when the British courts have declared the provision to be outwith the Convention?'

House of Commons, Second Reading

Hansard HC, 16 February 1998, Column 780

The Secretary of State for the Home Department (Mr Jack Straw): ... Clause 2 ensures that, in giving effect to those rights, our domestic courts and tribunals have regard to Strasbourg jurisprudence.

House of Lords, Report Stage

Hansard Hl, 19 January 1998, Column 1270

The Lord Chancellor (Lord Irvine of Lairg): As other noble Lords have said, the word 'binding' is the language of strict precedent but the Convention has no rule of precedent... We take the view that the expression 'take in account' is clear enough. Should a United Kingdom court ever have a case before it which is a precise mirror of one that has been previously considered by the European Court of Human Rights, which I doubt, it may be appropriate for it to apply the European court's findings directly to that case; but in real life cases are rarely as neat and tidy as that. The courts will often be faced with cases that involve factors perhaps specific to the United Kingdom which distinguish them from cases considered by the European Court ...

[Column 1271]

... it is important that our courts have the scope to apply that discretion so as to aid in the development of human rights law.

There may also be occasions when it would be right for the United Kingdom courts to depart from Strasbourg decisions. We must remember that the interpretation of the Convention rights develops over the years. Circumstances may therefore arise in which a judgment given by the European Court of Human Rights decades ago contains pronouncements which it would not be appropriate to apply to the letter in the circumstances of today in a particular set of circumstances affecting this country. The Bill would allow our courts to use their common sense in applying the European Court's judgment to such a case. We feel that to accept this amendment removes from the judges the flexibility and discretion that they require in developing human rights law… Clause 2 requires the courts to pay heed to all the judgments of the European Court of Human Rights regardless of whether they have been given in cases involving the United Kingdom.

SECTION 3: LEGISLATION

House of Lords, Second Reading

Hansard HL, 3 November 1997, Column 1230

The Lord Chancellor (Lord Irvine of Lairg): … Clause 3 provides that legislation, whenever enacted, must as far as possible be read and given effect in a way which is compatible with the Convention rights. This will ensure that, if it is possible to interpret a statute in two ways – one compatible with the Convention and one not – the courts will always choose the interpretation which is compatible. In practice, this will prove a strong form of incorporation … However, the Bill does not allow the courts to set aside or ignore Acts of Parliament. Clause 3 preserves the effect of primary legislation which is …

[Column 1231]

… incompatible with the Convention. It does the same for secondary legislation where it is inevitable incompatible because of the terms of the parent statute…

[Column 1294]

The Bill sets out a scheme for giving effect to the Convention rights which maximises the protection to individuals while retaining the fundamental principle of Parliamentary sovereignty. Clause 3 is the central part of this scheme. Clause 3(1) requires legislation to be read and given effect to so far as it is possible to do so in a way that is compatible with the Convention rights. Clause 3(2) provides that where it is not possible to give a compatible construction to primary legislation or to subordinate legislation whose incompatibility flows from the terms of the parent Act, that does not affect its validity, continuing operation or enforcement. This ensures that the courts are not empowered to strike down Acts of Parliament which they find to be incompatible with the Convention rights. Instead, clause 4 together with clause 10 introduces a new mechanism through which the courts can signal to the Government that a provision of legislation is, in their view, incompatible. It is then for government and Parliament to consider what action should be taken. I believe that this will prove to be an effective procedure and it is also one which accords with our traditions of Parliamentary sovereignty. That is why the Bill adopts it.

House of Commons, Second Reading

Hansard HC, 16 February 1998, Column 780

The Secretary of State for the Home Department (Mr Jack Straw): ... Clause 3 provides that legislation, whenever enacted, must as far as possible be read and given effect in such a way as to be compatible with Convention rights. We expect that, in almost all cases, the courts will be able to interpret legislation compatibly with the Convention. However, we need to provide for the rare cases where that cannot be done. Consistent with maintaining Parliamentary sovereignty, clause 3 therefore provides that if a provision of primary legislation cannot be interpreted compatibly with the Convention rights, that legislation will continue to have force and effect.

House of Commons, Committee Stage

Hansard HC, 3 June 1998, Column 421

The Secretary of State for the Home Department (Mr Jack Straw): ... we want the courts to strive to find an interpretation of legislation that is consistent with Convention rights, so far as the plain words of the ...

[Column 422]

... legislation allow, and only in the last resort to conclude that the legislation is simply incompatible with them....there was a time when all the courts could do to divine the intention of Parliament was to apply themselves to the words on the face of any Act. Now, following *Pepper v Hart*, they are able to look behind that and, not least, to look at the words used by Ministers. I do not think the courts will need to apply themselves to the words that I am about to use, but, for the avoidance of doubt, I will say that it is not our intention that the courts, in applying clause 3, should contort the meaning of words to produce implausible or incredible meanings. I am talking about plain words in what is actually a clear Bill with plain language – with the intention of Parliament set out in Hansard, should the courts wish to refer to it.

... Ever since the Wednesbury decision, the courts have chided others for being unreasonable, so it is difficult to imagine them not being reasonable. If we had used just the word 'reasonable', we would have created a subjective test. 'Possible' is different. It means, ...

[Column 423]

... 'What is the possible interpretation? Let us look at this set of words and the possible interpretations.'

SECTIONS 4 AND 5: DECLARATIONS OF INCOMPATIBILITY

House of Lords, Second Reading

Hansard HL, 3 November 1997, Column 1231

The Lord Chancellor (Lord Irvine of Lairg): ... Clause 4 provides for the rare cases where the courts may have to make declarations of incompatibility. Such declarations are serious. That is why clause 5 gives the Crown the right to have notice of any case where a court is considering making a declaration of incompatibility and the right to be joined as a party to the proceedings, so that it can make representations on the point.

A declaration of incompatibility will not itself change the law. The statute will continue to apply despite its incompatibility. But the declaration is very likely to prompt the government and Parliament to respond.

House of Commons, Second Reading

Hansard HC, 16 February 1997, Column 780

The Secretary of State for the Home Department (Mr Jack Straw): ... A declaration of incompatibility will not affect the continuing validity of the legislation in question. That would be contrary to the principle of the Bill. However, it will be a clear signal to Government and Parliament that, in the court's view, a provision of legislation does not conform to the standards of the Convention. To return to a matter that I discussed earlier, it is likely that the Government and Parliament would wish to respond to such a situation and would do so rapidly. We have discussed how that would operate and no doubt there will be further detailed discussions in committee on the floor of the House.

House of Commons, Third Reading

Hansard HC, 21 October 1998, Column 1306

Jack Straw: ... The right honourable and learned Gentleman asked me what would happen with the lower courts, and whether they would follow the judgment. No, they would not, because clause 4(6) is clear; a declaration does not affect the validity, continuing operation or enforcement of the provisions in respect of which it is given. There is absolute clarity there. In a judicial and political sense, the status quo ante would apply. Then, obviously, the Government would have to consider, and in most cases they would consider the position pretty rapidly. No time limit is set down, but the reverse could not apply. We could not, for example, say that the declaration of incompatibility would have force unless or until the Government said the reverse. That would create considerable uncertainty.

SECTION 7: PROCEEDINGS

House of Lords, Second Reading

Hansard HL, 3 November 1997, Column 1232

The Lord Chancellor (Lord Irvine of Lairg): If people believe that their Convention rights have been infringed by a public authority, what can they do about it? Under clause 7 they will be able to rely on Convention points in any legal proceedings involving a public authority; for example as part of a defence to criminal or civil proceedings, or when acting as plaintiff in civil proceedings, or in seeking judicial review, or on appeal. They will also be able to bring proceedings against public authorities purely on Convention grounds even if no other cause of action is open to them.

House of Lords, Second Reading

Hansard HC, 16 February 1998, Column 780

The Secretary of State for the Home Department (Mr Jack Straw): ... Clause 7 enables individuals who believe that they have been a victim of an unlawful act of a public authority to rely on the Convention rights in legal proceedings. They may do so in a number of ways: by bringing proceedings under the Bill in an appropriate court or tribunal; in seeking judicial review; as part of a defence against a criminal or civil action brought against them by a public authority; or in the course of an appeal. Clause 7 ensures that an individual will always have a means by which to raise his or her Convention rights. It is intended that existing court procedures will, wherever possible, be used for that purpose.

House of Commons, Second Reading

Hansard HC, 16 February 1998, Column 856

The Parliamentary Under-Secretary of State for the Home Department (Mr Mike O'Brien): ... My honourable Friend ... asked us to consider allowing organisations that are not themselves victims to bring class actions and to anticipate issues. We considered doing this but decided to follow the Convention practice and enable victims of breaches to raise issues as they occur.

House of Lords, Second Reading

Hansard HL, 24 November 1997, Column 830

The Lord Chancellor (Lord Irvine of Lairg): The purpose of the Bill is to give greater effect in our domestic law to the Convention rights. It is in keeping with this approach that persons should be able to rely ...

[Column 831]

... on the Convention rights before our domestic courts in precisely the same circumstances as they can rely upon them before the Strasbourg institutions. The wording of clause 7 therefore reflects the terms of the Convention, which stipulates that petitions to the European Commission (or to the European Court once the Eleventh Protocol comes into force) will be ruled inadmissible unless the applicant is the victim of the alleged violation.

I acknowledge that a consequence of that approach is that a narrower test will be applied for bringing applications by judicial review on Convention grounds than will continue to apply in applications for judicial review on other grounds. But interest groups will still be able to provide assistance to victims who bring cases under the Bill and to bring cases directly where they themselves are victims of an unlawful act.

I also point out that clause 7, consistently with the position in Strasbourg, also treats as victims those who are faced with the threat of public authority proposing to act in a way which would be unlawful under clause 6(1). So potential victims are included.

Interest groups will similarly be able to assist potential victims to bring challenges to action which is threatened before it is actually carried out.

Lord Goodhart: Can the noble and Learned Lord the Lord chancellor say what is the position of a public interest group which, having perfectly properly brought proceedings under clause 11 of the Bill on grounds …

[Column 832]

… which do not involve Convention rights, then finds that in those same proceedings it is unable to raise issues of Convention rights because of clause 7?

The Lord Chancellor: … I do not believe, for reasons I shall explain in a moment, that that consequence will follow.

… Essentially we believe the victim/potential victim test to be right. If there is unlawful action or if unlawful action is threatened then there will be victims or potential victims who will complain and who will in practice be supported by interest groups. If there are no victims, the issue is probably academic and the courts should not be troubled.

We are right to mirror the law as Strasbourg applies it.

… in relation to third-party intervention. The European Court of Human Rights rules of procedure allow non-parties such as national and international non-governmental organisations to make written submissions in the form of a brief. There is no reason why any change to primary legislation in this Bill is needed to allow the domestic courts to develop a similar practice in human rights cases, which is the answer to the noble Lord's question on how I would respond to the point that an interest group would have the right to be heard in a judicial review case under the English domestic test but that, if there was not a victim, could the individual interest group be heard on the Convention point? So now… I address an answer to that question.

This is a development – that is to say, allowing third parties to intervene and be heard – which has already begun in the higher courts of this country in public law cases. Provisions as to standing are quite different. They determine who can become parties to the proceedings. The standing rule which the Bill proposes in relation to Convention cases *simpliciter* is identical to that operated at Strasbourg; and why not? Is that not right in principle? It would not, however, prevent the acceptance by the courts in this country of non-governmental organisational briefs here any more than it does in Strasbourg.

Your Lordships' House, in its judicial capacity, has recently given leave for non-governmental organisations to intervene and file amicus briefs. It has done that in …

[Column 833]

… *R v Khan* for the benefit of Liberty and it has done that in *R v Secretary of State for the Home Department, ex p Venables* for the benefit of Justice. So it appears to me... that the natural position to take is to adopt the victim test as applied by Strasbourg when complaint is made of a denial of Convention rights, recognising that our courts will be ready to permit amicus written briefs from non-governmental organisations; that is to say briefs, but not to treat them as full parties.

[Column 834]

... Clause 7(1)(b) does not touch a third party who has not *ex hypothesi* been the victim of the infringment of a Convention right. It in no way precludes a third party from making submissions about the implication of Convention rights in written briefs if a written brief is invited or accepted by the court, as I believe will happen.

As regards oral interventions by a third party, I dare say that the courts will be equally hospitable to oral interventions provided that they are brief.

... It is not part of the intention of this Bill to alter the standing rules in relation to judicial review in either England or Scotland. It is part of the intention of this Bill to import the Strasbourg victim test in relation to complaints based solely on denial of Convention rights.

House of Commons, Committee Stage

Hansard HC, 24 June 1998, Column 1084

The Parliamentary Under-Secretary of State for the Home Department (Mr Mike O'Brien): ... We are appropriating the text of article 34 and the jurisprudence that goes with it. The intention is that a victim under the Bill should be in the same position as a victim in Strasbourg. A local ...

[Column 1085]

... authority cannot be a victim under clause 7 because it cannot be a victim in Strasbourg under current Strasbourg jurisprudence. On the definition, the Convention provides that

'The Commission may receive petitions ... from any person, non-governmental organisation or group of individuals claiming to be a victim of a violation by one of the High Contracting Parties of the rights set forth in this Convention.'

Applying the victim requirement, the basic approach of the Commission and the Court has been to require that the applicant must claim to be directly affected in some way by the matter complained of. In some cases, they have interpreted fairly flexibly the requirement for the applicant to be directly affected, although the jurisprudence on the issue is not always entirely consistent ... Applications have been allowed not only by the person immediately affected – sometimes referred to as the direct victim – but by indirect victims. Where there has been an alleged violation of the right to life and the direct victim is dead, for example, close relatives of the deceased can be treated as victims on the basis that they were indirectly affected by the alleged violation... Obviously, [family members] can be victims in appropriate circumstances. For example, a decision to deport someone might allow the family of the person to claim to be a victim of a violation of article 8 – the right to respect for family life. I can confirm that we have no intention of restricting guardians *ad litem* or...

[Column 1086]

... others who could normally undertake cases from doing so. Likewise, a case can be brought on behalf of a dead victim by his or her family or relatives. The best known case, of which we have all head, is the 'Death on the Rock' case, brought on behalf of a dead IRA terrorist shot in Gibraltar. That is the sort of area that we are considering. A person may be able to claim that he or she is directly affected as a consequence of a violation of the rights of someone else. Where complaints are brought by persons threatened by deportation, that may arise.

Under the provisions of the human rights Convention, many groups may feel that they have an interest in a particular issue and wish to assist the court. We are talking not only of Liberty, as there are a large number of different groups. For example, the Right to Life could produce a series of litigation cases, which might involve many interest groups that might want to assist the court. Interest groups, such as professional associations and NGOs, can bring an application in Strasbourg only if they can demonstrate that they themselves are victims of a breach – that is, that they are in some way affected by the measure complained of. It is not enough that the actual victim, whether a member of the organisation or not, consents to them acting on his behalf. In *B v United Kingdom*, both Mrs B and the Society for the Protection of the Unborn Child brought an application complaining of the way in which the law affected electoral expenses. The Commission ruled the application by SPUC inadmissible because it was not directly affected by the law – only Mrs B had been prosecuted. On the other hand, in *Council of Civil Service Unions v United Kingdom*, the Commission accepted that the CCSU was itself a victim of the GCHQ ban and could therefore bring an application, although it was rejected on different grounds. An NGO may represent its members in certain contexts and, in that case, it needs to identify them and produce the evidence of authority. In such circumstances, the NGO does not, however, thereby become a party itself.

Our courts will develop their own jurisprudence on the issue, taking account of Strasbourg cases and the Strasbourg jurisprudence. As a Government, our aim is to grant access to victims.

The Lord Chancellor: I well understand the reasons why noble Lords champion the sufficient interest test which applies in judicial review applications. But of course the provision in this Bill in no way affects that test of standing for judicial review which has been developed by the courts and not created by statute.

As regards the proposed statutory test, I believe that the concerns expressed about applying the victim test are misplaced. I say immediately to the noble Earl, Lord Russell, that there is nothing in our Bill which would prevent pressure groups –interest groups – from assisting and providing representations for victims who wish to bring cases forward.

There is a flexible Strasbourg jurisprudence on the victim test which I suggest the English courts would have no difficulty applying. Although I hesitate to take up time, and indeed abstain from doing so, I could cite example after example of an expansive approach by the Strasbourg court to the victim test.

As we have said a number of times, the purpose of the Bill is to give further effect in our domestic law to our Convention rights, and it is in keeping with that approach that a person should be able to rely on those rights before our courts in the same circumstances that they can rely upon them before the Strasbourg institutions, and not in different circumstances. Bringing rights home means exactly what it says – to mirror the approach taken by the Strasbourg court in interpreting Convention rights.

I acknowledge that as a consequence, and despite the flexibility of the Strasbourg test, a narrower test will apply for bringing applications on Convention grounds than in applications for judicial review on other grounds. But I venture to think that interest groups will plainly be able to provide assistance to victims who bring cases under the Bill, including, as I mentioned in Committee, the filing of amicus briefs. Interest groups themselves will be able to bring cases directly where they are victims of an unlawful act. I do not believe that different tests for Convention and non-Convention cases will cause any difficulties for the courts or prevent interest groups providing assistance to victims of unlawful acts.

House of Commons, Committee Stage

Hansard HC, 24 June 1998, Column 1083

The Parliamentary Under-Secretary of State for the Home Department (Mr Mike O'Brien): ... The purpose of the Bill is to give effect in our domestic law to the Convention rights. It is in keeping with that approach that people should be able to rely on those rights before our courts in the same circumstances as they can rely on them before the Strasbourg institutions. Clause 7 accordingly seeks to mirror the approach taken by Strasbourg – reliance on the Convention rights is restricted to victims or potential victims of unlawful acts and the definition of a victim for this purpose is tied to article 34 of the Convention as amended by the 11th Protocol ...

I acknowledge that, as a consequence, a narrower test will be applied for bringing applications by judicial review on Convention grounds than in applications for judicial review on other grounds. However, interest groups will still be able to provide assistance to victims who bring cases under the Bill, including the filing of amicus briefs. Interest groups will also be able to bring cases directly where they are victims of an unlawful act.

I do not believe that the different tests for Convention and non-Convention cases will cause undue difficulty for the courts, or prevent interest groups from helping individuals who are victims of unlawful acts.

... the Bill does not prevent interest groups from providing assistance to a victim once a case is brought.

House of Commons, Committee Stage

Hansard HC, 20 May 1998, Column 1094

The Parliamentary Under-Secretary of State for the Home Department (Mr Mike O'Brien): ... proceedings brought on Convention grounds alone and not under any pre-existing cause of action ... should be no different from other civil proceedings in having a limitation period ... our amendment relates only to proceedings under clause

7(1)(a). If a plaintiff proceeded under clause 7(1)(b) – that is to say, he brought proceedings under an existing cause of action and relied on his Convention rights as an additional argument in support of his case – the limitation period would be the one that applies in the normal way to the existing cause of action.

The Government amendment provides that proceedings under clause 7(1)(a) must be brought within one year, beginning with the date on which the act complained of took place, or within such longer period as the court or tribunal considers equitable, having regard to all the circumstances. However, that time limit is subject to any stricter time limit in relation to the procedure in question. The most obvious such case is judicial review. Assuming that the new rules of court that will be needed for the Bill provide that a procedure analogous to judicial review may ...

[Column 1095]

... be used for cases under clause 7(1)(a), it is reasonable that the time limit for that procedure – which is three months – should continue to apply. It would not be right for applicants who choose to bring their claims by way of judicial review to benefit from the longer 12-month period proposed for claims under the Bill ... There is no off-the-shelf answer to the question of how long the limitation period for claims under clause 7(1)(a) should be. What we have tried to do in our amendment is to strike a balance between the legitimate needs of the plaintiff and the legitimate needs of the defendant, which is what all limitation periods should do ... We believe that the right balance is provided by a 12-month period, with a power to extend it for the benefit of the complainant... We recognise ... that there may be circumstances where a rigid one-year cut-off could lead to injustice. Clause 7(5) does not therefore seek to provide a rigid limit, but enables a court to extend the period where it is appropriate to do so. There will be cases in which an individual has a good reason for delay. In judicial review cases, for example, the courts have extended time where the applicant has been seeking redress by other proper means, such as by pursuing internal grievance procedures, or where he has had to apply for legal aid. I have no doubt that the courts will continue to exercise their discretion so as to prevent prejudice to one party or the other where an application is made to extend time ... We do not wish to narrow the range of circumstances which might influence the court ...

[Column 1097]

It is not our intention to create a vast array of novel features that would allow litigants to pursue cases in courts in a way that the courts and Parliament had not intended. However, someone with a genuine human rights grievance will be entitled to pursue it under clause 7(1)(a), whether or not he is within the time limit for judicial review. We accept that that should be so. The ... one-year time limit for clause 7(1)(a) [is] so that the courts have time to make a judgment. We have not sought to constrain that time too much because clause 7(5)(b) allows the courts to decide when they wish to go beyond the 12-month period, should it be equitable to do so.

We are conscious that it is important that the person is allowed to pursue any action under clause 7(1)(a). We do not want to create an artificial time limit of three months... without giving the level of flexibility that is needed (which) would tie the procedure too tightly to the judicial review procedure. The courts will develop their own jurisprudence on this issue, over time.

Appeals before the Immigration Appeals Authority

The Lord Chancellor

18 November 1997 Column 505

... the thrust of the argument put forward by the noble Earl, Lord Russell, was that it should be possible in appeals to the special adjudicator under the 1993 Act to rely upon rights under the European Convention of Human Rights. It is the Government's intention that it should be possible to rely on those rights in appeals to the special adjudicator under the 1993 Act and we shall consider further whether any amendment to this Bill is needed to allow that result to be achieved.

Lord Williams of Mostyn moved Amendment No 30

Hansard HL 19 Jan 1998 Column 1360

Page 5 line 8, at end insert—

"(9A) The Minister who has power to make rules in relation to a particular tribunal may by order give that tribunal jurisdiction –
(a) to determine such questions arising in connection with the Convention rights, or
(b) to grant in respect of acts (or proposed acts) of public authorities which are (or would be) unlawful as a result of section 6(1) such relief or remedy of a kind that it has power to grant, as he considers appropriate
(9B) An order made under subsection (9A) may contain such incidental, supplemental, consequential or transitional provision as the Minister making it considers appropriate."

As your Lordships know, the amendments to clauses 7 and 20 respond to specific concerns expressed by the noble Earl, Lord Russell, in Committee. He referred to appeals in asylum cases heard by the special adjudicator under the Asylum and Immigration Appeals Act 1993 ... pointed out that the jurisdiction of the adjudicator was restricted under that Act to considering claims under the 1951 Convention on Refugees and suggested that the adjudicators should be allowed also to consider claims dependent on the European Convention of Human Rights. On that occasion, I indicated our preliminary view that the noble Earl was probably right and I also indicated – I paraphrase, bearing I mind the lateness of ...

[Column 1361]

... the hour – that we would see what we could do to attend to his concerns. We concluded that the noble Earl's analysis of the 1993 Act is correct.

A person appearing in difficult circumstances before the special adjudicator would not be able to rely on the Convention rights. He would not be left without any remedy under the Human Rights Bill, because he would be able to rely on those rights in separate proceedings under clause 7(1)(a) of the Bill. The better course, however, would be for him to be able to rely on Convention points at the time when the case was before the special adjudicator. I explained in Committee that that was our intention and that we would consider the form of amendment ...

... The effect of Amendment No 30 is to enable a Minister to confer jurisdiction on a tribunal to determine Convention issues or to grant a remedy where a public authority has acted incompatibly with the Convention rights. The jurisdiction is to be conferred by order. It will be in addition to the existing statutory provisions relating to tribunal jurisdiction. In the particular case of concern to the noble Earl, it will enable the Secretary of State to confer jurisdiction on the adjudicator to consider claims relating to Convention rights, notwithstanding the restriction in the 1993 Act, and to provide a remedy if a public authority acts in a way which is incompatible with those rights.

The intention would be to use the order-making power to extend the jurisdiction of the special adjudicators who hear asylum appeals so as to allow a person appealing on one of the grounds set out in section 8 of the 1993 Act to appeal also on the ground that his removal from the United Kingdom would be unlawful under clause 6(1) of the Human Rights Bill. An appellant who succeeded on that ground would not be granted asylum but would be irremovable from the United Kingdom and eligible for exceptional leave to remain. Therefore the effect of such an order would be to make the ECHR jurisdiction in asylum appeals consistent with that in non-asylum appeals under section 19 of the Immigration Act 1971.

The order conferring jurisdiction is to be subject to affirmative resolution under the scheme that we propose. We sought to make general provision of this kind rather than to operate directly on the Act of 1993. That is because we do not think it appropriate for a Bill of general application, such as this one, to remedy problems in a particular piece of legislation. Moreover, we are not certain that the problem identified by the noble Earl is necessarily confined to tribunal hearings in immigration appeals cases. We are not aware at present of similar problems arising from statutory restrictions on the jurisdiction of other tribunals, but if such problems do emerge we would look to a general provision which I hope the noble Earl can welcome because, although consonant with his approach, it goes beyond the ambit of his particular concern. We are looking for a general provision in order to deal with such problems.

[Column 1362]

I recognise that that is a short-term solution but, when a suitable opportunity arises, we will seek to amend the relevant primary legislation. On the basis of that explanation, which is as reasonably short as I can conventionally make it. I hope that the House will agree that the Government's amendments meet a mischief which was identified. I also hope that the noble Earl with think that this is an appropriate solution – perhaps a little more so than his solution – and on behalf not only of the Government but also of your Lordship's House, I thank the noble Earl for his persistence in identifying that gap, I beg to move.

Government Amendment No 129

Mr O'Brien, 24 June 1998, Column 1109

The power conferred by clause 7(13) has been included to cater for situations where the grounds on which proceedings may be brought before a tribunal are extremely narrowly defined either by statute or by restrictive judicial interpretation of statutory provision. In those rare cases, a tribunal would, unless its powers were suitably amplified, be precluded from determining issues relating to the Convention rights. The issue that prompted the inclusion of clause 7(13) is the constraints placed on special adjudicators hearing appeals under the Asylum and Immigration Appeals Act 1993.

It was pointed out in another place that the terms of the 1993 Act are such that they would prevent a special adjudicator hearing an asylum case from determining whether an appellant's removal from the United Kingdom would breach his Convention rights when such appeals were dealt with.

Even without subsection (13), an individual would not be left without a remedy under the Human Rights Bill, as he would be able to rely on the Convention rights in a subsequent application for judicial review. The better course is for him to rely on Convention rights at the time the case is before the special adjudicator. Clause 7(13) would allow that result to be achieved. In addition, as it has been cast in general terms, it could also be used to benefit other tribunals in the same position as the special adjudicator.

[Column 1110]

I come now to the special adjudicators and the Opposition's amendment, which involves an important point. The concern which prompted the inclusion of clause 7(13) was our wish to ensure that provision should be made to permit an appellant in an appeal under section 8 of the Asylum and Immigration Appeals Act 1993 to appeal also on the ground that the decision in question would be unlawful under section 6(1) of the Human Rights Act. As things stand, unless the appeal is a mixed appeal, the special adjudicator lacks the power to entertain that appeal.

Clause 7(13) will enable the Secretary of State to confer power on the special adjudicator to consider claims relating to the Convention rights, notwithstanding the restriction in the 1993 Act, and to provide a remedy if a public authority acts in a way that is incompatible with those rights. An appellant who succeeded in arguing that his removal from the United Kingdom would be unlawful under section 6(1) of the Human Rights Act would not be granted asylum, but would be irremovable from the United Kingdom and eligible for exceptional leave to remain.

[Column 1111]

The Opposition's amendment, by removing from clause 7(13) the scope to add to the remedies that a tribunal can grant, may in fact have a result, which I imagine Opposition Members do not intend. It might require a special adjudicator to grant a successful appellant asylum even where his appeal was based on Convention grounds, as the adjudicator would have no other remedy open to him.

Hansard HL 18 November 1997 Column 525

The Lord Chancellor: ... plans for judicial training are well in hand under the auspices of the Judicial Studies Board, under the chairmanship of Lord Justice Henry. The board is working on plans for judicial training at every level.

Counsel should not be spoon-fed. It is the duty of counsel to research their case and, if they have a Convention point which they desire to raise, they must equip themselves to do so and gain copies of any relevant reports that they desire to draw to the attention of the court. It is not the function of the state to do counsel's research for him.

... counsel are not to be spoon-fed but must educate themselves as part of a continuing process of self-education in developing areas of the law. It is intended that Convention rights and values shall permeate the work of the courts at all levels. It is up to counsel to get themselves up to speed in that endeavour.

As regards the unrepresented defendant, in this country it is usually a matter of choice because in the criminal courts legal aid will be available. But where a defendant insists upon defending himself, there is a well recognised and honourable tradition in the courts of the judge giving the defendant the maximum assistance that he can.

House of Lords, Second Reading

Hansard HL, 27 November 1997

The Lord Advocate (Lord Hardie): ... The unrepresented party, after all, is in need of greater assistance than the represented party in vindicating his rights and it is my understanding that the courts in Scotland and tribunals sitting there have a long and honourable tradition of support to the litigant who chooses to appear in his own behalf. Indeed, opposing counsel has a duty to draw to the attention of the court cases and authorities in favour of the opponent, particularly when the opponent is unrepresented.

SECTION 8: JUDICIAL REMEDIES

House of Lords, Second Reading

Hansard HL, 3 November 1997, Column 1232

The Lord Chancellor (Lord Irvine of Lairg): ... If a court or tribunal finds that a public authority has acted in a way which is incompatible with the Convention ... under clause 8 it may provide whatever remedy is available to it and which seems just and appropriate. That might include awarding damages against the public authority.

House of Lords, Committee Stage

Hansard HL, 24 November 1997, Column 844

The Lord Chancellor: Clause 8 provides the courts and tribunals with wide powers to grant such relief or remedy which they consider just and appropriate where they find that a public authority has acted unlawfully by virtue of clause 6(1) of the Bill. Clause 8(2) and (3) ... [is] a comprehensive and comprehensible code. However, it is necessary to put down certain limits on what remedies a court or tribunal can provide. Subsection (2) ... provides one such restriction ... [quoted] ... Quite clearly, this means that a criminal court will not be able to award damages for a Convention breach, even if it currently has the power to make a compensation order unless it also has the power to award damages in civil proceedings ...

[Column 855]

So as to make the intention plan, it is not the Bill's aim that, for example, the Crown Court should be able to make an award of damages where it finds, during the course of a trial, that a violation of a person's Convention rights has occurred. We believe that it is appropriate for an individual who considers that his rights have been infringed in such a case to pursue any matter of damages through the civil courts where this type of issue is normally dealt with; in other words, to pursue the matter in the courts that are accustomed to determining whether it is necessary and appropriate to award damages and what the proper amount should be. For that reason, we regard the inclusion of subsection (2) as an entirely proper part of the scheme.

We say that the Crown Court, in cases of crime, should not award damages. The remedy that the defendant wants in a criminal court is not to be convicted. We see very considerable practical difficulties about giving a new power to award damages to a criminal court in Convention cases. It would seem to me to open up the need for representation in the Crown Court to any person who it might appear in the course of criminal proceedings might be at risk of damages. We believe that that would be potentially disruptive of a criminal trial. Similarly a magistrates' court is a criminal court ... We believe that it is appropriate that the civil courts, which traditionally make awards of damages, should, alone, be enabled to make awards of damages in these Convention cases.

House of Lords, Committee Stage

Hansard HL, 18 November 1997, Column 479

The Lord Chancellor (Lord Irvine of Lairg): ... I cannot conceive of any state of affairs in which an English court, having held an Act to be unlawful because of its infringement of a Convention right, would under clause 8(1), be disabled from giving an effective remedy. I believe that the English law is rich in remedies and I cannot conceive of a case in which English law under clause 8(1) would be unable to provide an effective remedy.

However, during the earlier course of the debate I did not say that article 13 was incorporated. The debate is about the fact that it is not incorporated ... in my view the English courts ... would be able to have regard to article 13.

House of Lords, Report Stage

Hansard HL, 19 January 1998, Column 1266

The Lord Chancellor (Lord Irvine of Lairg): My Lords, I have not the least idea what the remedies the courts might develop outside clause 8 could be if article 13 was included ... Clause 8(1) is of the widest amplitude. No one is ...

[Column 1267]

... contending that it will not do the job. When we have challenged the proponents of the amendment on a number of occasions in Committee to say how clause 8 might not do the job, they have been unable to offer a single example. Therefore, the argument is all one way. What we have done is sufficient.

House of Commons, Second Reading

Hansard HC, 16 February 1998, Column 780

The Secretary of State for the Home Department (Mr Jack Straw): ... Clause 8 deals with remedies ... If a court or tribunal finds that a public authority has acted unlawfully, it may grant whatever remedy is available to it that it considers just and appropriate.

House of Commons, Committee Stage

Hansard HC, 20 May 1998, Column 979

Mr Garnier: Will the right hon. Gentleman give one or two examples of the remedies he envisages [under article 13] that would go beyond those set out in clause 8?

The Secretary of State for the Home Department (Mr Jack Straw): In considering article 13, the courts could decide to grant damages in more circumstances than we had envisaged. We had to consider that matter carefully, because of the effect on the public purse ... We had to think carefully about the scope of the remedies that we should provide.

SECTION 10: POWER TO TAKE REMEDIAL ACTION

House of Lords, Second Reading

Hansard HL, 3 November 1997, Column 1231

The Lord Chancellor (Lord Irvine of Lairg): ... if legislation has been declared incompatible, a prompt Parliamentary remedy should be available. Clauses 10 to 12 of the Bill provide how that is to be achieved. A Minister of the Crown will be able to make what is to be known as a remedial order. The order will be available in response to a declaration of incompatibility by the higher courts. It will also be available if legislation appears to a Minister to be incompatible because of a finding by the European Court of Human Rights.

We recognise that a power to amend primary legislation by means of a statutory instrument is not a power to be conferred or exercised lightly. Those clauses therefore place a number of procedural and other restrictions on its use. First, a remedial order must be approved by both Houses of Parliament. That will normally require it to be laid in draft and subject to the affirmative resolution procedure before it takes effect. In urgent cases, it will be possible to make the order without it being approved in that way, but even then it will cease to have effect after 40 days unless it is approved by Parliament. So we have built in as much Parliamentary scrutiny as possible.

In addition, the power to make a remedial order may be used only to remove an incompatibility or a possible incompatibility between legislation and the Convention. It may therefore be used only to protect human rights, not to infringe them. And the Bill also specifically provides that no person is to be guilty of a criminal offence solely as a result of any retrospective effect of a remedial order.

House of Commons, Second Reading

Hansard HC, 16 February 1998, Column 773

The Secretary of State for the Home Department (Mr Jack Straw): ... occasions on which the courts will declare an Act of this Parliament to be incompatible are rare; there will be very few such cases. Secondly, the purpose of remedial action is to try to resolve the current paralysis, which is to nobody's advantage. It is not to take away anyone's rights; it is to confer rights.

Section 10(1)(a)

House of Lords, Report Stage

Hansard HL, 29 January 1998, Column 393

Lord Williams of Mostyn: ... Amendments Nos 41 –[the words after 'right' in section 10(1)(a)] and 42 [which inserted the words after 'rights' in section 10(1)(b)] place limits on the power of a Minister to make a remedial order under clause 10 following a declaration of Convention incompatibility by a court. Both are specific responses to concerns expressed by your Lordships in Committee ...

House of Commons, Committee Stage

Hansard HC, 20 June 1998, Column 42

The Secretary of State for the Home Department (Mr Jack Straw): ... [O]ur intention is not that the procedure under clause 10 should be used to by-pass the will of the House, but simply to deal with practical problems that may arise ... Even on the most dismal interpretation of clause 10, the will of the House still prevails. It may be a truncated procedure, but it certainly does not give the courts the power to say what the law of the land should be ...

Section 10(2)

House of Commons, Committee Stage

Hansard HC, 24 June 1998, Column 1140

The Secretary of State for the Home Department (Mr Jack Straw): I am answering ad lib and without the benefit of a legal dictionary, but the situation that I described in the *Chahal* case, where the liberty of a subject would be adversely affected by a delay in producing primary legislation, was a compelling case. I am not certain that it would be an exceptional case, because one could ask, 'To what is it exceptional?' but it would certainly be a compelling case. Frankly, only in that situation would remedial orders be necessary and appropriate.

House of Commons, Third Reading

Hansard HC, 21 October 1998, Column 1300

The Secretary of State for the Home Department (Mr Jack Straw): The Government thought – there was no great argument about the matter, but it was important that we should deal with all the arguments – that it was important to enshrine Parliament's sovereignty in the Bill. We therefore developed the scheme of declarations of incompatibility. We did not propose that the Judicial committee of the House of Lords should have the power to override Acts of Parliament by stating that, because they were incompatible with the Convention, they were unenforceable and of no effect.

[Column 1301]

We said that the Judicial Committee of the House of Lords would be able to declare whether, in its opinion, an Act of Parliament was incompatible with the Convention, and subsequently to refer the matter back to the Government, which is answerable to Parliament. In the overwhelming majority of cases, regardless of which party was in government. I think that Ministers would examine the matter and say, 'A declaration of incompatibility has been made, and we shall have to accept it. We shall therefore have to remedy the defeat in the law spotted by the Judicial Committee of the House of Lords.' Therefore – as has been discussed in previous debates, and will be discussed again today – we have included in the Bill procedures for remedial orders. It is also always open to Ministers to introduce amending legislation in the normal way.

[Column 1330]

Mr Mike O'Brien: The requirement for compelling reasons in clause 10(2) is itself a response to concern expressed here and in another place about the remedial order provisions. It is there to make it absolutely clear that a remedial order is not a routine response in preference to fresh primary legislation. We would not want to go further ... and limit 'compelling reasons' to [likely jeopardy to national security, public health or the liberty of the individual]. There may be other circumstances that constitute compelling reasons sufficient to justify a remedial order: for example, a decision of the higher courts in relation to basic provisions of criminal procedure affecting the way in which, perhaps, all criminal cases must be handled. An example is a provision that might invalidate a crucial part of the codes of practice under the Police and Criminal Evidence Act 1984, or provisions relating to the detention of suspects. Therefore, there are a number of issues where we would want to proceed with care. We also might need to respond very quickly simply to avoid the criminal justice system in such cases either collapsing or not being able to deliver justice and proper convictions.

'Compelling' is a strong word. We see no need to define it by reference to particular categories. In both the outstanding cases ... put to me, our view is likely to be that those would not create the compelling reasons that would justify a remedial order. In any event, on those issues – electoral law and chastising children – everyone would expect primary legislation rather than a remedial order ...

[Column 1331]

It would be open to the Government to take no action in response to a declaration of incompatibility ... but, where a declaration is made, a Government who are committed to promoting human rights, as we are, will want to do something about the law in question. It is possible for primary legislation to be introduced and passed quickly, but the pressures on the timetable can make it very difficult to find a slot.

The power to make a remedial order is there for cases where there is a very good reason to amend the law following a declaration of incompatibility or a finding by the Strasbourg Court, but no suitable legislative vehicle is available. Where a remedial order is made or proposed, we accepted that the procedures for Parliamentary scrutiny needed to be strengthened. That is why the requirement to provide a document containing all the relevant information and a statement providing a summary of any representations on an order or draft order was added to Schedule 2 in Committee.

[Column 1357]

Mr Straw: Three sets of changes have been made as a result of concerns expressed … The first concerns remedial orders. We continue to believe that it should be possible to amend Acts of Parliament by a remedial order so as to bring them into line with the Convention rights, but we have … considerably restricted the circumstances in which they can be made, and we have significantly enhanced the Parliamentary opportunities for scrutiny of those orders.

[Column 1358]

We have explained that any response to a declaration of incompatibility by the courts, whether by fresh primary legislation or by a remedial order, is a matter on which the Government will propose, but it is for Parliament to dispose. One of the Bill's many strengths is that it promotes human rights while maintaining the sovereignty of Parliament and the separation of powers which underpins our constitutional arrangements.

SECTION 11: SAFEGUARD FOR EXISTING HUMAN RIGHTS

House of Lords, Report Stage

Hansard HL, 29 January 1998, Column 410

Lord Williams of Mostyn: … Clause 11 is simply to provide a saving for other human rights. It is there to ensure that if a person has existing rights, nothing in this Bill shall detract from them in any way …

[Column 411]

There are, of course, two kinds of relationship created in the Bill between Convention and domestic law: the interpretive principle in clauses 3 to 5, and the right to rely on Convention rights against a public authority in clauses 6 to 9. We do not wish to have any misunderstanding.

House of Commons, Second Reading

Hansard HC, 16 February 1998, Column 738

The Secretary of State for the Home Department (Mr Jack Straw): … Clause 11 confirms that a person's reliance on a Convention right does not restrict any other right or freedom that he enjoys under United Kingdom law.

SECTION 13: FREEDOM OF THOUGHT, CONSCIENCE AND RELIGION

House of Commons, Committee Stage

Hansard HC, 20 May 1998, Column 1020

The Secretary of State for the Home Department (Mr Jack Straw): ... Clause 13 would come into play in any case in which a court's determination of any question arising out of the Bill might affect the exercise by a religious organisation of the Convention right of freedom of thought, conscience and religion. In such a case, it provides for the court to have particular regard – not ...

[Column 1021]

... just to have regard, going back to the earlier debate, but to have particular regard – to the importance of that right. Its purpose is not to exempt Churches and other religious organisations from the scope of the Bill – they have not sought that – any more than from that of the Convention. It is to reassure them against the Bill being used to intrude upon genuinely religious beliefs or practices based on their beliefs. I emphasise the word 'practices', as well as 'beliefs'.

There is ample reassurance available on this point from Convention jurisprudence. Apart from stating the importance of the courts having due regard to article 9, clause 13 is designed to bring out the point that article 9 rights attach not only to individuals but to the Churches. The idea that Convention rights typically attach only to individuals and not the Churches caused considerable anxiety. I understood that, and that is why the new clause has been phrased so that the Churches have its protection as well as individuals.

There is Convention jurisprudence to the effect that a Church body or other association with religious objectives is capable of possessing and exercising the rights in article 9 as a representative of its members. Clause 13 will emphasise that point to our courts. The intention is to focus the courts' attention in any proceedings on the view generally held by the Church in question, and on its interest in protecting the integrity of the common faith of its members against attack, whether by outsiders or by individual dissidents. That is a significant protection.

... This section refers to the exercise of the right of freedom of thought, conscience and religion by a 'religious organisation', but leaves that expression undefined ... partly because no definition is readily available, at home or in Strasbourg.

We considered the issue with great care, and took the advice of Parliamentary counsel. I have already referred to the difficulty arising from this point in the amendments made in another place in discriminating between some religions and others. We are seeking to reflect precisely the Strasbourg case law. The Convention institutions have not offered a definition, but we are confident that the term 'religious organisation' is recognisable in terms of the Convention ...

The key concept that we are talking about is organisations with religious objectives.

SECTION 19: STATEMENTS OF COMPATIBILITY

House of Lords, Second Reading

Hansard HL, 3 November 1997, Column 1233

The Lord Chancellor (Lord Irvine of Lairg): … This section imposes a new requirement on government Ministers when introducing legislation. In future, they will have to make a statement either that the provisions of the legislation are compatible with the Convention or that they cannot make such a statement but nevertheless wish Parliament to proceed to consider the Bill.

Ministers will obviously want to make a positive statement whenever possible. That requirement should therefore have a significant impact on the scrutiny of draft legislation within government. Where such a statement cannot be made, Parliamentary scrutiny of the Bill would be intense.

House of Lords, Second Reading

Hansard HL, 27 November 1997, Column 1228

Lord Williams of Mostyn: The design of the Bill is to give the courts as much space as possible to protect human rights, short of a power to set aside or ignore Acts of Parliament. In the very rare cases where the higher courts will find it impossible to read and give effect to any statute in a way which is compatible with Convention rights, they …

[Column 1229]

… will be able to make a declaration of incompatibility. Then it is for Parliament to decide whether there should be remedial legislation. Parliament may, not must, and generally will, legislate. If a Minister's prior assessment of compatibility (under clause 19) is subsequently found by declaration of incompatibility by the courts to have been mistakes, it is hard to see how a Minister could withhold remedial action.

House of Commons, Second Reading

Hansard HC, 16 February 1998, Column 780

The Secretary of State for the Home Department (Mr Jack Straw): … Clause 19 is a further demonstration of our determination to improve compliance with Convention rights. It places a requirement on a Minister to publish a statement in relation to any Bill that he or she introduces. The statement will either be that the provisions of the legislation are compatible with Convention rights or that he or she cannot make such a statement, but that the Government nevertheless wish to proceed with the Bill.

I am sure that Ministers will want to make a positive statement whenever possible. The requirement to make a statement will have a significant impact on the scrutiny of draft legislation within Government and by Parliament. In my judgment, it will greatly assist Parliament's consideration of Bills by highlighting the potential implications for human rights.

House of Commons, Committee Stage

Hansard HC, 3 June 1998, Column 424

The Secretary of State for the Home Department (Mr Jack Straw): … Clause 8 would require the courts, in considering whether legislation was compatible with Convention rights, to have full regard to the margin of appreciation accorded to states by Strasbourg institutions. Presumably, that is intended to signal to the courts that they should recognise the primary responsibility of Governments for detailed decisions on how Convention rights are given effect in domestic law.

[Column 424]

The doctrine of the margin of appreciation – it is an important one – recognises that a state is allowed a certain measure of discretion, subject to European supervision, when it takes legislative, judicial or administrative action in respect of some Convention rights. In other words, it is best placed to decide in the first place whether –and, if so what – action is required.

My first point about the margin of appreciation is that it is more relevant to some Convention rights than to others. It is especially relevant to articles 8 to 11, which enable restrictions to be placed on rights where that is necessary in a democratic society, for any one of a number of reasons. It is less relevant to some of the other articles, for example, article 2 on the right to life and article 3 on the prohibition on torture or inhuman and degrading treatment or punishment. The doctrine of the margin of appreciation means allowing this country a margin of appreciation when it interprets our law and the actions of our Governments in an international court, perhaps the European Court of Human Rights. Through incorporation we are giving a profound margin of appreciation to British courts to interpret the Convention in accordance with British jurisprudence as well as European jurisprudence.

One of the frustrations of non-incorporation has been that our own judges have not been able to bring their intellectual skills and our great tradition of common law to bear on the development of European Convention jurisprudence …

The margin of appreciation is laid down in many commission and court judgments. Therefore, it is spelt out in the meaning of clause 2.

SPECIAL IMMIGRATION APPEALS COMMISSION BILL [HL]

Hansard HL, 7 July 1997, Column 481

Lord Williams of Mostyn: As I said previously, the main intention in providing appeal rights in the Bill has been to ensure that there is no risk of a breach of article 3 of the ECHR in cases where there is presently no right of appeal on national security grounds.

… We have, however, considered whether any other articles of the ECHR might require a right of appeal in some circumstances. As can be seen from my amendments, we have given particular thought to article 8, which deals, among other things, with the right to respect for family life.

Article 8 allows that national security considerations can justify interference with this right, but there is nevertheless a need to provide for an effective review of any decision to ensure that any interference is in accordance with the law and is necessary.

[Column 482]

For the ECHR rights arising from Article 8 considerations to be properly dealt with, the national security case underlying the refusal of entry clearance would need to be examined. If we do not provide a right of appeal to the new commission there would be a strong likelihood, following incorporation of the Convention at least, that a court of judicial review would insist on seeing the national security details.

... We believe ... that it would clearly be preferable for any consideration of the national security case to be dealt with by a commission which has been set up especially to deal with any such cases which arise.

Our amendments limit the new right of appeal in refusal of entry clearance cases to those cases where the right to family life is truly at issue ...

... those who believe that their rights under article 3 have been or would be violated will be able to rely on article 3 in domestic proceedings once incorporation has been achieved. That will be the case in respect of any alleged violation.

[Column 487]

One very important outcome of the judgment in *Chahal's* case is that it is clear that there can be no question of a balancing act between the risk to an individual and national security considerations. If there are good grounds for believing that a person will be an article 3 risk then the national security case for his or here removal is effectively – I put this bluntly – irrelevant.

Hansard HL, 5 June 1997, Column 733

The Parliamentary Under-Secretary of State, Home Office (Lord Williams of Mostyn): The security of the nation is a prime responsibility for this Government, as for any government. The threat from international terrorism is a real problem for the whole of the civilised world.

At the same time we must ensure that our procedures for dealing with such people meet accepted standards of fairness.

In the case of non-British citizens, an important weapon in our armoury in the fight against international terrorism – and against other activities which threaten our nation – is the ability, under the Immigration Act 1971, to exclude or deport the small number of foreign nationals who pose a significant risk. The powers are used sparingly. They are a vital part of our efforts to protect the United Kingdom from those who threaten us.

[Column 735]

In its judgment in *Chahal*, and in other cases involving national security considerations, the European Court of Human Rights has acknowledged that, where national security issues are at stake, consideration will almost inevitably have to be given to confidential material and that safeguards such as the ones included in the Bill may be essential. In such cases, what is needed is a remedy which is as effective as can be, given the threat to national security ...

[Column 738]

The decision of the European Court of Human Rights in *Chahal* demonstrated article 3's absolute nature. On the basis of the Government's plan to incorporate the European Convention on Human Rights into British law (article 3 which expressly rules out signatory countries from returning people to countries where there is a serious risk of their being tortured) can the Minister explain, first, how incorporation of the Convention would affect our ability to deport on national security grounds, secondly, what effect the Government consider incorporation would have on the provisions of the Bill, and, thirdly, how that would relate to and, indeed, work with the recent British initiative – adopted last December as a UN declaration – denying the protection of the 1951 Refugee Convention to terrorists?

... First, there is the very important question of whether the decision of the commission is to be binding on the Home Secretary ... that is intended that the decision should bind the Home Secretary, I respectfully suggest that that is a very significant advance in human rights terms.

I have to deal with article 3, which is another important question. There is no danger that new procedures will result in a person being returned to a place in which he or she will be at real risk of being subjected to torture or cruel and degrading treatment. article 3 of the Convention on Human Rights prohibits us from returning a person to a place where there are substantial grounds of believing that such real risk would subsist. The absolute nature of article 3 ... was determined by *Chahal*.

[Column 753]

Article 3 is an absolute obligation ... terrorists will benefit from the provision of article 3 because it is an absolute obligation which has been specified by the European Court ...

[Column 754]

Detention of an asylum seeker is only used as a last resort. Temporary admission is granted wherever possible. Only around 1.5 per cent ... of asylum seekers are detained. The majority of those – 75 to 80 per cent – will have had their applications refused. Almost every asylum seeker has the right to apply to an independent adjudicator for bail. We do not incarcerate people on mere suspicion alone ... There are various ways, as is well known, of challenging detention by various applications for habeas corpus, applications for bail or judicial review.

We are conscious of the fact that lengthy periods of detention are undesirable and in many cases plain wrong. One of the aspects at which the Government are looking is the length of detention, the use of bail, the use of chief immigration officer's bail, the alternatives to detention consistent with other interests, when detention should be used, whether prisons ought to be used for detention and what is the place of bail hostels

Index